Regulating Religion

This book focuses on government regulation of religious institutions in South Africa. Part 1 explains the meaning of government regulation for religious communities by providing a brief overview of the relationship between church and state, the right to freedom of religion and the legal status of religious organisations. With reference to case examples, this section highlights the importance of religious autonomy and the right to self-determination of religious institutions and non-interference by the state in the internal affairs of the organisation. No fundamental rights are however absolute and the section concludes with a discussion on the limitation of rights and an overview of the relevant constitutional provisions and anti-discrimination laws in place relevant to religious organisations, in the context of equality and non-discrimination. Part 2 discusses in more detail the daily rights, responsibilities and freedoms associated with the right to freedom of religion within some specific spheres of society where regulation of religion has occurred or is necessary or has proved to be problematic. It includes those related to the role of religion in society; the relations between religion and state institutions; education; finance; family matters; employment law; planning law; broadcast media and general governance issues.

Helena Van Coller is Associate Professor of Law, Rhodes University, South Africa.

ICLARS Series on Law and Religion

The *ICLARS Series on Law and Religion* is a new series designed to provide a forum for the rapidly expanding field of research in law and religion. The series is published in association with the International Consortium for Law and Religion Studies, an international network of scholars and experts of law and religion founded in 2007 with the aim of providing a place where information, data and opinions can easily be exchanged among members and made available to the broader scientific community. The series aims to become a primary source for students and scholars while presenting authors with a valuable means to reach a wide and growing readership.

Other titles in this series:

Lutheran Theology and Secular Law
The Work of the Modern State
Edited by Marie A. Failinger and Ronald W. Duty

Religious Freedom and the Law
Emerging Contexts for Freedom for and from Religion
Edited by Brett G. Scharffs, Asher Maoz and Ashley Isaacson Woolley

Religion, Pluralism, and Reconciling Difference
Edited by W. Cole Durham, Jr. and Donlu Thayer

Religious Literacy, Law and History
Perspectives on European Pluralist Societies
Edited by Alberto Melloni and Francesca Cadeddu

Regulating Religion
State Governance of Religious Institutions in South Africa
Helena Van Coller

Religious Rights within the Family
From Coerced Manifestation to Dispute Resolution in France, England and Hong Kong
Esther Erlings

For more information about this series, please visit: www.routledge.com/ICLARS-Series-on-Law-and-Religion/book-series/ICLARS

Regulating Religion

State Governance of Religious Institutions in South Africa

Helena Van Coller

Routledge
Taylor & Francis Group
LONDON AND NEW YORK

First published 2020
by Routledge
2 Park Square, Milton Park, Abingdon, Oxon OX14 4RN

and by Routledge
605 Third Avenue, New York, NY 10017

First issued in paperback 2020

Routledge is an imprint of the Taylor & Francis Group, an informa business

British Library Cataloguing-in-Publication Data
A catalogue record for this book is available from the British Library

Library of Congress Cataloging-in-Publication Data
A catalog record has been requested for this book

ISBN 13: 978-0-367-72696-6 (pbk)
ISBN 13: 978-1-138-29871-2 (hbk)

Typeset in Galliard
by Taylor & Francis Books

Regulating Religion

State Governance of Religious Institutions in South Africa

Helena Van Coller

Routledge
Taylor & Francis Group
LONDON AND NEW YORK

First published 2020
by Routledge
2 Park Square, Milton Park, Abingdon, Oxon OX14 4RN

and by Routledge
605 Third Avenue, New York, NY 10017

First issued in paperback 2020

Routledge is an imprint of the Taylor & Francis Group, an informa business

British Library Cataloguing-in-Publication Data
A catalogue record for this book is available from the British Library

Library of Congress Cataloging-in-Publication Data
A catalog record has been requested for this book

ISBN 13: 978-0-367-72696-6 (pbk)
ISBN 13: 978-1-138-29871-2 (hbk)

Typeset in Galliard
by Taylor & Francis Books

Contents

Preface

South Africa is a multi-religious country and is home to a wide variety of religious traditions. Religion has been legislated since the middle of the 1600s through various legislative enactments. Most sought to uphold and protect certain religious tenets as opposed to regulating them. This has however changed over the years, and religious institutions are subject to and are being regulated through numerous laws and regulations. The preamble of the South African Charter of Religious Rights and Freedoms highlights the fact that the constitutional recognition and protection of the right to freedom of religion is an important mechanism for the *equitable regulation* of the relationship between the state and religious institutions. However, religious communities and leaders argue that they are already 'over-regulated', which can create the danger of violating communities' right to freedom of religion.

Recently, the Commission for the Promotion and Protection of the Rights of Cultural, Religious and Linguistic Communities (CRL Rights Commission) published a report on the *Commercialisation of Religion and Abuse of People's Belief Systems.* The proposals made by the Commission in its report originated from various newspaper reports and complaints by individual believers as well as religious institutions relating to abuses taking place in certain religious institutions. This report calls for far-reaching regulation of religious organisations and religious 'practitioners' in South Africa and proposes that legislation be introduced to this end. The intersection between religion and the law has been the subject matter of some controversy for many years now.

The title of this book says it all – *State Governance of Religious Institutions in South Africa.* Never has this topic been more relevant than now. The book is not a complete and systematic study of all aspects relating to religious institutions in South Africa or the regulation thereof, nor was it intended to be. With this monograph, I took the liberty of focussing on relevant issues as well as topics of interest to me, associated with religious regulation. Some I have come across in my years working in this area and through numerous law and religion conferences, others through conversations with colleagues and ordinary believers. With this book and through the various examples, I hope to provide some insights into how the relationship between state and religious institutions in South Africa is, or should be, regulated in different spheres of society. What does government regulation of religion exactly mean for religious communities in South Africa? What is the role that government needs to play in protecting and promoting the religious rights and freedoms of communities in South Africa? What does freedom of religion mean to religious communities and what are the daily rights, responsibilities and freedoms that are associated with this right?

The book falls into two main parts. Part 1, consisting of Chapters 1 to 4, focuses on some general themes relating to relevant issues of law and religion and sets out the background, introduction and general context of the theme within a South African context. Part 2, consisting of Chapters 5 to 11, will discuss in more detail the rights, responsibilities and freedoms associated with this right within some specific spheres of society where regulation of religion has occurred or is necessary, or has proved to be problematic.

Chapter 1 presents some important background material and provides a short overview of the development of the relationship between state and church in South Africa. The enactment of the new Constitution brought a new approach to the relationship between church and state, but also between law and religion in South Africa. We saw a shift from an approach where churches and religious organisations knew no real freedom of religion during these periods, towards one with full recognition of and protection of religious freedom.

Chapter 2 aims to give a description of the meaning of 'religious institution' or 'religious community' for purposes of the right to freedom of religion and the subsequent government regulation of religious institutions in South Africa. The chapter will also address the importance of the right to acquire and maintain legal personality and the implications for religious institutions. Chapter 3 shows the importance of collective religious rights and outlines the constitutional provisions aimed at protecting the rights of religious institutions. The chapter also addresses the importance of religious autonomy for religious organisations and highlights the fact that the state is under a duty to respect these rights and should create the opportunity and space for individuals and religious institutions to enjoy these rights fully, with as little state regulation as possible. Where the state or other role-players interfere with the autonomy of religious organisations, reference will often be made to the right to equality, and non-discrimination or different fundamental rights will have to be balanced against each other. Chapter 4 addresses the right to equality and non-discrimination in relation to religious organisations and illustrates how various fundamental rights, such as the right to freedom of religion, may be limited in accordance with section 36 of the Constitution.

Part 2 of the book, Chapters 5 to 11, outlines the various rights that religious institutions and members enjoy as part of the duty that rests on the state to give effect to the right of freedom of religion, and to protecting and promoting the collective autonomy of religious institutions. Each chapter will briefly look at how the state can or has limited these rights through government regulation in a particular area. Chapter 5 discusses the right to worship in community with others as an important part of the collective right to freedom of religion. Some of the religious practices and rituals include aspects of burial rights; circumcision and rites of passage; aspects relating to witchcraft practices; ritual slaughter and dietary practices; religious equipment and symbols; and religious holidays. Chapter 6 focuses on religion in education, with reference to important legislation such as the Schools Act and relevant dress and disciplinary codes. It will address important aspects of religious observances, such as religious dress, jewellery, hairstyles, headscarves and religious symbols, in both public and independent schools.

Section 16 of the Constitution guarantees the right to freedom of expression. Chapter 7 will address this right and the relevant laws and regulations enacted to prevent the dissemination of religion in a manner that is offensive to others, such as laws against blasphemy and hate speech. Chapter 8 will focus on the recognition of religious or other marriages and unions in South Africa. The discussion will focus on civil unions and religious marriages, with specific reference to marriages in accordance with Muslim and Hindu rites. Chapter 9 outlines the relevant financial laws and regulations applicable to religious institutions. Financial abuses, misappropriation of funds and non-compliance with financial legislation are but some of the issues highlighted by the CRL Rights Commission in its report. The chapter will explain the current legislative framework relevant to religious institutions, with a particular emphasis on financial requirements, and will briefly outline some aspects of financial regulation in the non-profit context. The chapter will conclude with examples relating to financial abuses and non-compliance with the relevant laws, and proposals for the financial regulation of the religious sector.

Chapter 10 outlines some issues associated with the position, status and duties of religious leaders. The chapter will address the employment status of religious leaders. With reference to the position in different churches, the discussion will also focus on discrimination and the right of religious institutions to appoint office holders. The chapter will conclude with a brief example of access to public institutions by religious ministers in the form of chaplaincies. Chapter 11 will conclude with Part 2, with some last examples of religious exemptions that have not been discussed in any of the other sections. Some relate to individual claims of religious accommodation but may be of importance to religious institutions and their members. Examples relate to abortion and the compulsory prevention or treatment of disease, and last, reasonable accommodation in relation to the taking of an oath and military service.

List of cases

Amod v Multilateral Motor Vehicle Accident Fund 1999 (4) SA 1319 (SCA)
Antonie v Governing Body, Settlers High School 2002 4 SA 738 (C)
Association of Welfare Organisations and Non-Governmental Organisations v MEC for Social Development Free State and Others (1719/2010) [2010] ZAFSHC 73 (5 August 2010)
Biserica Adeverat Ortodoxa din Moldova v Moldova, no 952/03 (2007)
Bishop Mlibo Ngewu v The Anglican Church of Southern Africa and Ten Others [2016] ZAKZPHC 88
Bredell v Pienaar 1922 CPD 578
Cassim v Molife 1908 TS 748
Christian Education South Africa v Minister of Education 2000 (4) SA 757 (CC)
Church of Scientology Moscow v Russia, no 18147/02 (2007)
Church of the Province of Southern Africa (Diocese of Cape Town) v CCMA & others [2001] 11 BLLR 1213 (LC) 1223
Corporation of the Presiding Bishop of the Church of Jesus Christ of Latter-Day Saints v Amos 483 U.S 327 (1987)
Daniels v Campbell NO and Others 2004 (5) SA 331 (CC)
Dawood and Another v Minister of Home Affairs and Others; Shalabi and Another v Minister of Home Affairs and Others; Thomas and Another v Minister of Home Affairs and Others 2000 (3) SA 936
De Lange v Presiding Bishop of the Methodist Church of Southern Africa for the time being and Another 2016 (2) SA 1 (CC)
De Lange v Presiding Bishop, Methodist Church of Southern Africa 2015 (1) SA 106 (SCA)
De Vos v Die Ringskommissie van die Ring van die NG Kerk, Bloemfontein and Another 1952 (2) SA 83 (O)
Department of Correctional Services & another and Another v Police and Prisons Civil Rights Union (POPCRU) and Others 2013 (4) SA 176 (SCA)
Dlamini and Another v Joosten And Others 2006 (3) SA 342 (SCA)
Ex Parte Chairperson of the Constitutional Assembly: In re Certification of the Amended Text of the Constitution of the Republic of South Africa, 1996 1997 (2) SA 97 (CC)
Ex Parte Johannesburg Congregation of the Apostolic Church 1968 (3) SA 377 (W)

Fortuin v Church of Christ Mission of the Republic of South Africa (3626/15) [2016] ZAECPEHC 18

Garden Cities Incorporated Association Not For Gain v Northpine Islamic Society 1999 2 SA 268 (C)

Gauteng Provincial Legislature In re: Gauteng School Education Bill of 1995 1996 (3) SA 165

Gold Circle (Pty) Ltd v Premier, KwaZulu-Natal 2005 4 SA 402 (D)

Govender v Ragavayah NO and Others 2009 (3) SA 178 (D)

Grundling v Van Rensburg NO 1984 (3) SA 207 (W)

Harksen v Lane NO and Others 1998 (1) SA 300

Hartman v Chairman, Board for Religious Objection, and others 1987 (1) SA 922 (O)

Hasan and Chaush v Bulgaria (2002) 34 EHRR 554

Hasan and Chaush v Bulgaria App. No. 30985/96 62 (2000)

Hay v B 2003 (3) SA 492 (W)

Hennessey v Durban Town Council 1923 NPD 317

Holy Synod of the Bulgarian Orthodox Church (Metropolitan Inokentiy) v Bulgaria, nos 412/03 and 35677/04 (2009)

In re Certification of the Constitution of the Republic of South Africa 1996, 1996 (10) BCLR 1253 (CC)

Islamic Unity Convention v Independent Broadcasting Authority and Others (2002 (4) SA 294

Jamiat Ul-Ulama of Transvaal v Johncom Media Investment Ltd and Others (1127/06) [2006] ZAGPHC 12 (3 February 2006)

Jamile v African Congregational Church 1971 SA 836 (D)

Kievits Kroon Country Estate (Pty) Ltd v Mmoledi 2014 (1) SA 585 (SCA)

Leela Förderkreis eV v Germany, no 58911/01 (2008)

Life Healthcare Group (Pty) Ltd and Another v JMS (as parent and guardian of the infant child MT) and Another (34758/2014) [2014] ZAGPJHC 299 (20 October 2014)

Macdonald v Free Presbyterian Church of Scotland [2010] UKEAT S/0034/09/ BI (10 February 2010)

Macdonald v Free Presbyterian Church of Scotland 2009 ET S/11071 (28 May 2009)

Malebjoe v Bantu Methodist Church of South Africa 1957 (4) SA 465 (W)

Manoussakis v Greece 1996-IV Eur. Ct. H.R 1346

MEC for Education: KwaZulu-Natal and Others v Pillay 2008 (1) SA 474 (CC)

Metropolitan Church of Bessarabia and others v Moldova 45701/99 [2001] ECHR 860 (13 December 2001)

Minister of Education & Another v Syfrets Trust Ltd NO & Another 2006 (4) SA 25 (CC)

Minister of Home Affairs v Fourie; Lesbian and Gay Equality Project v Minister of Home Affairs 2006 (1) SA 524 (CC)

Moloi v St John Apostolic Faith Mission 1954 (3) SA 940 (T)

Moosa N.O. and Others v Minister of Justice and Correctional Services and Others 2018 (5) SA 13 (CC)

Morrison v Standard Building Society 1932 AD 229

Moscow Branch of the Salvation Army v Russia, no 72881/01 (2006)
National Coalition for Gay and Lesbian Equality v Minister of Justice 1999 (1) SA 6 (CC)
National Sugar Refining and Allied Industries Union obo Mngomezulu v Tongaat Hulett Sugar Ltd (Darnall) [2016] 11 BALR 1172 (NBCSMRI)
Nederduitse Gereformeerde Kerk in Afrika (OVS) en Nederduitse Gereformeerde Kerk in Afrika
(Phororo) v Verenigende Gereformeerde Kerk in Suider-Afrika 1999 (2) SA 156 (SCA)
Nhlabathi and Others v Fick [2003] 2 All SA 323 (LCC)
Nkosi and Another v Bührmann 2002 1 SA 372 (SCA)
Obergefell v. Hodges, 576 US (2015)
Odendaal v Kerkraad van die Gemeente Bloemfontein-Wes van die NG Kerk in OVS en Andere 1960 (1) SA 160 (O)
Organisasie vir Godsdienste-Onderrig en Demokrasie v Laerskool Randhart and Others 2017 (6) SA 129 (GJ)
Peach & Co v The Jewish Congregation of Johannesburg 1894 SAR 345
Prenn v Simmonds [1971] 3 All ER 237 (HL) 239J
Prince v President of the Law Society, Cape of Good Hope 1998 (8) BCLR 976 (C)
Prince v President, Cape Law Society 2000 (3) SA 845 (SCA)
Prince v President, Cape Law Society and Others 2002 (2) SA 794 (CC)
R v Webb 1934 AD 493
Radebe and Others v Principal of Leseding Technical School and Others (1821/2013) [2013] ZAFSHC 111 (30 May 2013)
Regina v Chieff Rabbi of the United Hebrew Congregations of Great Britain and the Commonwealth, ex parte Wachmann (1992) 1 WLR 1036 (QB)
Religionsgemeinschaft der Zeugen Jehovahs v Austria, no 40825/98 (2008)
Rescue Committee Dutch Reformed Church v Mertheze 1926 CPD 298
Roberts v United States Jaycees 468 US 609 (1984)
Ryland v Edros 1997 (2) SA 690 (C); *Khan v Khan* 2005 (2) SA 272 (T)
S v Färber 1985 (1) SA 340 (O)
S v Lawrence; S v Negal; S v Solberg 1997 10 BCLR 1348 (CC); 1997 2 SACR 540 (CC)
SACTWU v Berg River Textiles [2012] JOL 28114 (LC)
Schreuder v Nederduitse Gereformeerde Kerk Wilgespruit & andere 1999 BLLR 713 (LC)
Seedat's Executors v The Master (Natal) 1917 AD 302
Shillings CC v Cronje 1988 (2) SA 402 (A)
Singh v Ramparsad 2007 (3) SA 445 (DCLD)
Smit NO and Others v King Goodwill Zwelithini Kabhekuzulu and Others (10237/2009) [2009]
ZAKZPHC 75 (4 December 2009)
South African Human Rights Commission obo South African Jewish Board of Deputies v Masuku and Another 2018 (3) SA 291 (GJ)
Strydom v Nederduitse Gereformeerde Gemeente Moreleta Park 2009 4 SA 510 (T)

Supreme Holy Council of the Muslim Community v Bulgaria, no 39023/97 (2004)
Svyato-Mykhaylviska Parafi ya v Ukraine, no 77703/01 (2007)
Taylor v Kurstag 2005 (1) SA 362 (W)
The Nederduitsche Hervormde Church v The Nederduitsche Hervormde of Gereformeerde Church 1893 CLJ 327
Theron v Ring van Wellington van die NG Sendingkerk in Suid-Afrika 1976 (2) SA 1 (SCA)
Turner v Jockey Club of South Africa 1974 (3) SA 633 (SCA)
Twelve Apostle Church in Christ and Another v Twelve Apostle Church in Christ and Another (AR 488/2009) [2010] ZAKZPHC 5 (15 February 2010)
United Methodist Church of South Africa v Sokufundumala 1989 (4) SA 1055 (O)
Universal Church of the Kingdom of God v Myeni and Others (DA 3/14) [2015] ZALAC 31 (28 July 2015)
Van Heerden v Minister of Finance 2004 6 SA 121 (CC)
Van Loggerenberg and another v 94.7 Highveld Stereo 2004 (5) BCLR 561 (BCT)
Venter v Den Kerkeraad der Gereformeerde Kerk te Bethulie 1879 OVS 4
Volks NO v Robinson and Others 2005 (5) BCLR 446 (CC)
Wagenaar v United Reformed Church SA [2005] 1 BALR 127 (CCMA)
Webb & Co Ltd v Northern Rifles 1908 TS 462
Wittman v Deutscher Schulverein 1998 (4) SA 423 (T)
Women's Legal Centre Trust v President of the Republic of South Africa and Others, Faro v Bignham N.O. and Others, Esau v Esau and Others (22481/2014, 4466/2013, 13877/2015) [2018] ZAWCHC 109 (31 August 2018)
Yiba and Others v African Gospel Church 1999 (2) SA 949 (C)

Part 1

1 Introduction and Background

Church and state relationship in South Africa

Brief historical overview

In South Africa, between 1652 and 1795, the government followed a Constantinian model in respect of the relationship between church and state. This approach focused not only on government protection of the church, but also on government control over the church. As pointed out by Hiemstra:[1]

> The basic structure proposed by the Constantinian model is that political authorities are understood to be dominant over church authorities. Firstly, this means political authorities often assist, influence, and sometimes fully control church authority. Secondly, the state's control includes advancing and supporting 'true religion' through the use of its coercive power.

Although there is no state religion established by law in South Africa, it has not always been the case. In 1795, the Cape came under the control of the British and the occupation continued until 1803 when the Batavian Republic took control of the Cape Colony in 1803 until 1806. JA de Mist was appointed the Commissioner-General and with his publication of the 'Church Order of the Mist', he was of the view that no civilised society could exist without religion.[2] According to section 4 of the *Provisioneele Kerken-Orde voor de Bataafsche Volksplanting aan de Kaap de Goede Hoop* of 1804 (Church Order of 25 July 1804), De Mist decreed that 'no ecclesiastical bodies other than those that operated in the Cape when the Batavian Republic took control of the colony in 1803 would be permitted to conduct religious ceremonies or hold public gatherings'.[3] Although De Mist saw it as the government's duty to protect church associations, it could only be achieved

1 JL Hiemstra 'Church, State and the Kingdom of God, an Overview' *REC Focus, Quarterly Journal from the REC Commissions* (2005) *5(2)* 28.
2 P Coertzen 'The Position of Churches in South Africa under a New Constitution' in H Warnink (ed) *Legal Position of Churches* (2001) 37–38.
3 J Van der Vyver 'Religion' in WA Joubert and TJ Scott (eds) The Law of South Africa (2003) *23(1)* para 149.

within the boundaries of firm and just principles based on law and order. The effect of the Church Order of De Mist was in essence not the separation of church and state, but rather the total control of the state over the church.[4] According to Jooste,[5] this had the further effect that the church was seen as a mere voluntary association. A further shift in control and the relationship between church and state came in 1806, when the Cape Colony again was under British control. On 22 July 1843, the Dutch Reformed Church submitted Ordinance 7 of 1843 to the Legislative Council for consideration. This Ordinance was seen as a 'code of law more adapted to the present circumstances of the Church and the Colony, than those comprised in the Church Ordinance of Commissioner-General De Mist'.[6]

Section 8 of the Ordinance was of particular importance for the future position of the church, stating that 'all church laws and regulations will legally be seen as the laws of a mere *voluntary association*, which are legally binding only on them who voluntary subject themselves to the said laws and regulations' [own emphasis]. In a report by Sir William Porter in relation to this Ordinance, the views were expressed even more explicitly:

> The Church laws are to be viewed as the rules of a mere voluntary association. It is not said, indeed that the D.R. Church is such a mere voluntary association; a position which her members would deny and which it would have been improper to lay down. But to declare that her legislation shall be judged of just as if she were such an association, is, I conceive a sound principle and with a legislation so limited, she cannot possibly do harm.[7]

The influence of English law also made its way into the decisions of the courts. In the 1922 case of *Bredell v Pienaar*,[8] the Dutch Reformed Church was described by Watermeyer J as a voluntary association with reference to section 8 of the subsequently repealed Dutch Reformed Church of South Africa Ordinance 7 of 1843 (Cape) and the rules and regulations of the church were thus that of a voluntary association.[9] The period up and until 1994 (including the 1910 Union of South Africa; the period of National Party control with its accompanying 'apartheid' policies and the birth of the Republic in 1960), was still characterised by the earlier Constantinian approach to a greater or lesser degree. Churches and religious organisations knew no real freedom of religion during these periods.[10]

4 Coertzen *The Position of Churches* 37–38.
5 JP Jooste *Die Geskiedenis van die Gereformeerde Kerk in Suid-Afrika, 1859–1959* (1959) 15.
6 P Coertzen *The Position of Churches* 39.
7 FE O'Brien Geldenhuys *Die Regsposisie van Kerkraad, Ring en Sinode onder die Gereformeerde Stelsel van Kerkregering soos toegepas in die Gefedereerde Ned Geref Kerke in Suid-Afrika* (1951) 348.
8 *Bredell v Pienaar* 1922 CPD 578, 581.
9 Van der Vyver The Law of South Africa para 150–151.
10 P Coertzen 'Grappling with Religious Differences' *Brigham Young University Law Review* (2008) 785–788.

A new approach – the constitutionally protected right to freedom of religion

Constitutional change in South Africa took effect on 27 April 1994, when an interim constitution came into force. This was a transitional constitution, aimed at setting out the procedures for the negotiation of a final constitution. After lengthy negotiations, the Constitutional Assembly adopted the final constitution on 8 May 1996, which was certified by the Constitutional Court and signed into law on 4 February 1997. In 1990, during a National Inter-Faith Conference, South African religious groupings got together and adopted a Declaration on Religious Rights and Responsibilities, explaining in concrete terms what the right to freedom of religion meant for religious believers.[11] A compromise between a too strict separation between church and state and an approach of endorsing or favouring one religion over others was evident in the drafting of sections 15 and 31 of the Constitution. It does not prevent the state from recognising or supporting religion, but in addition requires the state to treat religions equally. Read together, these two provisions entrench the right of individuals and religious communities to exercise their religion freely. These two provisions have been described as 'complementary and mutually supportive spheres'.[12]

In the South African context, Currie and De Waal[13] argue that the debate about the meaning of 'religion' is unnecessary, because section 15 of the Constitution, apart from protecting the right to freedom of religion, also protects the rights to freedom of conscience, thought, belief and opinion. Section 15 protects a wide range of world-views, including agnosticism and atheism or the freedom to reject any religious beliefs. The South African Constitutional Court in *National Coalition for Gay and Lesbian Equality v Minister of Justice*[14] observed: 'Religious practices are protected because they are considered to be central to human identity and hence to human dignity'.[15] Similarly, in *Christian Education South Africa v Minister of Education*[16] the same court described the practice of religion as one of the hallmarks of an open, democratic and free society that awakens the 'concepts of self-worth and human dignity which form the cornerstone of human rights'.

Those who advocated for religious freedom called for both religious tolerance as well as a secular state which did not give preference to one particular religion over others. According to Currie and De Waal,[17] the interpretation of the right to freedom of religion still reflects its historical origins in that it is interpreted in relation to the extent to which the state recognises a religion and how it provides for the freedom to exercise or how it establishes that religion. The drafters of the

11 I Currie and J De Waal *The Bill of Rights Handbook* 6 ed (2013) 315.
12 Currie and De Waal *The Bill of Rights Handbook* 316.
13 Currie and De Waal *The Bill of Rights Handbook* 316.
14 *National Coalition for Gay and Lesbian Equality v Minister of Justice* 1999 (1) SA 6 (CC).
15 *National Coalition* para 26.
16 *Christian Education South Africa v Minister of Education* 2000 (4) SA 757 (CC) para 36.
17 Currie and De Waal *The Bill of Rights Handbook* 315.

Constitution was aware of the dangers associated with a too strict separation between church and state, but similarly one that is too close to the church, as was the case during the apartheid regime. Particularly in relation to religion and religious diversity, the Constitution has been described as one of 'profound toleration and accommodation'.[18] Various provisions in the Constitution support this view and the Constitutional Court, through its decisions, has emphasised the important role of religion, not only in society, but also the importance for the state as a component of our constitutional democracy.

Section 15 of the Constitution provides that everyone has the right to freedom of conscience, religion, thought, belief and opinion. However, individuals and community may not exercise the right in a manner inconsistent with the other provisions of the Bill of Rights. Section 15 includes different aspects of religious freedom, such as the freedom of religious choice, freedom of religious observance, freedom of religious teaching and freedom to propagate a religion.[19] The right to freedom of religious choice is an individual right and does not relate to the practice of religion in community with others. The other components associated with section 15 may receive additional protection under section 31 of the Constitution. Section 31 provides that persons belonging to cultural, religious or linguistic communities may not be denied the right, with other members of that community, to enjoy their culture, practise their religion and use their language, and to form, join or maintain cultural, religious and linguistic associations and other organs of civil society, also including indigenous communities. However, the observance of these religious rights must relate to the practice of a religion in community with other practitioners or believers. According to Currie and De Waal,[20] this will exclude atheism and agnosticism, since those beliefs are only held by individual believers or non-believers and are not communally practised.

Religious institutions as juristic persons are afforded numerous rights under the Bill of Rights,[21] including the right to freedom religion (section 15); freedom of assembly (section 17); freedom of association (section 18); the right to self-determination (sections 31 and 235). The Constitution also makes provision for a Commission for the Promotion and Protection of the Rights of Cultural, Religious and Linguistic Communities (sections 181 (1)(c) and 185–186). The Constitution also envisaged the establishment of a Pan South African Language Board charged, inter alia, with promoting and ensuring respect for languages used for religious purposes in South Africa, such as Arabic, Hebrew, Sanskrit and others (section 6(5)(b)(ii)). Unfortunately it has been reported in 2016 that this constitutionally mandated Board, which was established in 1996, has 'done little to fulfil its mandate. So much so that the Minister of Arts and Culture dissolved the

18 J Van der Vyver 'Equality and Sovereignty of Religious Institutions: A South African Perspective' *Santa Clara Journal of International Law* (2012) *10(1)* 157.

19 See Currie and De Waal *Bill of Rights Handbook* 633.

20 Currie and De Waal *Bill of Rights Handbook* 633.

21 Section 8(4).

board in January after a damning report by the Auditor-General that suggests wide-scale corruption and mismanagement'.[22]

According to Van der Vyver,[23] church and state relations also implicate constitutional provision associated with the establishment of religion, including the reference to deity (the Preamble[24] and Schedule 2[25]); freedom of religion, belief and opinion (section 15(1)); religious observances in state and state-aided institutions (section 15(2)), and the establishment of parochial schools (sections 29(3) and (4)); marriages concluded under a system of religion (section 15(3)); equality before the law and equal protection and benefit of the law (sections 9(1) and (2)), and non-discrimination on ground of religion (sections 9(3)-(5)); unlawful conduct in the name of religious beliefs; and resolution of legal disputes that involve doctrinal issues. Various other rights relate to religion in some way or other: the right to freedom of expression (section 16); freedom of movement (section 21); the rights to assemble, demonstrate, picket and present petitions (section 17); and numerous other rights.

Section 9 of the Constitution further provides for the right to equality before the law and the right to equal protection and benefit of the law, and non-discrimination on various grounds, including ethnic or social origin and culture. Section 9(1) of the Constitution, guaranteeing everyone's equality before and equal protection and benefit of the law, is also significant. Read with section 9(3), it explicitly prohibits unfair discrimination against anyone on the grounds of, among others, religion, conscience and belief. 'Equality' also includes the equal treatment of minority religions and their adherents. In order to give effect to section 9(4) of the Constitution, the South African Parliament passed the Promotion of Equality and Prevention of Unfair Discrimination Act of 2000 (PEPUDA). Indigenous people and communities may therefore not be discriminated against on basis of race, culture, religion or any of the grounds envisaged in section 9(3) of the Constitution. Section 7(2) of the Constitution further makes it clear that the state must not only respect and protect the rights in the Bill of Rights, but also promote and fulfil them. It further emphasises the relevance of customary law, in that the Bill of Rights does not deny the existence of any other rights or freedoms that are recognised or conferred by common law, customary law or legislation, to the extent that they are consistent with the Bill.[26] When interpreting the Bill of Rights, a court must also promote the values that underlie an open and democratic society based on human dignity, equality and freedom, and must consider international law.[27]

22 M Thamm 'Multilingualism: Pan South African Language Board going Nowhere Slowly, Haemorrhaging Millions' *Daily Maverick* (25 February 2016).

23 J Van der Vyver 'Constitutional Perspective of Church-State Relations in South Africa' *Brigham Young University Law Review* (2001) *1999(2)* 649.

24 'May God protect our people… God bless South Africa'.

25 In relation to an oath – 'So help me God'.

26 Constitution of the Republic of South Africa, 1996, section 39(3).

27 Constitution of the Republic of South Africa, 1996, section 39(1).

Section 234 provides that 'in order to deepen the culture of democracy established by the Constitution, Parliament may adopt Charters of Rights consistent with the provisions of the Constitution'. Any such charter of rights will then have the force of law. The Constitution envisages that the rights in the Constitution may be further extended, supplemented and given content by way of such additional charters. The South African Charter of Religious Rights and Freedoms (SACRRF) is a document that defines the freedoms, rights, responsibilities and relationship between the 'state' of South Africa and her citizens concerning religious belief.[28] The Charter expresses what freedom of religion means to those of religious belief and religious organisations within a South African context and the daily rights, responsibilities and freedoms that are associated with this right. These include the right to gather in community to observe religious belief, freedom of expression regarding religion, the right of citizens to make choices according to their convictions, the right to change their faith, the right to be educated in their religion, the right to educate their children in accordance with their philosophical and religious convictions, and the right to refuse to perform certain duties or assist in activities that violate their religious beliefs.

The above Charter was first signed at a public ceremony in Johannesburg on 21 October 2010, and signatories continue to be added to the open document. Signatories include religious groups and organisations, human rights organisations, legal and academic entities and media bodies. If passed into law, the charter will ensure that the rights of religious believers are clearly defined and protected under the law of South Africa. The Charter may be used as a legal instrument even as the current climate of understanding and tolerance between government and religion may alter. After the public signing of the SACRRF, a Council for the Protection and Promotion of Religious Rights and Freedoms was established to oversee the process of the Charter being formally enacted into South African law. The passing of the SACRRF into law will mean that religious believers have legal impartiality and protection to practise all elements of religious belief under the Constitution. The SACRRF is the first public charter to be developed under section 234 of the Constitution of South Africa.[29] The Charter gives content to the right to freedom of religion and is therefore instrumental in regulating the relationship between church (religion) and state in South Africa.

Noteworthy in this provision is the reference to the right to change one's religion or belief, and this section was therefore included in sections 1 and 2 of the Religious Charter.[30] In general, the description of freedom of religion in the

28 The South African Charter of Religious Rights and Freedoms, Explanatory notes on the Charter, 16 May 2016, 4. Online at: www.crlcommission.org.za/docs/sacrrf.pdf [Accessed: 9 November 2016].

29 See further Charter 4–5.

30 1. Every person (which includes an institution) has the right to believe according to their own religious or philosophical beliefs or convictions, and to choose which faith, worldview, religion, or religious institution to subscribe to, affiliate with or belong to. 2. No person may be forced to believe, what to believe or what not to believe, or to act against their convictions.

South African Constitution is quite basic compared to the description in both the Universal Declaration of Human Rights[31] and the Universal Declaration.[32] It places a huge responsibility on both religious communities as well as the courts to interpret and give content to this right.

Section 15 of the Constitution further includes section 15(2)[33] and section 15 (3).[34] According to Du Plessis,[35] the mere inclusion of these two provisions, in particular section 15(2):

> contradicts any depiction of the South African State as a secular State. South Africa is rather a religion-neutral State whose constitutional provisions on the right to religious freedom sustain religion without preferring any particular faith or denomination.[36]

Section 15(2) requires that any religious observances at state or state-aided institutions, must be conducted on an equitable basis and attendance should be free and voluntary. State or state-aided institutions include institutions such as schools, hospitals, prisons and so forth. Relevant to section 15(2) of the Constitution is section 29(3) that provides for the right to establish and maintain, at their own expense, independent educational institutions, provided that they do not discriminate on the basis of race, are registered with the state and maintain standards that are not inferior to standards at comparable public. This can include religious schools.[37] Section 15(2) has a significant impact on the relationship between state and church, more particularly, the state and religious institutions in South Africa. This seems to be quite problematic for religious institutions in South Africa, since appropriate legislation and policies are made by public authorities and could potentially infringe the right to freedom of religion of religious institutions. These

2.1. Every person has the right to change their faith, religion, convictions or religious institution, or to form a new religious community or religious institution.

31 Universal Declaration of Human Rights, 10 December 1948, 217A (III)..

32 Council of Europe, European Convention for the Protection of Human Rights and Fundamental Freedoms.

33 (2) Religious observances may be conducted at state or state-aided institutions, provided that-
(a) those observances follow rules made by the appropriate public authorities;
(b) they are conducted on an equitable basis; and
(c) attendance at them is free and voluntary.

34 (3) (a) This section does not prevent legislation recognising-
(i) marriages concluded under any tradition, or a system of religious, personal or
(ii) systems of personal and family law under any tradition, or adhered to by persons professing a particular religion.

35 LM du Plessis 'Current Problems Concerning Church and State Relationships and Religious Freedom in South Africa. The Viewpoint of a Constitutional Lawyer' in H Warnink (ed) *Legal Position of Churches and Church Autonomy* (2001) *19* and further.

36 See further J Van der Vyver 'Godsdiensvryheid: Sekularisasie of Politieke Neutraliteit?' *Woord en Daad* (2000) 3–5.

37 See for more detail Chapter 6 on 'Religion in education'.

concerns have therefore been taken up by communities and have found their way into the Charter of Religious Rights.[38]

Any constitutional right, including the right to freedom of religion, can however be limited in accordance with section 36 of the Constitution (the limitation clause). The section will assess whether any limitation is reasonable and justifiable in an open and democratic society based on human dignity, equality and freedom, by taking into account certain factors, such as the nature of the right; the importance of the purpose of the limitation; the nature and extent of the limitation; the relation between the limitation and its purpose; and less restrictive means to achieve the purpose.[39] Section 8(2) of the Bill of Rights further provides for the horizontal application of the Bill of Rights in appropriate circumstances. Section 8 (4) states that a juristic person (including a religious organisation) is entitled to the rights in the Bill of Rights to the extent required by the nature of the rights and the nature of that juristic person. In accordance with our common law, and explained in the next chapter, religious organisations are seen as a juristic person. Included in this definition are all associations, societies, church denominations and locally organised congregations. Although freedom of religion is by its very nature an individual right, it can be exercised either individually or in community with others. Section 15, read together with section 31 of the Constitution, entrenches an individual right to freedom of religion as well as the collective right to freedom of religion. The collective aspect of the right to freedom of religion will be discussed in more detail in Chapter 3.

It is safe to say that South African society is a society with no strict secular character, but rather a society where recognition is given to the wide variety of

38 9. Every religious institution has the right to institutional freedom of religion.
9.1 Every religious institution has the right (a) to determine its own confessions, doctrines and ordinances, (b) to decide for itself in all matters regarding its doctrines and ordinances, and (c) in accordance with the principles of tolerance, fairness, openness and accountability to regulate its own internal affairs, including organisational structures and procedures, the ordination, conditions of service, discipline and dismissal of office-bearers and members, the appointment, conditions of employment towards and members, the appointment, conditions of employment and dismissal of employees and volunteers, and membership requirements.
9.2 Every religious institution is recognised and protected as an institution that has authority over its own affairs, and towards which the state, through its governing institutions, is responsible for just, constructive and impartial government in the interest of everybody.
9.3 The state, including the judiciary, must respect the authority of every religious institution over its own affairs, and may not regulate or prescribe matters of doctrine and ordinances.
9.4 The confidentiality of the internal affairs and communications of a religious institution must be respected. The privileged nature of any religious communication that has been made with an expectation of confidentiality must be respected insofar as the interest of justice permits.
9.5 Every religious institution is subject to the law of the land A religious institution must be able to justify any non-observance of a law resulting from the exercise of the rights in this Charter.

39 The limitation of rights will be discussed in more detail in Chapter 4.

religious traditions and space in which they can interact and express their different religious beliefs and practices, even in the public sphere. This is also a view supported by the European Court, as expressed in the case of *Serif v Greece*:[40]

> Although the Court recognises that it is possible that tension is created in situations where a religious or any other community becomes divided, it considers that this is one of the unavoidable consequences of pluralism. The role of the authorities in such circumstances is not to remove the cause of tension by eliminating pluralism, but to ensure that the competing groups tolerate each other.

This approach is further supported and confirmed by the South African Government in its 2003 National Policy on Religion in Education. In the foreword to this policy it is explicitly stated that South Africa does not have a state religion and confirms the fact that 'our country is not a secular state where there is a very strict separation between religion and the state'. The policy recognises the rich and diverse religious heritage of South Africa and adopts a 'cooperative model that accepts our rich heritage and the possibility of creative inter-action between schools and faith whilst, protecting our young people from religious discrimination or coercion'.

The introduction to the policy outlines four different models for structuring the relationship between religion and the state in South Africa. The first model is based on the theocratic model, where the state identifies or associates with only one particular religion. Another model is a form of repressionist model. In this model, the state would seek to limit or even eliminate religion from the public sphere, which would go against a pluralistic and religiously active society such as South Africa. Many countries, such as France, adopted another model, one where there is strict neutrality or impartiality towards all religions or religious views. Such a country is neither religious nor anti-religious and there is a strict separation between the religious and the secular spheres. Often no form of religious expression is allowed in the public sphere. This approach has been criticised as follows:

> Drawing strict separation between religion and the secular state is extremely difficult to implement in practice, since there is considerable interchange between religion and public life. Furthermore, a strict separation between the two spheres of religion and state is not desirable, since without the commitment and engagement of religious bodies it is difficult to see us improving the quality of life of all our people.[41]

40 J Murdoch *Freedom of Thought, Conscience and Religion. A Guide to the Implementation of Article 9 of the European Convention of Human Rights. Human Rights Handbook. No 9* (2007) 44.

41 Introduction to the 2003 *National Policy on Religion in Education.*

In the preferred cooperative model, there is interaction and cooperation between the state and religion. In line with section 7(2) of the Constitution, the state is expected not only to respect and protect the rights in the Bill of Rights, but also to promote and fulfil them. Bilchitz and Williams[42] are in favour of a model of 'positive recognition', rather than mere accommodation. Some features of this model include equal worth of individuals, regardless of their differences and that individuals must be protected from coercion by the state. In this model the state must create enabling conditions for the positive expression of identity, without necessarily constructing religious structures for religious communities, but creating a space where people and communities can do so for themselves. The state should refrain from imposing a separation between itself and religion, and must allow for religion to enter the public domain, subject to the requirement that it must be done on an equal basis and show equal respect for the rights of all religious followers. This means that certain accommodation, advantages and exemptions may be conferred on some groups as long as it is fair and not to the disadvantage of others. Within this model, neutrality is interpreted as equal recognition of all religions by the state and not a complete withdrawal of religion from the public sphere.

Conclusion

From the discussion above it is quite clear that the South African Constitution never envisioned an absolute separation between the state and religion. It does not prohibit people from any form of religious practices in the public sphere, because that will clearly constitute an infringement of their right to religious freedom, equality and human dignity. The Constitution creates a framework for accommodating rather than suppressing religion and religious differences. The Constitutional Court has interpreted the right to religious freedom to extend to the public domain, rejecting the idea that there should be no interaction between the state and religion. This will be emphasised further in the rest of the chapters through the various examples and judgments of the South African courts. Various authors have also argued that the Constitution envisioned an accommodation model where the state and religious communities work together to ensure that everyone is afforded the right to practise their religion without infringing on the rights of others.[43] A cooperative model for structuring the relationship between religion and the state in South Africa combines 'constitutional separation and mutual recognition'[44] and is the preferred model for a democratic and pluralistic

42 D Bilchitz and A Williams 'Religion and the Public Sphere: Towards a Model that Positively Recognises Diversity' *South African Journal of Human Rights* (2012) *28* 170.

43 LM du Plessis 'Freedom of or Freedom from Religion? An Overview of Issues Pertinent to the Constitutional Protection of Religious Rights and Freedoms in the New South Africa' *Brigham Young University Law Review* (2001) 450; Bilchitz and Williams 2012 South African Journal on Human Rights 164.

44 2003 *National Policy on Religion in Education* para 4.

society like South Africa. The South African Constitution recognises our pluralistic society where people hold very diverse convictions and beliefs. This calls for an accommodative approach towards people's differing beliefs, as recently expressed and confirmed by the court in the case of *Organisasie vir Godsdienste-Onderrig en Demokrasie v Laerskool Randhart*:[45]

> This fits a twin theme often raised during argument, and accepted by all, namely first, that we are not a secular State and, second, that in this country our diversity is celebrated, not tolerated.

Bibliography

Bilchitz D and A Williams 'Religion and the Public Sphere: Towards a Model that Positively Recognises Diversity' *South African Journal on Human Rights* (2012) 28146.

Coertzen P 'The Position of Churches in South Africa under a New Constitution' in H Warnink (ed) *Legal Position of Churches* (2001) 37–38.

Coertzen P 'Grappling with Religious Differences' *Brigham Young University Law Review* (2008) 3785–788.

Council of Europe, European Convention for the Protection of Human Rights and Fundamental Freedoms, as amended, 4 November 1950.

Currie I and J de Waal *The Bill of Rights Handbook* 6 ed (2013) Cape Town: Juta.

Du Plessis LM 'Current Problems Concerning Church and State Relationships and Religious Freedom in South Africa. The Viewpoint of a Constitutional Lawyer' in H Warnink (ed) *Legal Position of Churches and Church Autonomy* (2001) 13–33Leuven: Peeters.

Du Plessis LM 'Freedom of or Freedom from Religion? An Overview of Issues Pertinent to the Constitutional Protection of Religious Rights and Freedoms in the New South Africa' *Brigham Young University Law Review* (2001) 2439–466.

Hiemstra JL 'Church, State and the Kingdom of God, an Overview' *REC Focus, Quarterly Journal from the REC Commissions* (2005) 5(2) 3–49.

Jooste JP *Die geskiedenis van die Gereformeerde Kerk in Suid-Afrika, 1859–1959* (1959) Potchefstroom: Sinode Gereformeerde Kerk in Suid-Afrika.

Murdoch J *Freedom of Thought, Conscience and Religion. A Guide to the Implementation of Article 9 of the European Convention of Human Rights. Human Rights Handbook. No 9* (2007) Strasbourg: European Council.

National Policy on Religion and Education. 2003. Online at: https://www.gov.za/documents/national-policy-religion-and-education

O'Brien Geldenhuys FE *Die Regsposisie van Kerkraad, Ring en Sinode onder die Gereformeerde stelsel van Kerkregering soos toegepas in die Gefedereerde Ned Geref Kerke in Suid-Afrika* (1951) Pretoria: Van Schaik.

Thamm M 'Multilingualism: Pan South African Language Board going Nowhere Slowly, Haemorrhaging Millions' *Daily Maverick* (25 February 2016).

United Nations General Assembly, Universal Declaration of Human Rights, 10 December 1948, 217A (III).

45 *Organisasie vir Godsdienste-Onderrig en Demokrasie v Laerskool Randhart and Others* 2017 (6) SA 129 (GJ) para 95.

Van der Vyver J 'Godsdiensvryheid: Sekularisasie of Politieke Neutraliteit?' *Woord en Daad* (2000) Somer 3–5.

Van der Vyver J 'Constitutional Perspective of Church-State Relations in South Africa' *Brigham Young University Law Review* (2001) 1999(2) 635–673.

Van der Vyver J 'Religion' in WA Joubert and TJ Scott (eds) *The Law of South Africa* (2003) 23:141–163Durban: Butterworths.

Van der Vyver, J. 2012. 'Equality and Sovereignty of Religious Institutions: A South African Perspective' *Santa Clara Journal of International Law* (2012) 10(1) 147–169.

2 The nature and legal status of religious institutions

Introduction

Religious pluralism pre-supposes various definitions and interpretations of 'religion' and 'the scope of religious pluralism … alone has resulted in such a multiplicity and diversity of ideas about what is a "religion" or a "religious belief" that no simple formula seems able to accommodate them all'.[1] This view equally applies to the interpretation of 'religious organisation'. As expressed by Cohen[2] as follows:

> The question is: what is a religious institution? Is it just a church or also a monastery or a hospital? Is it just a synagogue or also a private mikve (ritual pool) or yeshiva (Talmudic academy)? Is it a church library, a church-run women's club? What about other Christian denominations, the Muslims, the Druze and Bahai? There is no end to it. In the 'Holy Land', everything is someone's religious institution.

For religious organisations to be able to exercise their rights and obligations in governing their internal affairs, it is important to give an overview of the meaning and status of religious organisations for the purposes of this discussion and to outline some important features. The last section will briefly outline some implications for religious institutions as juristic persons, particularly in relation to religious disputes.

The nature and meaning of 'religious organisation'

Louche et al[3] confirm that what constitutes a religious organisation is not in itself self-evident. Even within a particular religion, the legal and organisational

1 Quoted from JMT Labuschagne 'Die Begrip "Godsdiens" in Godsdiensvryheid: 'n Bewussynsantropologiese Ekskursie na die Evolusiekern van die Reg' *De Jure Law Journal* (1997) 118–119.

2 R Cohen 'Israel and the Holy See Negotiate: A Case Study in Diplomacy Across Religions' *The Hague Journal of Diplomacy* (2010) *5(3)* 227.

3 C Louche, D Arenas and KC van Cranenburgh 'From Preaching to Investing: Attitudes of Religious Organisations Towards Responsible Investment' *Journal of Business Ethics* (2012) *110(3)* 303.

structure may vary. Most countries provide for a specific organisational structure for religious organisations, the so-called *sui generis* religious organisation, whether referred to as a church, organisation, association or the like. Such an organisation is not only regarded and observed as being of a religious nature, but, according to Potz and Wieshaider,[4] it can lay claim to 'the guaranteed autonomy to freely administer its internal affairs' and:

> it is most likely linked with additional rights which are not necessarily considered to be the core of the exercise of religion, but very often go together as a result of co-operation between the State and the religious community in coping with societal challenges.

A religious community is described as:

> A group of people who follow a particular system of belief, morality and worship, either in recognition of a divine being, or in the pursuit of spiritual development, or in the expression of a sense of belonging through social custom and ritual.[5]

Rivers[6] uses the term 'organized religions' to describe the law as it applies to 'religious organizations', religious associations, religious bodies and the like. Religious organisations are further described as 'mediating structures' according to Berger and Neuhaus,[7] referring to institutions that stand between the individual and his or her private life, and institutions of public life, helping the individual to mediate between the private and the public spheres.

The meaning of 'religion' is also important for purposes of the collective right to freedom of religion in determining when an organisation will be treated as 'religious' in order to qualify for the protection afforded by the Constitution. For reasons of practicality and to empower the courts to efficiently deal with religious disputes, Van der Schyff[8] rightly proposes a functional, rather than a purely

4 R Potz and W Wieshaider 'Religious Entities as Legal Persons – Parts of Western and Central Europe' in L Friedner *Churches and Other Religious Organisations as Legal Persons* (2007) 30.

5 A South African Declaration on Religious Rights and Responsibilities, accepted and assented to during a National Inter-religious Conference, held in November 1992 under the auspices of the South African Chapter of the World Conference on Religion and Peace (WCRP-SA). See further LM du Plessis 'Current Problems Concerning Church and State Relationships and Religious Freedom in South Africa. The Viewpoint of a Constitutional Lawyer' in H Warnink (ed) *Legal Position of Churches and Church Autonomy* (2001)*15* and further.

6 J Rivers *The Law of Organized Religions* (2010) vii.

7 As cited by R Ahdar 'Religious Group Autonomy, Gay Ordination, and Human Rights Law' in R O'Dair and A Lewis (eds) *Law and Religion: Current Legal Issues* (2001) *4* 279.

8 G Van der Schyff 'The Legal Definition of Religion and its Application' *South African Law Journal* (2002) *119* 289.

philosophical or theological, approach. In a legal context, this discussion will follow the functional approach in defining and qualifying a religious institution in accordance with certain qualities and characteristics. According to Van der Schyff, the following characteristics must at least be present in order to qualify as 'religion':

> a belief in a supreme being, a belief in a transcendental reality, a moral code, a worldly view that describes the human role in the universe and in terms of which an individual organizes and manages his life, holy rituals and festivals, worship and prayers, holy scriptures and texts and the existence of a social organization that supports and develops the said beliefs system.[9]

The latter is of great importance for religious institutions.

In order to attach certain activities to specific organisations, a classification system can come in handy. In the United States, for example, a very comprehensive classification system, the National Taxonomy of Exempt Entities (NTEE), is used in order to classify non-profit organisations. The National Centre for Charitable Statistics developed the system. The International Classification of Non-profit Organisations (ICNPO) classifies non-profit institutions by primary area of activity. The *United Nations (UN) Handbook on Non-profit Institutions in the System of National Accounts* recommends this system. The ICNPO provides for the classification of distinct and separate units and groups, rather than organisations in general. Organisations often consist of different units or establishments which may have their own activity. The ICNPO therefore provides for different units and establishments and groups them into 12 main activity groups, subdivided into 24 sub-groups. Group 10 focuses on 'Religion' and includes the following:

> organisations promoting religious beliefs and administering religious services and rituals; includes churches, mosques, synagogues, temples, shrines, seminaries, monasteries and similar religious institutions, in addition to related associations and auxiliaries of such organisations.[10]

This system specifically distinguishes churches and religious organisations from all other organisations. Group 10 further differentiates between congregations on the one hand and associations of congregations on the other hand. Congregations includes organisations such as 'churches, synagogues, temples, mosques, shrines, monasteries, seminaries and similar organisations promoting religious beliefs and administering religious services and rituals'. Associations of congregations include other associations and 'auxiliaries of religious congregations and organisations supporting and promoting religious beliefs, services and rituals'.[11] 'Religious

9 Van der Schyff 2002 *South African Law Journal* 290.

10 See L Salamon and K Anheier 'In Search of the Non-profit Sector. II: The Problem of Classification' *Voluntas* (1992) *3(3)* 297.

11 Salamon and Anheier 1992 *Voluntas* 297.

organisations' is a very broad concept and can include congregations on the one hand but also more general religious organisations as faith-based organisations on the other hand. Jeavons[12] argues that it would be wrong to classify congregations as faith-based organisations, since a pastor, rabbi, imam or minister would rarely see themselves as leaders of faith-based organisations, but rather as leaders of a church, temple, synagogue or mosque. The primary function of these organisations is to worship. The term 'church' is also used very broadly to refer to different types of religious organisations, which includes synagogues, temples, mosques and other organisations with church-type characteristics. Congregations on the other hand are also involved in various service activities, but often as a manifestation of their religion and belief, and described as 'the basic units of organized religious life in almost every spiritual tradition visible…'.[13]

Although authors may disagree with each other on the exact meaning of 'religion', I think most agree on the importance of religion in society. As correctly pointed out by the German Theologian Rudolf Otto: 'religion is as much a matter of fact as the reality of humanity itself'.[14] Justice Albie Sachs highlighted the important role of religious organisations in the case of *Minister of Home Affairs v Fourie*:

> Religious bodies play a large and important part in public life, through schools, hospitals and poverty relief programmes. They command ethical behaviour from their members and bear witness to the exercise of power by state and private agencies; they promote music, art and theatre; they provide halls for community activities, and conduct a great variety of social activities for their members and the general public. They are part of the fabric of public life, and constitute active elements of the diverse and pluralistic nation contemplated by the Constitution. Religion is not just a question of belief or doctrine. It is part of a people's temper and culture, and for many believers a significant part of their way of life. Religious organisations constitute important sectors of national life and accordingly have a right to express themselves to government and the courts on the great issues of the day. They are active participants in public affairs fully entitled to have their say with regard to the way law is made and applied.[15]

The Constitutional Court in *Taylor v Kurstag*[16] states with reference to Witte[17] that:

12 TH Jeavons 'The Vitality and Independence of Religious Organizations' *Society* (2003) *40(2)* 27.

13 Jeavons 2003 *Society* 27.

14 R Otto *Das Schaudern ist der Menschheit bestes Teil. Wie auch die Welt ihm das Gefühl verteuere, Ergriffen fühlt er tief das Ungeheuere.* [The Idea of the Holy: an Inquiry into the Non-rational Factor in the Idea of the Divine and its Relation to the Rational] [1923] (translated by Harvey JW) (1917) 154.

15 *Minister of Home Affairs and Another v Fourie and Another* 2006 (1) SA 524 (CC) para 90.

16 *Taylor v Kurstag* 2005 (1) SA 362 (W) para 37.

17 J Witte 'The South African Experiment in Religious Human Rights' *Journal for Juridical Science* (1993) *18(1)* 24–25.

> active religious rights require that individuals be allowed to exercise their religious beliefs privately and groups be allowed to engage in private worship assembly. More fully conceived, active religious rights embrace an individual's ability to engage in religious assembly, religious speech, religious worship, observance of religious laws and ritual, payment of religious taxes, and the like. They also embrace a religious institution's power to promulgate and enforce internal religious laws of order, organisation, and orthodoxy, to train, select, and discipline religious officials, to establish and maintain institutions of worship, charity, and education, to acquire, use, and dispose of property and literature used in worship and rituals, to communicate with co-believers and proselytes, and many other affirmative acts in manifestation of the beliefs of the institution.

According to Van Dijkhorst J in *Wittman v Deutscher Schülverein*,[18] 'religion' is not a neutral concept and encompasses a 'system of faith and worship [as] the human recognition of superhuman controlling power and especially of a personal God or gods entitled to obedience and worship'. Freedom of 'religion' as interpreted in accordance with section 9 of the European Convention also applies to the individual or collective exercise of religion only if it forms part of an established religious practice.[19] The European Court of Justice in *Metropolitan Church of Bessarabia*,[20] however, emphasised the view that 'in principle the right to freedom of religion [...] excludes assessment by the State of the legitimacy of religious beliefs or the ways in which those beliefs are expressed'.[21] This view will receive further attention in the next chapter, with reference to collective religious rights and section 31 of the Constitution. As far as a conceptualisation goes, the discussion will use the concept of 'religious institution' in accordance with the South African Charter of Religious Rights and Freedoms (SACRRF). Reference to 'every person' in the Charter thus includes a religious organisation or institution and includes any reference to church, religious entity, institution and community. The courts will ultimately have to judge whether a specific religious institution qualifies as 'religious' for purposes of the right to freedom of religion, based on the nature of the institution, aims and objectives, functioning and characteristics.

For religious organisations to be able to exercise their rights and obligations in governing their internal affairs, their legal status is important, as well as the type of organisation under which they operate, in order to be able comply with the legislative requirements for that specific type of organisation.

18 *Wittman v Deutscher Schülverein* 1998 (4) SA 423 (T) 449.

19 BP Vermeulen and MJ Kanne 'Kerk en Staat en de Mensenrechten' in LC van Drimmelen and TJ Van der Ploeg (ed) *Kerk en Recht* (2004) 78.

20 *Metropolitan Church of Bessarabia and others v Moldova*, no. 45701/99, Reports 2001-XII.

21 Vermeulen and Kanne *Kerk en Recht* 79.

Legal status

Introduction

As illustrated in the previous discussion, churches and religious organisations function as voluntary associations in civil society, as either churches or congregations in support and development of religious convictions and practices, or as faith-based community or service organisations. Faith-based organisations are often non-profit organisations that are involved in some or other form of service delivery, including religious education, charity, elderly care, health services and missionary work. The term civil society is interpreted in many ways and no one definition exists. Civil society encompasses the way in which communities provide services, organise and undertake various activities. Civil society also includes school governing bodies, academics, students, faith-based organisations (FBOs), special interest organisations, professional associations, trade unions and many others. One view sees the sector as occupying the space between the state, the market and the family. Often referred to as the 'voluntary sector', and in South Africa the 'non-profit' sector, it comprises non-profit organisations (NPOs) registered in terms of the South African Non-Profit Organisations Act 71 of 1997.[22] Non-governmental organisations (NGOs), community-based organisations (CBOs), civil society organisations (CSO) and faith-based organisations (FBO) are all collectively known as non-profit organisations (NPOs). Different forms of NPOs are available and in South Africa, churches or religious organisations often operate as trusts, companies or voluntary associations. In relation to trusts, the Trust Property Control Act 57 of 1988 makes it possible to set up a non-profit trust that obliges the trustees to administer the trust in the interest of the beneficiaries. Religious organisations can also register as a non-profit company. The non-profit company is a legal person and administered in terms of the Companies Act 71 of 2008. Most often, religious organisations or churches operate as voluntary associations established in terms of the common law. These three kinds of entities may then voluntary register as NPOs in terms of the Non-profit Organisations Act with the Department of Social Development.

The right to legal personality

The right to legal personality is an essential component of the right to freedom of religion and emphasises the rights of self-governance and self-regulation of churches and religious organisations. This view was highlighted by the European Court of Human Rights in the case of *Metropolitan Church of Bessarabia and others v Moldova*.[23] Moldovan law only afforded legal personality to recognised

22 Coalition on Civil Society Resource Mobilisation 'Critical Perspectives on Sustainability of the South African Civil Society Sector' *Johannesburg: Charities Aid Foundation Southern Africa* (2012) 9. Online at: www.cafsouthernafrica.org/pdf/caf_report%28perspectives_on_sustainability_report_2012%29.pdf [Accessed 14 March 2015].

23 *Metropolitan Church of Bessarabia and others v Moldova* 45701/99 [2001] ECHR 860 (13 December 2001).

religious denominations. By denying the Church legal personality, it violated its right to freedom of religion. As expressed by the court:

> not being recognised, the applicant Church cannot operate. In particular, its priests may not conduct divine service, its members may not meet to practice their religion and, not having legal personality, it is not entitled to judicial protection of its assets. The court therefore considers that the government's refusal to recognise the applicant Church [...] constituted interference with the right of the applicant Church and the other applicants to freedom of religion, as guaranteed by Article 9§1 of the Convention.

Similar approaches have been taken by South African courts, although Jansen JA in the case of *Theron v Ring van Wellington van die N.G. Sendingkerk in SA*,[24] confirmed the position that the legitimacy and effect of internal church rules are not dependent on its legal personality. The church as a legal person has the legal capacity to possess legal rights and duties, distinct from its members. They can own property, resolve their own disputes and sue or be sued in their own name. Without juristic personality, a church association could not sue its members, as explained as follows:

> Thus, if a church member's negligence caused fire damage to a church, neither the church nor the church's insurance Company, as a subrogee of the insured church, could sue the members. It also meant that a church association could not be sued by its members ... Finally, since an association could not sue or be sued, it generally was held an association's members were personally responsible for the acts of other members or agents of the association committed in the course of the association's business.[25]

In South Africa, churches and religious associations can acquire legal personality through various means. In the first instance, they can acquire juristic personality through governmental approval in terms of legislation, such as universities.[26] Earlier legislation recognised various church denominations as juristic persons. Section 3 of The Apostolic Faith Mission of South Africa (Private) Act,[27] described the Apostolic Faith Mission as a juristic person in the following words:

> The church shall be a body corporate with perpetual succession, capable of suing and being sued in its own name, and of acquiring rights and incurring obligations, distinct from its members.

24 *Theron v Ring van Wellington van die N.G. Sendingkerk in SA* 1976 (2) SA 1 (SCA) 13.
25 RR Hammar *Pastor, Church and Law* (1983) 128.
26 Van der Vyver J 'Religion' in WA Joubert and TJ Scott (eds) *LAWSA* (2003) 23(1) para 151.
27 The Apostolic Faith Mission of South Africa (Private) Act 24 of 1961 (SA), as amended.

The Methodist Church of Southern Africa Private Act 111 of 1978 had a similar provision in relation to the Methodist Church of South Africa.[28] However, Parliament repealed both statutes in 2008.[29]

In the second instance, a church can acquire juristic personality by registering under an Act of Parliament, such as companies under the Companies Act 71 of 2008 or other profit-making societies. An example is FOR SA, a non-profit, non-denominational Christian organisation, whose ethos is Bible-based. It is registered as a non-profit company (NPC) in terms of the Companies Act 71 of 2008, and is also currently in the process of being registered as a public benefit organisation (PBO) in terms of the Income Tax Act 58 of 1962. Their vision is to be a voice for the Christian Church in South Africa to government and to society, on issues affecting the rights of religious communities in South Africa.

Third, churches can acquire juristic personality by means of a mere reference to it in their respective constitutions or church orders. Thus, this is where a church acquires legal personality under the common law as a *universitas*. The focus of the remainder of the discussion will be on this aspect. Pienaar[30] distinguishes between a *universitas* as a corporate body under the common law and an unincorporated association of persons. Although a *universitas* is not incorporated through legislation or formal registration, it is still a corporate body and not an unincorporated association of persons.[31] According to the court in *Shillings CC v Cronje*,[32] the term 'unincorporated' refers to 'an association which does not have legal *persona* separate from its constituent members'. In relation to the common law *universitas*, the nature and purpose of the association, together with its constitution, determines whether it is in fact a juristic person. Expressed by the court as follows:

> An association of individuals does not always require the special sanction of the State in order to hold property and to sue in its separate name in South Africa. In order to determine whether an association of individuals is a corporate body, which can sue in its own name, the court has to consider the nature and the objects of the association as well as the constitution, and if these show that it possesses the characteristics of a corporation or *universitas*, then it can sue in its own name.[33]

The mere reference to the legal personality of the various organs or bodies in the internal constitution or church order is sufficient for legal personality.[34] However, the South African courts have not been consistent in its approach.

28 See section 3 of The Methodist Church of Southern Africa Private Act 111 of 1978.
29 See the Methodist Church of Southern Africa (Private) Act Repeal Act 45 of 2008 and The Apostolic Faith Mission of South Africa (Private) Act Repeal Act 47 of 2008.
30 GJ Pienaar 'Regspersone as Staatsorgane en Nie-staatsorgane ingevolge die Grondwet' *PER/PELJ* (1998) 152.
31 Pienaar 1998 *PER/PELJ* 152.
32 *Shillings CC v Cronje* 1988 (2) SA 402 (A) 419F.
33 *Morrison v Standard Building Society* 1932 AD 229.
34 See further Van der Vyver *LAWSA* Vol 23 para 150.

View of the courts

As early as 1908, in the case of *Cassim v Molife*,[35] the court held that 'being a religious body, the authorities are unanimous that it is *ipso jure a universitas*'. However, it was clear that the courts did not apply this view consistently or had consensus in relation to the characteristics or legal implications of such a juristic person. In the same year, in the case of *Webb & Co Ltd v Northern Rifles*,[36] the court described a *universitas* as:

> An universitas personarum in Roman-Dutch law is a legal fiction, an aggregation of individuals forming a person or entity, having the capacity of acquiring rights and incurring obligations to a great extent as a human being, to be distinguished from a mere association of individuals forming it, its capacity to acquire rights or incur obligations is distinct from that of its members, which are acquired or incurred for the body as a whole, and not for the individual members.

With reference to *Webb v Northern Rifles*, the KwaZulu-Natal High Court recently confirmed this view by declaring that the Twelve Apostle Church in Christ, by reference to the constitution of its mother church:

> provided for perpetual succession and that the mother church could sue and be sued in its own name. It is clear that the mother church was a voluntary association. In my view it was that form of voluntary association known as a *universitas*.[37]

Under the influence of English law, the Dutch Reformed Church was described as a voluntary association in terms of the colonial legislation of the time, with reference to the 1922 case of *Bredell v Pienaar*.[38] In *Theron v Ring van Wellington*,[39] the court confirmed the view that our courts have always treated churches as voluntary associations, and based its decision on the 1843 Ordinance in terms of which the rules and regulation of the Dutch Reformed Church:

> shall be regarded in law in like manner as the rules and regulations of a merely voluntary association, and shall be capable of affecting the persons or properties of such persons only as shall be found in the course of any action or suit before any competent Court to have subscribed, agreed to, adopted or recognised the said rules and regulations or some of them in such manner as

35 *Cassim v Molife* 1908 TS 748, 750.
36 *Webb & Co Ltd v Northern Rifles* 1908 TS 462, 464–465.
37 *Twelve Apostle Church in Christ and Another v Twelve Apostle Church in Christ and Another* (AR 488/2009) [2010] ZAKZPHC 5 (15 February 2010) para 7.
38 *Bredell v Pienaar* 1922 CPD 578, 581. See earlier reference under Chapter 1.
39 *Theron v Ring van Wellington van die N.G. Sendingkerk in SA* 1976 (2) SA 1 (SCA) 25G.

> to be bound thereby in virtue of the ordinary legal principles applicable to cases of express or implied contract.

Although it seems clear that, from a legal point of view, the church is a juristic person with its own rights and duties flowing from an internal constitution, our courts have not always followed this line of reasoning. In English law, churches do not constitute corporate bodies with legal personality, but church property vests in a statutory body. This also used to be the practice in relation to the Dutch Reformed Church, as seen in the case of *Rescue Committee Dutch Reformed Church v Mertheze*,[40] where the Cape Provincial Division of the Supreme Court held that the Dutch Reformed Mission Church was not a legal person and that 'such an association [unincorporated association] is not regarded as having any legal personality'.[41] The courts took a similar approach in relation to other denominations such as the African Mission Society, where the court in *Cassim v Molife*[42] held that:

> I am not satisfied that the society thus formed was a *universitas*. There is nothing to show that it was intended that the society should hold property apart from its members.[43]

In much earlier decisions, however, the courts recognised the legal personality of the church and its various organs.[44] In 1893, the court described the Dutch Reformed Church in South Africa (NHK – Nederduitse Hervormde Kerk) as a juristic person, in the case of *The Nederduitsche Hervormde Church v The Nederduitsche Hervormde of Gereformeerde Church*.[45] Similarly, the court recognised the Jewish Congregation of Johannesburg[46] as a juristic person. In an *obiter dictum* decision by J Brink in *De Vos v Die Ringkommissie van die Ring van die N.G. Kerk Bloemfontein*,[47] the courts seem to reach a turning point in relation to how they viewed the juristic personality of churches. The court held that there is much to be said for the proposition that the Dutch Reformed Church was in fact a legal person.[48] Subsequent legislation, although in the preface, proceeded on the

40 *Rescue Committee Dutch Reformed Church v Mertheze* 1926 CPD 298, 300.
41 *Rescue Committee Dutch Reformed Church* 300.
42 *Cassim v Molife* 748.
43 *Cassim v Molife* 752.
44 *Venter v Den Kerkeraad der Gereformeerde Kerk te Bethulie* 1879 OVS 4, 6.
45 *The Nederduitsche Hervormde Church v The Nederduitsche Hervormde of Gereformeerde Church* 1893 CLJ 327, 335. See further Van der Vyver The Law of South Africa para 151.
46 See *Peach & Co v The Jewish Congregation of Johannesburg* 1894 SAR 345.
47 *De Vos v Die Ringkommissie van die Ring van die N.G. Kerk Bloemfontein* 1952 (2) SA 83 (O) 84; 93.
48 See further *Malebjoe v Bantu Methodist Church of South Africa* 1957 (4) SA 465 (W) for the recognition of the Bantu Methodust Church of South Africa as a *universitas*, as well as the Apostolic Faith Mission in the case of *Moloi v St John Apostolic Faith Mission* 1954 (3) SA 940 (T).

assumption that the Dutch Reformed Church was 'an autonomous body corporate'.[49] This view was further emphasised in the 1968 case of the Johannesburg Congregation of the Apostolic Church,[50] where the court explicitly declared the Johannesburg Apostolic Church as an *universitas personarum*, capable of acquiring and owning its own property, distinct from its members. The court confirmed the position of the church as a *universitas* under the common law in the following words:

> It is not necessary that an association should be created by statute or registered in terms of a statute to possess the attributes of a juristic person. It can derive that quality from the common law, and the answer as to whether it does possess the characteristics of a juristic person which exists apart from its members must always be sought in the rules or constitution. These will show the nature and objects of the association. If it has perpetual succession, that is to say if the association continues to exist although the members may change from day to day and the governing body may change from time to time, and if the constitution provides that it may own property apart from its members, then it will be a *universitas.*[51]

In a recent judgment of the Supreme Court of Appeal in *Nederduitse Gereformeerde Kerk in Afrika en die Verenigde Gereformeerde Kerk in Suider-Afrika*,[52] the court confirmed the view that our courts have consistently recognised congregations of different denominations as juristic persons. Subsequently, they held that the local congregation of the Dutch Reformed Church in Africa (DRCA) must be recognised as a juristic person, who is the lawful owner of its property and finances. The court took a similar approach in relation to the Apostolic Faith Mission, the Bantu Methodist Church and the African Congregation Church.[53] In relation to the Apostolic Faith Mission, the court held that:

> With regard to the first point I have come to the conclusion that the respondent [St John Apostolic Faith Mission] is a legal *persona*. The tests have been laid down on numerous occasions and there is no need for me to do more than refer to the cases of *Webb and Co v Northern Rifles*, 1908 T.S. 462, and *Morrison v Standard Building Society*, 1932 AD 229. The essentials are the holding of property apart from the individual members and the possession of

49 Dutch Reformed Church in South Africa (Repeal of Laws) (Private) Act 22 of 1961. In its Preamble it states that – Whereas the Dutch Reformed Church in South Africa is an *autonomous body corporate* and as such is entitled to make laws and regulations for the control and management of its own affairs [own emphasis]. See further Van der Vyver *LAWSA* 23 para 150.

50 *Ex Parte Johannesburg Congregation of the Apostolic Church* 1968 (3) SA 377 (W).

51 *Ex Parte Johannesburg* 377.

52 *Nederduitse Gereformeerde Kerk in Afrika (OVS) en Nederduitse Gereformeerde Kerk in Afrika (Phororo) v Verenigende Gereformeerde Kerk in Suider-Afrika* (536/96) 1999 (2) SA 156 (SCA).

53 Van der Vyver The Law of South Africa para 150.

> perpetual succession. As far as that is concerned it appears to me that the respondent does comply with these requirements.[54]

In relation to the Bantu Methodist Church, the court based its decision on section 189 of the Church's constitution that states:

> (i) That all movable and immovable property presently owned by the church and held for and on its behalf and all movable and immovable property hereafter acquired by the church shall be transferred into the names of the president and three trustees.

And further, section 194, that states:

> The church may sue or be sued in its own name and the authority to institute or defend any legal proceedings, including arbitration proceedings, shall be signed and executed on its behalf by the president for the time being referred to in clause 189 hereof.

The court also confirmed one of the most important characteristics of a *universitas*, namely 'the capacity to acquire certain rights as apart from the rights of the individuals forming it, and perpetual succession'.[55] The court held that:

> It is quite clear from the provisions of the constitution relating to membership and to expulsion which it is not necessary to set out in full, that the church goes on even although the existing members leave it. I have come to the conclusion that this is a religious body which the individuals created, a body corporate to hold property and that the body continues even if all the members at the present time leave it.[56]

Implications for religious institutions in relation to religious disputes

In *Jamile v African Congregational Church*,[57] the court held that '[t]he respondent Church is a body corporate which, in terms of its constitution, may be sued in any competent court of law in its own name'.[58] Flowing from this right is the fundamental principle that all law-making bodies of churches and religious institutions should abide by the law as laid down in their respective church orders, rules and regulations.[59] South Africa is a richly diverse society, and this statement

54 According to Murray J in *Moloi v St John Apostolic Faith Mission* 942.
55 Sien *Webb & Co. Ltd v Northern Rifles* 1908 TS 462, 465; *Morrison v Standard Building Society* 1932 AD 229, 238.
56 *Malebjoe v Bantu Methodist Church of SA* 467.
57 *Jamile v African Congregational Church* 1971 SA 836 (D).
58 *Jamile v African Congregational Church* 836.
59 HJ van Eikema *Hoofdlijnen der Rechtssociologie en de Materiële Indeling van Publiek- en Privaatrecht* (1983) 101.

pertains to religious diversity as well. As is the case in any religiously diverse society, it is inevitable that members of different religious communities who hold different religious views and have practices will experience conflicts within, but also outside these communities. Often these disputes end up in court, and although it is widely accepted that courts, and even the state, should not force religious associations to exercise their religion in a particular way, they are not automatically exempt from procedural constitutional and other legislative provisions and measures.

South African courts have always been willing to review not only the actions of public bodies but also the decisions of private entities. Judicial review was often limited to the rules of natural justice, particularly in the context of religious institutions. The principles of natural justice was applicable, it was argued, because these domestic tribunals 'wield powers as great as, if not greater than, any exercised by courts of law. They can deprive a man of his livelihood'.[60] It is possible to subject private actors to the requirements of lawfulness, procedural fairness and rationality. Under the new constitutional dispensation, the common law principles still applies, but only in the field described as 'private administrative law'. This view is further supported by a recent judgment in *Fortuin v Church of Christ Mission of the Republic of South Africa*,[61] where the court was confronted with a case where a religious minister sought judicial review of the church's decision to dis-fellowship him from the performance of his pastoral duties as an ordained minister of his church. An important aspect that arose from the said case focused on the power of a court to review decisions taken by a church and the element of fairness. In order to establish whether the respondents in the *Fortuin* case followed fair or equitable procedures as contemplated in their own constitution, the court embarked upon an investigation into the powers to review a decision taken by a religious association.[62] In this regard, the applicant argued that the court has common law jurisdiction to review the decision of a domestic tribunal where it has disregarded its own rules or did not adhere to the fundamental principles of fairness. The court consequently held there was ample authority to empower it to interfere with the decision because the religious institution flouted fundamental principles of fairness. It was clear from the evidence that the church failed to follow procedural fairness as required by its own constitution and, consequently, the court set aside the decision by the church to dis-fellowship and suspend the applicant. Therefore, the *Fortuin* case aligned itself with numerous cases[63] that

60 DM Pretorius 'The Defence of the Realm: Contract and Natural Justice' *South African Law Journal* (2002) *119* 376.

61 *Fortuin v Church of Christ Mission of the Republic of South Africa* (3626/15) [2016] ZAECPEHC 18.

62 For a more detailed discussion of the *Fortuin* case, see EH van Coller 'Regsgeskille en die Kerk: Lesse te Leer uit die Saak van Johannes Fortuin en die Church of Christ Mission/Legal Disputes and What the Church can Learn from the Case of Fortuin v Church of Christ Mission of the Republic of South Africa and Others' *LitNet Akademies* (2017) *14(3)* 592–617.

63 See cases such as *De Vos v Die Ringskommissie van die Ring van die N.G. Kerk, Bloemfontein and Another* 1952 (2) SA 83 (O); *Odendaal v Kerkraad van die Gemeente Bloemfontein-Wes van die N.G. Kerk in OVS en Andere* 1960 (1) SA 160

have supported the understanding that civil courts have the authority to interpret a church order and to adjudicate accordingly by means of judicial review. However, courts generally support the position that they should act with deference in respect of church customs, doctrine and interpretations. The KwaZulu-Natal High Court supported this view in a recent judgment in the case of Bishop Ngewu and the Anglican Church of Southern Africa. The court *Bishop Mlibo Ngewu*[64] confirmed the view that:

> It is common cause between the parties that this court can review proceedings of the Church if there has been non-compliance with the Church's Constitution and/or Canons or with the principles of natural justice.[65]

As early as the case of *Odendaal v Loggerenberg*,[66] the court confirmed its authority to review the decisions of domestic tribunals. According to the court, it was common cause that a court of law will interfere with the decision of a domestic tribunal, only when there was a violation of the rules or constitution of the association or where elementary principles of fairness was ignored and the accused was in fact prejudiced as a result of the violation. Further, in *United Methodist Church of South Africa v Sokufundumala*,[67] where the congregation terminated a minister of the Methodist Church's service unilateral, the court held that the respondent had the right to state his case and that the church did not comply with the rules of natural justice. The court also confirmed the earlier view of Steyn J in *Turner v Jockey Club of South Africa*[68] where Botha JA emphasised that the rules of natural justice do not require a domestic tribunal to follow the strict procedural and technical rules of a court of law, but that:

> [T]hey do require such a tribunal to adopt a procedure which would afford the person charged a proper hearing by the tribunal, and an opportunity of producing his evidence and of correcting or contradicting any prejudicial statement or allegation made against him. The tribunal is required to listen fairly to both sides and to observe 'the principles of fair play'. [...] In addition to what may be described as the procedural requirements, the fundamental principles of justice require a domestic tribunal to discharge its duties honestly and impartially. [...] They require also that the tribunal's finding of the facts

(O) and *Theron v Ring van Wellington van die N.G. Sendingkerk in Suid-Afrika* 1976 (2) SA 1 (SCA) that confirm the position and serves as authority for the fact that civil courts do have the authority to interpret the constitution or church order of a religious institution and to act accordingly.

64 *Bishop Mlibo Ngewu v The Anglican Church of Southern Africa and Ten Others* [2016] ZAKZPHC 88.

65 *Bishop Mlibo Ngewu* para 33.

66 *Odendaal v Loggerenberg* 719C-E.

67 *United Methodist Church of South Africa v Sokufundumala* 1989 (4) SA 1055 (O).

68 *Turner v Jockey Club of South Africa* 1974 (3) SA 633 (SCA) 646F.

> on which its decision is to be based shall be 'fair and bona fide'. [...] It is, in other words, 'under an obligation to act honestly and in good faith'.

The court concluded that the respondent in *United Methodist Church* did not get a fair hearing and an opportunity to state his case, and the decision was accordingly set aside.

In *Yiba and Others v African Gospel Church*,[69] the court further confirmed the principles applicable to the nature of the relationship between voluntary associations and its members, and the interpretation of its constitution in the context of disciplinary action. The constitution, together with the rules and regulations, form the agreement that sets out the nature and scope of authority of the organisation, as well as the functionaries and members of the organisation. The organisation explicitly undertakes to treat members fairly in accordance with the rules and regulations of the constitution, and they cannot ignore these rules. The question that comes to mind is: what exactly is regulated by the organisations' constitution? In the context of churches and religious organisations, the church order or constitution determines that the particular organisation is regulated by means of internal church or organisational rules, compiled by the institution itself and not the state. According to Van der Vyver:

> It is not for state institutions to judge the substance, or the truth or falsity, of religious belief per se. However, it is a vital function of government to resolve, through its judicial arm, disputes pertaining to the rights and obligations of its subjects. Courts of law ought not to shy away from that function merely because those rights and obligations cannot in a given case be established without doctrinal issues.[70]

The Supreme Court of Appeal confirmed that an appropriate interpretation of a church order should include an interpretation where words are interpreted in the context of its nature and purpose, and that the relationship between words should be looked at in the context of the church order as a whole.[71] The court is in favour of the approach taken by Lord Wilberforce in *Prenn v Simmonds*,[72] where the court was of the view that the broad contextual background includes the so-called 'matrix of facts', in which the church order is set when interpreting the church order. According to the court:

> the time has long passed when agreements, even those under seal, were isolated from the matrix of facts in which they were set and interpreted purely on internal linguistic considerations [...] We must enquire beyond the language

69 *Yiba and Others v African Gospel Church* 1999 (2) SA 949 (C).

70 J Van der Vyver 'Constitutional Perspective of Church-State Relations in South Africa' *Brigham Young University Law Review* (2001) *1999(2)* 670.

71 *Nederduitse Gereformeerde Kerk in Afrika (OVS)*.

72 *Prenn v Simmonds* [1971] 3 All ER 237 (HL) 239J.

> and see what the circumstances were with reference to which the words were used, and the object, appearing from those circumstances, which the person using them had in view.

It is not always easy to determine which matters (suspension, dismissal, co-ownership and decision-making) are regulated by church law and which by the civil law. The church order and constitution play an important role in assisting the courts to determine the scope of interference and review when they challenge the lawfulness of a decision. Because disciplinary action in various churches goes hand in hand with the particular religious doctrines and convictions of the church, courts should act with deference. Courts should assess each case on its own merits and therefore the particular factual context is of the utmost importance. In addition, associations do not have any inherent power to discipline members. The respective constitution, rules and regulations of the association must provide for that. An association must therefore exercise its disciplinary authority in accordance with the said rules and regulations, and a court shall not interfere where an association has acted in accordance with its own rules. A court will however interfere where a domestic tribunal has not acted within the scope of its own rules, or has not exercised its discretion properly or has acted *ultra vires* and therefore outside the scope of its authority. Because a dismissal or suspension is one of the most severe forms of punishment, the constitution has to explicitly provide for it. An organisation, or a church for that matter, cannot suspend a member if it is contrary to its rules, and a member can also not be dismissed by another organ other than the one authorised to do so.[73]

Conclusion

This chapter has illustrated that the concept of a 'religious organisations' is very broad. It includes different types of religious organisations and institutions. This term is therefore very generic in nature, and 'wide enough to cover the various churches, religious societies or religious congregations under whatever name they wished to describe themselves ... [and also] ... that each religious denomination should be respected when it says what its ethos is'.[74] The discussion supports and will follow this approach throughout the various chapters.

Through the various case examples it became clear that South African courts, in particular the later decisions, acknowledge and recognise churches and religious institutions as juristic persons. This approach has found its way into various provisions in internal constitutions and church orders of various churches and denominations. The reference to a church as a voluntary association points to the body as an association with legal personality, who is the lawful owner of its property and is in charge of its own finances. The body exists independently and

73 See for instance *Yiba and Others v African Gospel Church* 960D-961H.

74 P Colton 'Religious Entities as Legal Persons – Ireland' in L Friedner *Churches and Other Religious Organisations as Legal Persons* (2007) 128.

distinctly from its members. The competencies of a church or religious organisation, in particular, must be determined in light of the rules and regulations set out in its own internal constitution or church order, but also in terms of the rules applicable to all voluntary associations, in general.

Religious associations must make sure that they follow their own rules and procedures and that their internal church orders and rules provide for the necessary procedural guarantees in order to give effect to the basic requirements of a fair hearing. However, courts should act with deference in respect of church customs and interpretations. Domestic tribunals must exercise their functions in accordance with the requirements as laid down in the constitution, but also in accordance with the rules of natural justice.

Bibliography

A South African Declaration on Religious Rights and Responsibilities, accepted and assented to during a National Inter-religious Conference, held in November 1992 under the auspices of the South African Chapter of the World Conference on Religion and Peace (WCRP-SA).

Ahdar R 'Religious Group Autonomy, Gay Ordination, and Human Rights Law' in R O'Dair and A Lewis (eds) *Law and Religion: Current Legal Issues* (2001) 4:276–296.

Coalition on Civil Society Resource Mobilisation *Critical Perspectives on Sustainability of the South African Civil Society Sector* (2012) Johannesburg: Charities Aid Foundation Southern Africa.

Cohen R 'Israel and the Holy See Negotiate: A Case Study in Diplomacy across Religions" *The Hague Journal of Diplomacy* (2010) 5(3) 213–234.

Colton P 'Religious Entities as Legal Persons – Ireland' in L Friedner *Churches and Other Religious Organisations as Legal Persons* (2007) 125–138 Leuven: Peeters.

Du PlessisLM 'Current Problems Concerning Church and State Relationships and Religious Freedom in South Africa. The Viewpoint of a Constitutional Lawyer' in H Warnink (ed) *Legal Position of Churches and Church Autonomy* (2001) 13–33 Leuven: Peeters.

Labuschagne JMT 'Die Begrip "Godsdiens" in Godsdiensvryheid: 'n Bewussynsantropologiese Ekskursie na die Evolusiekern van die Reg' *De Jure Law Journal* (1997) 118–119.

Louche C, D Arenas and KC van Cranenburgh 'From Preaching to Investing: Attitudes of Religious Organisations Towards Responsible Investment' *Journal of Business Ethics* (2012) 110(3) 301–320.

Hammar RR *Pastor, Church and Law* (1983) Springfield, Missouri: Gospel Publishing House.

Jeavons TH 'The Vitality and Independence of Religious Organizations' *Society* (2003) 40 (2) 27–36.

Otto R *Das Schaudern ist der Menschheit bestes Teil. Wie auch die Welt ihm das Gefühl verteuere, ergriffen fühlt er tief das Ungeheuere* (1917) [The Idea of the Holy: an Inquiry into the Non-rational Factor in the Idea of the Divine and its Relation to the Rational] (1923) (translated by HarveyJW) London: Oxford University Press.

Pienaar GJ 'Regspersone as Staatsorgane en Nie-staatsorgane ingevolge die Grondwet' *PER/PELJ* (1998) 1(1) 152.

Potz R and W Wieshaider 'Religious Entities as Legal Persons – Parts of Western and Central Europe' in L Friedner *Churches and Other Religious Organisations as Legal Persons* (2007) 27–36 Leuven: Peeters.

Pretorius DM 'The Defence of the Realm: Contract and Natural Justice' *South African Law Journal* (2002) 119374.

Rivers J *The Law of Organized Religions* (2010) London: Oxford University Press.

Salamon L and K Anheier'In Search of the Non-profit Sector. II: The Problem of Classification' *Voluntas* (1992) 3(3) 297–309.

Van Coller EH 'Regsgeskille en die Kerk: Lesse te Leer uit die Saak van Johannes Fortuin en die Church of Christ Mission / Legal Disputes and What the Church can Learn from the Case of Fortuin v Church of Christ Mission of the Republic of South Africa and Others' *LitNet Akademies* (2017) 14(3) 592–617.

Van der Schyff G 'The Legal Definition of Religion and its Application' *South African Law Journal* (2002) 119(2) 288–294.

Van de Vyver J 'Constitutional Perspective of Church-State Relations in South Africa' *Brigham Young University Law Review* (2001) *1999(2)* 635–673.

Van der Vyver J 'Religion' in WA Joubert and TJ Scott (eds) *The Law of South Africa* (2003) 23:141–163Durban: Butterworths.

Van Eikema Hommes HJ *Hoofdlijnen der Rechtssociologie en de Materiële Indeling van Publiek- en Privaatrecht* (1983) Zwolle: WEJ Tjeenk Willink.

Vermeulen BP and MJ Kanne 'Kerk en Staat en de Mensenrechten' in LC van Drimmelen and TJ Van der Ploeg (eds) *Kerk en Recht* (2004) Utrecht: LEMMA BV.

Witte J 'The South African Experiment in Religious Human Rights' *Journal for Juridical Science* (1993) 18(1) 1–32.

3 Collective religious rights and religious autonomy

Introduction

Rivers[1] describes the collective aspect of the right to freedom religion as a 'set of rights, immunities, privileges, and powers held by a religious association as such'. The religious organisation is entitled to determine and administer their own internal religious affairs without interference from the state. In this manner the community or organisation structures their religious life according to their own needs and their own moral and religious precepts. This aspect of the right to freedom of religion is not merely an aggregation of individual freedoms but the rights and freedoms asserted by the religious organisation as a group. The importance of religious autonomy for religious organisations was further highlighted by the European Court in the case of *Hasan*,[2] by emphasising the fact that religious communities traditionally and universally exist in organised structures and 'were the organisational life of the community not protected by Article 9 of the Convention, all other aspects of the individual's freedom of religion would become vulnerable'. The protection of religious group autonomy thus also protects and gives meaning to individual religious rights, expressed as follows:

> Individual belief would lack its richness, its connectedness, and much of its character-building and meaning-given power if it were cut off from the extended life off religious communities.[3]

Similarly, in the South African context, the rights protected by section 31 of the Constitution have been described as significant both for individuals and for the communities they constitute. 'If the community as community dies, whether through destruction or assimilation, there would be nothing left in respect of which the individual could exercise associational rights'.[4] As outlined in Chapter 1,

1 J Rivers *The Law of Organized Religions* (2010) 231
2 *Hasan and Chaush v Bulgaria* (2002) 34 EHRR 554 para 62.
3 WC Durham Jr 'The Right to Autonomy in Religious Affairs: A Comparative View' in Robbers (ed) *Church Autonomy* (2001) 713.
4 *Christian Education South Africa v Minister of Education* 2000 (4) SA 757 (CC) para 23.

the right to freedom of religion entrenched in the Constitution includes the right to have a belief, to express such belief publicly and to manifest such belief by worship and practice, teaching and dissemination. The last element is of particular importance for collective religious rights. The collective aspect of the right to freedom of religion is underlined by article 18(1) of the International Covenant on Civil and Political Rights (ICCPR) which emphasises that the right to freedom of thought, conscience and religion includes the freedom 'either individually or in community with others and in public or private, to manifest his religion or belief in worship, observance, practice and teaching'. As pointed out by the South African Constitutional Court:

> Just as it is difficult to postulate a firm divide between religious thought and action based on religious belief, so it is not easy to separate the individual religious conscience from the collective setting in which it is frequently expressed. Religious practice often involves interaction with fellow believers. It usually has both an individual and a collective dimension and is often articulated through activities that are traditional and structured, and frequently ritualistic and ceremonial.[5]

Read together with the right to freedom of association (section 18) and the rights of religious communities (section 31), the right to freedom of religion further guarantees a degree of autonomy for religious communities to manifest their beliefs and run their affairs without interference. This chapter will first outline the collective or institutional aspect of the right to freedom of religion. The last section will focus on the aspect of religious autonomy in that religious associations have the right to structure themselves in accordance with their own religious precepts, free from state interference.

Collective religious rights

The interim Constitution contained 34 Constitutional Principles (CPs) in schedule 4. A new constitutional text passed by the Constitutional Assembly in terms of chapter 5 of the interim Constitution had to comply with these CPs. CP XII stated that collective rights of self-determination in forming, joining and maintaining organs of civil society, including linguistic, cultural and religious associations, should be recognised and protected.[6] In *Ex Parte Chairperson of the Constitutional Assembly: In re Certification of the Amended Text of the Constitution of the Republic of South Africa*,[7] the Constitutional Court considered the argument that the wording of section 31[8] did not comply with the requirements of CP XII, which required that:

5 *Christian Education South Africa* para 19.
6 *Christian Education South Africa* para 19.
7 *Ex Parte Chairperson of the Constitutional Assembly: In re Certification of the Amended Text of the Constitution of the Republic of South Africa*, 1996 1997 (2) SA 97 (CC).
8 Section 31 of the Constitution provides that persons belonging to cultural, religious or linguistic communities may not be denied the right, with other members of that community, to enjoy their culture, practise their religion and use their language, and

> Collective rights of self-determination in forming, joining and maintaining organs of civil society, including linguistic, cultural and religious associations, shall, on the basis of non-discrimination and free association, be recognised and protected.

The court noted:

> Having regard to the CPs as a whole, the '(c)ollective rights of self-determination' mentioned in CP XII are associational individual rights, namely those rights which cannot be fully or properly exercised by individuals otherwise than in association with others of like disposition. The concept 'self-determination' is circumscribed both by what is stated to be the object of self-determination, namely 'forming, joining and maintaining organs of civil society' as well as by CP which requires the state for which the Constitution has to provide, to be 'one sovereign State'. In this context 'self-determination' does not embody any notion of political independence or separateness. It clearly relates to what may be done by way of the autonomous exercise of these associational individual rights, in the civil society of one sovereign State.[9]

Section 31(1)(b) specifically includes reference to the right to form, join and maintain 'other organs of civil society'. Because of this inclusion, the court held that the objects of the section 31 (amended text) rights do not differ from the objects of the CP XII rights of self-determination and that both sets of objects comprise various activities in relation to organs of civil society. Although the subjects of the CP XII rights were unspecified and therefore unrestricted, section 31 confers them on persons belonging to cultural, religious and linguistic communities. For those communities not expressly protected by section 31, the court held that the clear protection of other rights of association coupled with the generous standing provisions protect the rights of collective self-determination stipulated by the CP for those communities.[10] The court also noted that a protective constitutional framework for civil society is enhanced by institutional structures such as the Public Protector, the Human Rights Commission, the Commission for the Promotion and Protection of Rights of Cultural, Religious and Linguistic Communities, and the Commission for Gender Equality.[11] With reference to these institutional structures and the express protection of rights of association in the amended text of the Constitution, together with the procedural provisions governing their enforcement, the court was happy to conclude that the requirements of CP XII have been met by the provisions of section 31.[12]

to form, join or maintain cultural, religious and linguistic associations and other organs of civil society.

9 *Ex Parte Chairperson of the Constitutional Assembly* para 24.

10 *Ex Parte Chairperson of the Constitutional Assembly* para 26.

11 *Ex Parte Chairperson of the Constitutional Assembly* para 25.

12 *Ex Parte Chairperson of the Constitutional Assembly* para 27.

The Constitutional Court in *Christian Education*[13] confirmed that the Constitution does comply with these Principles and highlighted the fact that rights of belief are first spelt out fully as individual rights in sections 15 of the Constitution, even though they have a community dimension and are frequently exercised in a community setting. Section 31 then emphasises the protection given to members of communities united by a shared language, culture or religion. Section 31 of the Constitution reflects Section 27 of the International Convention on Civil and Political Rights (ICCPR) to which South Africa is a party. Article 27 of the ICCPR is the most widely accepted legally binding provision on minorities and provides the basis and inspiration for the UN Declaration on Minorities. Article 27 reads:

> In those States in which ethnic, religious or linguistic minorities exist, persons belonging to such minorities shall not be denied the right in community with the other members of their group, to enjoy their own culture, to profess and practise their own religion, or to use their own language.

Section 31 does not refer to the recipients of the protection as 'minorities', but rather as those who belong to a specific cultural, religious or linguistic community. Section 31 further uses the word 'cultural' community, rather than 'ethnic minority'.[14] Following the approach used in article 27, the court confirmed that the protection of diversity is not effected through merely giving legal personality to groups as such. The court held that the protection of the constitutional values of pluralism and diversity is achieved through the 'double mechanism of positively enabling individuals to join with other individuals of their community, and negatively enjoining the state not to deny them the rights collectively to profess and practise their own religion'.[15] The word 'community' in section 31 refers to an aggregation of people, with a particular quality of relationship. Currie and De Waal[16] suggest that the meaning of 'minorities' in section 27 of the Declaration on Minorities could be used to interpret 'community', in that the purpose of section 31 is to protect the same values of pluralism and tolerance that section 27 seeks to protect. In line with that, a community, for the purposes of section 31, should be an identifiable group, united by a common religion and members of the group should identify themselves as part of the group and should also be identifiable as such by other members. Therefore, section 31 protects the practice of religion, in particular the communal aspects of religious practice, rather than religious beliefs or its purely private aspects. Section 18 of the Universal Declaration of Human Rights[17] explicitly affirms that freedom to manifest a religion or belief may be exercised either alone or in community with others.

13 *Christian Education South Africa* para 23.
14 *Christian Education South Africa* para 23.
15 *Christian Education South Africa* para 23.
16 I Currie and J De Waal *The Bill of Rights Handbook* 6 ed (2013) 628–629.
17 Universal Declaration of Human Rights, 10 December 1948, 217A (III).

> Everyone has the right to freedom of thought, conscience and religion; this right includes freedom to change his religion or belief, and freedom, either alone or in community with others and in public or private, to manifest his religion or belief in teaching, practice, worship and observance.[18]

International Law has also started to put more emphasis on protecting the rights of religious associations and has seen a shift from only the individual protection of religious rights to also include collective approaches to issues of religious rights.[19] Religious associations are now clearly protected under the European Convention and case law confirms this position.[20] In the case of *Hasan and Chaush v Bulgaria*,[21] the European Court confirmed that:

> religious communities traditionally and universally exist in the form of organised structures. They abide by rules which are often seen by followers as being of a divine origin. Religious ceremonies have their meaning and sacred value for the believers if they have been conducted by ministers empowered for that purpose in compliance with these rules. The personality of the religious ministers is undoubtedly of importance to every member of the community. Participation in the life of the community is thus a manifestation of one's religion, protected by article 9 of the Convention.[22]

Important aspects of the collective right to freedom of religion include the right of a religious organisation to be able to register as a juristic person (as outlined in Chapter 2) and to be exempted from laws of general application where it is in the interest of protecting the right to freedom of religion. On an international level, both are protected under article 9 of the European Convention for the Protection of Human Rights and Fundamental Freedoms (ECHR). The right to freedom of association is a correlative right, which supports and forms part of a variety of other rights and freedoms, in particular the right to religious freedom (both the individual as well as the collective aspect). It guarantees persons the right to associate and form organisations in whichever way they choose. This ties in with the discussion in Chapter 2, where it was illustrated that religious institutions function as voluntary associations in civil society. The important relationship between the right to freedom of association and the right to freedom of religion was outlined by the European Court as follows:

18 Article 8 of the Council of Europe, Framework Convention for the Protection of National Minorities of 1995 also included reference to the right to establish 'religious institutions, organisations and associations'.
19 See further Rivers *The Law of Organized Religions* 37 and further.
20 For recent developments and a general discussion of freedom of religion under the Convention, see for instance I Leigh 'Balancing Religious Autonomy and Other Human Rights under the European Convention' *Oxford Journal of Law and Religion* (2012) 1(1) 109.
21 *Hasan and Chaush v Bulgaria* App. No. 30985/96 62 (2000).
22 *Hasan and Chaush v Bulgaria* App. No. 30985/96 62.

> Where the organisation of the religious community is at issue, Article 9 must be interpreted in the light of Article 11 of the Convention which safeguards associative life against unjustified State interference [...] Were the organisational life of the community not protected by Article 9 of the Convention, all other aspects of the individual's freedom of religion would become vulnerable.[23]

In *Metropolitan Church of Bessarabia and others v Moldova*,[24] Moldova had refused to register the Metropolitan Church of Bessarabia and the court reinforced the decision in *Hasan and Chaush* with reference to article 9, and stated:

> In addition one of the means of exercising the right to manifest one's religion, especially for a religious community, in its collective dimension, is the possibility of ensuring judicial protection of the community, its members and its assets, so that article 9 must be seen not only in the light of article 11, but also in the light of article 6.[25]

It has been stated that 'associational rights safeguard primordial religious and cultural attachments from undue state interference'.[26] Section 18 of the South African Constitution guarantees everyone the right to freedom of association. The right to freedom of association is one of the most fundamental rights in a democratic society and is a right that allows citizens to join associations, without interference by the state, in order to attain various ends.[27] One aspect of this right incorporates the right of individuals as members of particular organisations to decide freely with whom they want to associate, whether for social, political or religious reasons, as a manifestation of a particular freedom of culture, belief or religion. This associational right encompasses certain membership and admission requirements. Woolman[28] refers to this as 'capture [which] justifies the ability of associations to control their association through selective membership policies, the manner in which they order their internal affairs and the discharge of members or users'.

23 *Hasan and Chaush v Bulgaria* App. No. 30985/96 62.
24 *Metropolitan Church of Bessarabia and others v Moldova* 45701/99 [2001] ECHR 860 (13 December 2001).
25 See further *Supreme Holy Council of the Muslim Community v Bulgaria*, no 39023/97 (2004); *Moscow Branch of the Salvation Army v Russia*, no 72881/01 (2006); *Biserica Adeverat Ortodoxa din Moldova v Moldova*, no 952/03 (2007); *Church of Scientology Moscow v Russia*, no 18147/02 (2007); *Svyato-Mykhaylviska Parafi ya v Ukraine*, no 77703/01 (2007); *Religionsgemeinschaft der Zeugen Jehovahs v Austria*, no 40825/98 (2008); *Leela Förderkreis e.V. v Germany*, no 58911/01 (2008); *Holy Synod of the Bulgarian Orthodox Church (Metropolitan Inokentiy) v Bulgaria*, nos 412/03 and 35677/04 (2009).
26 S Woolman 'Association' in I Currie and J De Waal : *Handbook* (2005) 421.
27 As quoted from H Cheadle and D Davis *South African Constitutional Law: The Bill of Rights* (2002) 251.
28 S Woolman 'On the Fragility of Associational Life: A Constitutional Liberal's Response to Patrick Lenta' *SAJHR* (2009) 25(2) 287.

Two South African High Court decisions considered the right to freedom of association specifically in the context of religious associations. The court in both *Taylor v Kurstag*[29] and *Wittman v Deutscher Schulverein*[30] recognised the right of religious organisations:

> to have one's life shaped in a manner that does not readily permit the alteration of either belief or act and that to be a member of a liberal society is to live in a state committed to not so readily dictating the ends of its citizens.[31]

That does not give religious organisations a blank cheque to act however they want. The state can still interfere with the functioning of such an organisation. It merely means that the state should recognise and respect the religious nature of the organisation and should afford the organisation an appropriate amount of deference. The case of *Taylor v Kurstag* is of particular importance for the institutional right to freedom of religion applicable to religious institutions in South Africa. It also illustrates the important connection between the right to institutional freedom of religion (section 31) and the right to freedom of association (section 18).

In *Taylor v Kurstag*, a member of the Jewish community was excommunicated by the relevant Jewish Church authority, the *Beth Din*, by means of a *Cherem*. He applied for the setting aside of the *Cherem* in that it not only violated his right to freedom of association in accordance with section 18, but also that it violated his institutional right to freedom of religion, in particular the right to practise his religion and maintain religious associations with fellow members of his faith. The court enquired into whether the limitation of his rights could be justified by reference to the associational rights of the community. Other than the minority decision of Ngcobo J in *Prince v President, Cape Law Society*[32] where he stated: '[i]t is undesirable for courts to enter into the debate whether a particular practice is central to a religion unless there is a genuine dispute as to the centrality of a practice', the court in *Kurstag* confirmed that the *Cherem* forms part of the Jewish religion and that as part of the particular religion, a member is bound by it and that 'they are not coerced; assumption of the obligation is consensual'.[33] The nature of the organisation is also important and according to the court, in deciding the fairness of the process, held that the nature of the institution should be taken into account: 'A religious tribunal is subject to the discipline of the Constitution, but its being a religious body giving effect to the associational rights of its members, must be accounted for'.[34] Consequently, the court had to determine whether there was a violation of the individual's rights and whether the *Cherem* should be lifted. Although the *Cherem* might have severe consequences on a

29 *Taylor v Kurstag* 2005 (1) SA 362 (W).
30 *Wittman v Deutscher Schulverein* 1998 (4) SA 423 (T).
31 Woolman *Bill of Rights Handbook* 442.
32 *Prince v President, Cape Law Society* 2002 (2) SA 794 (CC) para 42.
33 *Taylor v Kurstag* para 35.
34 *Taylor v Kurstag* para 63.

particular member's position within the Jewish faith and the particular community, the court confirmed that the question involved religious doctrine and that 'the threshold for intervention is and should be high' and that if the court should interfere

> it would be impossible for voluntary organisations, particularly religious communities, to require conformity with particular values and to impose sanctions for their contravention. The members of the faith, exercising their own rights in terms of s 31, have the right to protect the integrity of their common bond by disciplining those who do not conform.[35]

In the absence of bias or bad faith on the part of the *Beth Din*, the court upheld the constitutionality of its *Cherem*.[36] The court concluded that the limitation on the applicant's rights was reasonable and justifiable as a failure to enforce its rulings would result in the Jewish faith not being able to protect the integrity of Jewish law. The associational rights of the organisation took precedence over the personal rights of the individual. In reaching its conclusion, the court assessed the full extent of the limitation on the rights of the applicant and weighed this against the associational rights of the organisation.

The right to freedom of association also incorporates the right of everyone to decide to join any organisation of choice. In the context of the horizontal application of the Bill of Rights, it means that no one may be discriminated against on one or more of the grounds listed in section 9 of the Constitution, including race, gender, sexual orientation or religion. If a religious organisation can proof that discriminatory practices or admission policies are lawfully designed for the protection and promotion of a particular communities' cultural or religious precepts and principles, the right to freedom of association of the particular organisations to set discriminatory admission requirements should trump other considerations.[37] The right to equality and non-discrimination will be discussed in more detail in the next chapter.

In Chapter 2, the right of a religious organisation to own property and to have legal personality was shown to be an important aspect of the collective right to religious freedom. Of similar importance, as expressed by the European Court in *Manoussakis v Greece*,[38] is that the collective right to freedom of religion also 'excludes any discretion on the part of the State to determine whether religious beliefs or the means used to express such beliefs are legitimate'. In the same way that the European Court has emphasised the importance of religious autonomy for religious communities, the existence of religious associations 'to enable collective action, and the need for the State to remain neutral and impartial in exercising

35 *Taylor v Kurstag* para 58.
36 *Taylor v Kurstag* para 62.
37 The issue of equality and non-discrimination will be discussed in more detail in Chapter 4.
38 *Manoussakis v Greece* 1996-IV Eur. Ct. H.R 1346 para 28.

its regulatory power over them'[39] is of particular importance to religious communities in South Africa. The next section will discuss the aspect of religious autonomy in more detail.

Religious autonomy

In the case of *Corporation of the Presiding Bishop of the Church of Jesus Christ of Latter-Day Saints v Amos*,[40] Justice Brennan explains judicial deference to religious organisations' control over their internal affairs by referring to the importance of 'self-definition'.[41] He is of the view that a religious community:

> Represents an ongoing tradition of shared beliefs, an organic entity not reducible to a mere aggregation of individuals. Determining that certain activities are in furtherance of an organization's religious mission, and that only those committed to that mission should conduct them, is thus a means by which a religious community defines itself. Solicitude for a church's ability to do so reflects the idea that furtherance of the autonomy of religious organizations often furthers individual religious freedom as well.

Apart from the fact that the right to freedom of religion can be exercised in community with others, it can also be a collective group right, such as the right to self-determination of a religious community. Van der Vyver[42] distinguishes between the competence of a church institution to regulate and administer its own affairs, which is an institutional group right and the collective group right, which is a right that belongs to every member of the group and which can be exercised separately or jointly with other members of the group. The institutional group right vests in the social institution and is exercised by the collective entity through its agents. The right of a church to internal sphere sovereignty is, according to him, an example of an institutional group right. Thus, where there is state interference in the internal affairs of non-state institutions, the interference violates the internal sphere sovereignty of the entity concerned. Sphere sovereignty also implies the relationship between two or more distinct social entities, such as state and church.[43]

The South African Religious Charter (SACRRF)[44] guarantees every religious institution the right to institutional freedom of religion, including the right to

39 Rivers *The Law of Organized Religions* 53.
40 *Corporation of the Presiding Bishop of the Church of Jesus Christ of Latter-Day Saints v Amos* 483 U.S. 327 (1987).
41 R Ahdar 'Religious Group Autonomy, Gay Ordination, and Human Rights Law' in R O'Dair and A Lewis (eds) *Law and Religion: Current Legal Issues* (2001) 4:285.
42 J van der Vyver 'Equality and Sovereignty of Religious Institutions: A South African Perspective' *Santa Clara Journal of International Law* (2012) 10(1) 149.
43 See also J van der Vyver 'Limitations of Freedom of Religion or Belief: International Law Perspectives' *Emory International Law Journal* (2005) 19(1) 525.
44 Sections 9, 9.1, 9.2 and 9.3 of the South African Charter of Religious Rights and Freedoms (SACRRF).

determine its own doctrines, and to regulate its own internal affairs, including organisational structures and procedures. Every religious institution is recognised and protected as having authority over its own affairs, and the state, including the judiciary, must respect the authority of every religious institution over its own affairs, and may not regulate or prescribe matters of doctrine and ordinances. The term 'management of own religious affairs' can be interpreted in many ways. According to Krishnaswami,[45] it refers to matters that fall within the dogma of a religious institution and matters that pertain to faith, ritual and doctrine. This can include the organisational structure of an institution, its membership and spiritual administration. According to him, this means that in countries where the state and religion are separate, a maximum freedom in the management of religious affairs must be assured to all faiths. According to this view, 'all religions are automatically treated equally in such countries; and the very idea of separation implies at least a minimum of intervention — if not complete non-intervention — in the management of religious affairs'.[46] As pointed out by Frederick Gedicks:[47]

> In liberal society, the government has no competence to determine moral ends. In theory, at least, the goals of liberal democratic government must depend on the value held by those it governs – values that originate outside of government in churches, families, political parties, trade unions, private schools, and other voluntary associations. In the absence of these groups, government and society would be deprived of the enriching world-views that these groups contribute.

Religious associations have the right to structure themselves in accordance with their religious precepts and the degree of autonomy which each faith enjoys in the management of its religious affairs is determined by the state. Both the regulation and the protection of religious freedom in society rests with the state. Government legislation determines the scope of religious freedom for individuals as well as the collective autonomy of religious organisations. As pointed out by Doe and Jeremy,[48] through its laws, the state regulates religion 'in the distribution of entitlements', such as the various rights and privileges of religious organisations and their members. The state also regulates religion by setting limits to the exercise of these rights, through various duties, prohibitions and conditions. These rights and duties often come in conflict with each other, especially where the right to freedom of religion comes in conflict with other human rights, particularly through relevant equality and anti-discrimination laws. Ahdar[49] argues that anti-discrimination laws

45 A Krishnaswami *Study of Discrimination in the Matter of Religious Rights and Practices* (1960) 48.

46 Krishnaswami *Study of Discrimination* 49.

47 F Gedicks 'Toward a Constitutional Jurisprudence of Religious Group Rights' *Wisconsin Law Review* (1989) 99(1) 116.

48 N Doe and A Jeremy 'Justification for Religious Autonomy' in R O'Dair and A Lewis (eds) *Law and Religion: Current Legal Issues* (2001) 4: 422.

49 Ahdar *Religious Group Autonomy* 275.

and human rights 'may have a chilling effect' upon religious groups' determination on leadership and, in turn, subvert those groups' very vision.

In the English case of *Wachmann*,[50] the Chief Rabbi disciplined the applicant, an Orthodox rabbi, declaring him 'morally and religiously fit to hold his rabbinical office'.[51] Wachmann's employment was terminated and he sought judicial review.[52] Some of the most important functions of the Chief Rabbi included the responsibility 'to advise and rule on matters of Jewish law, ritual, and doctrine, [...] to certify religious officiants as religiously and morally fit (or unfit) to hold their respective offices within their congregation'.[53] Simon Brown J observed that 'the court would never be prepared to rule on questions of Jewish law'.[54] The High Court refused the application for review on the basis that the Chief Rabbi's discharge of his religious functions was not seen as public in nature. He explained the functions of the Chief Rabbi as 'essentially intimate, spiritual and religious functions which the government could not and would not seek to discharge in his place were he to abdicate his regulatory responsibility'.[55] The judge went further to state that a court is hardly in a position to regulate religious functions and to determine whether someone is morally and religiously fit to carry out the religious functions of his office. He concluded by stating:

> The court must inevitably be wary of entering so self-evidently sensitive an area, straying across the well-recognised divide between church and state. One cannot, therefore, escape the conclusion that if judicial review lies here, then one way or another this secular court must inevitably be drawn into adjudicating upon matters intimate to a religious community.[56]

According to Barrie,[57] the Queen's Bench Divisions' approach to judicial review of the disciplinary function of the Chief Rabbi came as a surprise. He relies on the case of *Grundling v Van Rensburg*[58] and authors such as Wiechers, Baxter, Boulle et al and the common law approach relating to the reviewability of disciplinary proceedings of religious associations. This approach in *Wachmann* must however also be seen in the context of the doctrine of non-entanglement into doctrinal issues, as applied in South Africa, where courts must exercise deference and respect religious organisations and churches' 'autonomous sphere'. This is also in line with the decision of Malan J in *Taylor v Kurstag*,[59] where the court accepted that the

50 *Regina v Chieff Rabbi of the United Hebrew Congregations of Great Britain and the Commonwealth, ex parte Wachmann* (1992) 1 WLR 1036 (QB).
51 *Ex Parte Wachman* 1038.
52 GN Barrie 'Judicial Review of Disciplinary Action of Ecclesiastical Body' *Journal of South African Law* (1993) 339; Ahdar *Religious Group Autonomy* 281.
53 Barrie 1993 *Journal of South African Law* 339.
54 Ahdar *Religious Group Autonomy* 281.
55 *Ex parte Wachmann* 1042.
56 *Ex parte Wachmann* 1043.
57 Barrie 1993 *Journal of South African Law* 338–339.
58 *Grundling v Van Rensburg NO* 1984 (3) SA 207 (W).
59 *Taylor v Kurstag* para 61.

decision by the Jewish *Beth Din* is subject to judicial review, but emphasised the importance of judicial deference, when the court stated the following:

> Although the decision of the Beth Din are subject to judicial scrutiny, just as those of any other faith are, the values embodied in the doctrines of entanglement and the reluctance to interfere in matters of faith, whether procedural or otherwise, cannot be discarded [...]

After the decision in *Wachmann*, English courts are in favour of an approach where there is 'no governmental interest in the functioning of religious organizations, judicial supervision is rare'.[60]

In a recent judgment by the Supreme Court of Appeal in *De Lange v Presiding Bishop, Methodist Church of Southern Africa*,[61] the court was confronted with a dispute relating to the sexual orientation of a spiritual leader. The Supreme Court of Appeal dismissed De Lange's appeal and she was granted leave to appeal to the Constitutional Court. In the Constitutional Court, De Lange argued that the church's reliance on the rule proscribing ministers from entering into same-sex marriages contravened her right to equality under the Constitution, which prohibits unfair discrimination based on marital status or sexual orientation. During the course of its judgment in the Supreme Court of Appeal, the court emphasised the nature of the dispute and that the issues in dispute went to sensitive matters of church doctrine and governance and that these were issues:

> that the Church should be left to determine domestically, as far as is possible, without interference from the Court. The Court should only become involved in the dispute where it is strictly necessary to do so. Even then, I am advised and submit that it will refrain from determining doctrinal issues, in order to avoid religious entanglement.[62]

The court went on to say that protecting the autonomy of religious associations was considered a central aspect of protecting religious rights and that such protection had been described as 'vital to a conscience-honouring social order'.[63] Although the court made it clear that it was not necessary for it to deal with the collision between the rights to freedom of association and religious freedom, on the one hand, and the right to equality, on the other, it still took the view 'that a proper respect for freedom of religion precludes our courts from pronouncing on matters of religious doctrine, which fall within the exclusive realm of the Church'.[64] Her appeal to the Constitutional Court was dismissed, mainly because the court found that De Lange had unequivocally disavowed her unfair

60 M Hill 'Judicial Approaches to Religious Disputes' in R O'Dair and A Lewis (eds) *Law and Religion* (2001) 410.

61 *De Lange v Presiding Bishop, Methodist Church of Southern Africa* 2015 (1) SA 106 (SCA).

62 *De Lange* SCA para 30.

63 *De Lange* SCA para 31.

64 *De Lange* SCA para 39.

discrimination claim before the High Court and should first have approached the Equality Court to hear the discrimination claim.[65] However, in concurring with the approach taken in the Supreme Court of Appeal, Van der Westhuizen J acknowledged the fact that fundamental rights and values often compete and that they need to be weighed, balanced and limited. With reference to the 'doctrine of entanglement', he held:

> It is of course one thing to say that the Constitution with its values and rights reaches everywhere, but quite another to expect the courts to make rulings and orders regarding people's private lives and personal preferences. Courts are not necessarily the best instruments to balance competing rights and values in intimate spheres where emotions and convictions determine choices and association. In this case the Supreme Court of Appeal, relying on the 'doctrine of entanglement', held that the dispute at issue was quintessentially one which a secular court should try to avoid, if possible.[66]

Conclusion

As a carrier of the right to freedom of religion, religious institutions have the autonomy to implement their own religious doctrines and beliefs. This chapter has shown that there are a number of constitutional provisions designed to protect the rights of members of communities. They all aim to underline the constitutional value of acknowledging diversity and pluralism in society. The protection of diversity also requires that 'associations should not always be expected to conform to public principles, including non-discrimination, when those principles clash with the convictions of members, and the state should refrain as far as possible from interfering with the internal affairs of associations'.[67] Taken together, these rights have been described as rights that:

> affirm the right of people to be who they are without being forced to subordinate themselves to the cultural and religious norms of others, and highlight the importance of individuals and communities being able to enjoy what has been called the 'right to be different'. In each case, space has been found for members of communities to depart from a general norm. These provisions collectively and separately acknowledge the rich tapestry constituted by civil society, indicating in particular that language, culture and religion constitute a strong weave in the overall pattern.[68]

65 *De Lange v Presiding Bishop of the Methodist Church of Southern Africa for the time being and Another* 2016 (2) SA 1 (CC) para 30.
66 *De Lange* CC para 79.
67 As quoted by Brennan J in *Roberts v United States Jaycees* 468 US 609 (1984) and referred to by P Lenta 'Taking Diversity Seriously: Religious Associations and Work-Related Discrimination' *SALJ* (2009) 126(4) 832.
68 *Christian Education South Africa* par 24.

The state is under a duty to respect these rights and to create the opportunity and space for individuals and religious institutions to enjoy these rights fully, with as little state regulation as possible. In terms of section 7 of the Constitution, the state has a constitutional obligation to 'respect, protect, promote and fulfil' the institutional freedom of religious institutions to govern their own affairs free from interference by the state. Although the right to freedom of religion is not unlimited, interference should be limited to 'protecting vulnerable members of society from readily discernible, serious harm and then only to the extent permitted by s 36 of the Constitution'.[69] The aspect of limitation of rights will be discussed in the next chapter.

Bibliography

Ahdar R 'Religious Group Autonomy, Gay Ordination, and Human Rights Law' in R O'Dair and A Lewis (eds) *Law and Religion: Current Legal Issues* (2001) 4:276–296.

Barrie GN 'Judicial Review of Disciplinary Action of Ecclesiastical Body' *Journal of South African Law* (1993) 339.

Cheadle H and D Davis *South African Constitutional Law: The Bill of Rights* (2002) Durban: Butterworth.

Comments on the CRL Rights Commission's Report on the 'Commercialisation' of Religion, submitted by Freedom of Religion South Africa (FOR SA) and the South African Council for the Protection and Promotion of Religious Rights and Freedoms (28 February 2017).

Currie I and J de Waal *The Bill of Rights Handbook* 6 ed (2013) Cape Town: Juta.

Doe N and A Jeremy 'Justification for Religious Autonomy' in R O'Dair and A Lewis (eds) *Law and Religion: Current Legal Issues* (2001) 4:422.

Durham W Cole Jr 'The Right to Autonomy in Religious Affairs: A Comparative View' in Robbers (ed) *Church Autonomy* (2001) 686–714Frankfurt/M: Peter Lang.

Gedicks F 'Toward a Constitutional Jurisprudence of Religious Group Rights' *Wisconsin Law Review* (1989) 99(1) 99–169.

Hill M 'Judicial Approaches to Religious Disputes' in R O'Dair and A Lewis (eds) *Law and Religion: Current Legal Issues* (2001) 4:410.

Krishnaswami A *Study of Discrimination in the Matter of Religious Rights and Practices* (1960) New York: United Nations Publication.

Leigh I 'Balancing Religious Autonomy and Other Human Rights under the European Convention' *Oxford Journal of Law and Religion* (2012) 1(1) 109–125.

Lenta P 'Taking Diversity Seriously: Religious Associations and Work-Related Discrimination' *South African Law Journal* (2009) 126(4) 827–860.

Rivers J *The Law of Organized Religions* (2010) London: Oxford University Press.

The Council of Europe, *TheFramework Convention for the Protection of National Minorities* (FCNM), 1 February 1995, ETS 157.

Universal Declaration of Human Rights, 10 December 1948, 217A (III).

69 Comments on the CRL Rights Commission's Report on the 'Commercialisation' of Religion, submitted by Freedom of Religion South Africa (FOR SA) and the South African Council for the Protection and Promotion of Religious Rights and Freedoms (28 February 2017) 13.

Van der Vyver J 'Equality and Sovereignty of Religious Institutions: A South African Perspective' *Santa Clara Journal of International Law* (2012) 10(1) 147–169.

Van der Vyver J 'Limitations of Freedom of Religion or Belief: International Law perspectives' *Emory International Law Journal* (2005) 19(1) 499–537.

Woolman S 'Association' in I Currie and J De Waal *Bill of Rights Handbook* (2005) Cape Town: Juta.

Woolman S 'On the Fragility of Associational Life: A Constitutional Liberal's Response to Patrick Lenta' *South African Journal on Human Rights* (2009) 25(2) 287–305.

4 Conflict of rights

Introduction

As was pointed out in Chapter 3, section 31(2) of the Constitution makes it clear that any rights relating to religious communities (to enjoy, practice their religion and form, join and maintain religious associations), may not be exercised in a manner inconsistent with any provision of the Bill of Rights. These qualifications serve a double purpose. According to the Constitutional Court, 'the first is to prevent protected associational rights of members of communities from being used to "privatise" constitutionally offensive group practices and thereby immunise them from external legislative regulation or judicial control'.[1] This is particularly where associations make use of practices to abuse the notion of pluralism in order to discriminate and achieve exclusivity, privilege and domination. A second purpose, according to the court, relates to 'oppressive features of internal relationships primarily within the communities concerned', and where the application of section 8, which regulates the horizontal application of the Bill of Rights, might be particularly relevant. Section 8(4)[2] extends the protection of the Bill of Rights to juristic persons, 'to the extent required by the nature of the rights and the nature of that juristic person'.

Where a religious institution requires its clergy to be heterosexual or a church refuses to appoint women as priests or ministers, the prohibition against unfair discrimination may be violated and section 9 of the Constitution will be relevant. The state can however also compel religious institutions to appoint gay or women clergy that goes against the religious views of the organisation or church. In such a case, the institutional aspect of the right to freedom of religion may be violated and the right to equality will then have to be balanced against the right to freedom of religion. Where the state interferes with the autonomy of religious organisations, reference will often be made to anti-discrimination laws. The balancing of different fundamental rights will take place under section 36 of the Constitution. It is thus clear that article 15 (freedom of religion), article 18 (freedom of

1 *Christian Education South Africa v Minister of Education* 2000 (4) SA 757 (CC) para 26.

2 A juristic person is entitled to the rights in the Bill of Rights to the extent required by the nature of the rights and the nature of that juristic person.

association) and article 31 (right to associate in religious communities) of the Constitution are extremely important in respect of religious institutions and the degree of interference by the state in the internal affairs of the association (membership, activities etc.). Government interference can occur as a result of discriminatory practices by the organisation, but only in accordance with article 36 of the Constitution. Examples include activities or provisions in the organisations' constitution that are in conflict with the principles of a society based on human dignity, equality and freedom; where membership is declined on the basis of discriminatory practices and where the internal affairs of the institution are not conducted in accordance with democratic principles.[3] This chapter will first discuss the right to equality and non-discrimination in relation to religious institutions and then outline how various fundamental rights, such as the right to freedom of religion, may be limited in accordance with section 36 of the Constitution.

Equality and non-discrimination

Section 9 of the Constitution is the equality clause and states that everyone is equal before the law and has the right to equal protection and benefit of the law. It further prohibits anyone, including the state, from unfairly discriminating against anyone on any of the listed grounds. These grounds include race, gender, sex, pregnancy, marital status, ethnic or social origin, colour, sexual orientation, age, disability, religion, conscience, belief, culture, language and birth.

In *Harksen v Lane*[4] and later decisions such as *Van Heerden v Minister of Finance*,[5] the Constitutional Court refined the test to be followed in determining whether section 9 of the Bill of Rights is violated. *Harksen v Lane* provides for two different tests to be applied, one in relation to section 9(1) and one in relation to section 9(3). Section 9(1) guarantees equal protection and benefit of the law to everyone. The question here is whether there is differentiation between people or categories of people? If so, does the differentiation bear a rational connection to a legitimate governmental purpose? If it does, then there is no violation of s 9(1). However, even if there is a rational relationship, it is still necessary to determine whether, despite such rationality, the differentiation nevertheless amounts to unfair discrimination. If there is no rational connection, then there is a violation of s 9(1) and the enquiry moves onto the prohibition of discrimination under s 9(3) of the Constitution. The question here is whether the differentiation amounts to 'unfair discrimination'? A two-stage analysis is followed to determine whether the differentiation amounts to unfair discrimination, namely does the differentiation amount to discrimination and whether the discrimination is unfair? If it had been found to have been on one of the listed grounds, unfairness would be presumed and discrimination is established. If the discrimination was found to be unfair then

3 G Pienaar 'Konstitusionele Voorskrifte rakende Regspersone' *THRHR* (1997) 60: 576- 577.

4 *Harksen v Lane NO and Others* 1998 (1) SA 300.

5 *Van Heerden v Minister of Finance* 2004 6 SA 121 (CC).

a determination would have to be made as to whether the provision could be justified under the limitations clause, section 36. The section 36 analysis will be discussed in more detail in the next section. Any differentiation based on, for instance, sexual orientation, will be deemed for legal purposes to be unfair discrimination, unless it can be proven that the differentiation is reasonable and justifiable in an open and democratic society based on human dignity, equality and freedom.

A decision by the South African Human Rights Commission (SAHRC) in the ATKV/Goudinie matter can serve as a good example. The 'Afrikaanse Taal- en Kultuurvereniging' (ATKV), came into existence in 1930 as a cultural organisation of which membership was only open to whites until the 1980s. The ATKV runs and operates five holiday resorts in South Africa, open to all members of the public, but the activities at the resorts promote the Afrikaans language and Christian values. ATKV members receive a 30 per cent discount at the resort, while other members of the public must pay full price. On the question of whether the admission requirements of the ATKV constituted unfair discrimination, Dr Kok argued on behalf of the ATKV that the admission requirements did constitute discrimination on religious grounds, but that the discrimination was fair in that it served a legitimate and lawful purpose of promoting the religious grounds and commitment of the ATKV to Christian values. He then argued that the admission requirements did not constitute unfair discrimination. The issue before the SAHRC was whether an organisation, like the ATKV, which was not only a language organisation, but also a cultural and religious organisation, can limit its membership to members of one particular faith (in this instance, Christians). Membership was refused to members that would have qualified on language or cultural grounds; it was excluded as a result of their belief (in this instance, Muslims). The ATKV requires all its members to commit to upholding the Christian faith and to promote, advance and develop the Afrikaans language and culture. The applicants, being of the Muslim faith, did not wish to subscribe to the founding principles of the ATKV. They alleged that they were being unfairly discriminated against on the basis of religion. The Commission found that while the practices of ATKV were in fact discriminatory, they were not unfair as the organisation permitted non-Christian and non-Afrikaners to attend their resorts. The Commission also found that the ATKV are entitled to set particular religious convictions as admission requirements and consequently to exclude certain members on religious grounds.[6]

Religious institutions have not been exempted from the unfair discrimination provisions in the Constitution, and some may say it is unfortunate. Discrimination in relation to gender and especially sexual orientation are still upheld in various churches. Imposing these constitutional proscriptions of unfair discrimination on religious institutions would, according to Van der Vyver,[7] amount to political

6 South African Human Rights Commission (SAHRC) Report *Public Inquiry Exclusionary Policies of Voluntary Associations: Constitutional Considerations* (2006) 32 available at www.sahrc.org.za.

7 J van der Vyver 'Equality and Sovereignty of Religious Institutions: A South African Perspective' *Santa Clara Journal of International Law* (2012) 10(1) 158.

totalitarianism, which 'becomes evident when state authority extends into the private enclave of non-State societal circles, such as family life, academic institutions and the sovereign sphere of churches'. A dismissed employee or a learner suspended from school for not complying with a rule or regulation, often relies on anti-discrimination laws, rather than a claim for exemption from a particular regulation. This is often the case with particular dress codes, such as wearing headscarves or dreadlocks.[8] The claim will be that the condition imposed by the employer or the school that they should refrain from wearing certain accessories, constitutes discrimination.

Section 5 of the Employment Equity Act 55 of 1998 requires employers to eliminate unfair discrimination in any employment policy or practice. Section 6(1) prohibits both direct and indirect discrimination.[9] Often a rule or regulation does not target a particular group, but it may have a disproportionate impact on individuals because of their membership of a specific group. According to Lenta,[10] it would be unlawful for employers to 'impose standardized rules about uniforms, dress and appearance with which religious groups cannot comply, unless compelling reasons can be offered in support of these rules'. Where a rule or requirement is disproportionately burdensome on members of a particular religious group, it can point towards indirect discrimination against that religious group. As outlined by Krishnaswami:[11]

> Viewed from this angle it may be seen that certain limitations imposed upon particular manifestations of religion or belief, although apparently conceived in general terms, may in fact tend to affect only a particular group, or to affect it more than others. This consideration cannot be ignored when deciding whether or not a particular limitation is legitimate. Only when public authorities refrain from making any adverse distinctions against, or giving undue preferences to, individuals or groups, will they comply with their duty as concerns non-discrimination.

Legislation is often quite clear when it comes to discrimination by the state and when we look at section 9(3) of the Constitution,[12] we see that:

> (3) The state may not unfairly discriminate directly or indirectly against anyone on one or more grounds, including race, gender, sex, pregnancy,

8 See Chapter 5 and Chapter 6 for a further discussion on religious dress in the context of education and in the workplace.

9 'No person may unfairly discriminate, either directly or indirectly, against an employee, in any employment policy or practice, on one or more grounds, including race, gender, sex, pregnancy, marital status, family responsibility, ethnic or social origin, colour, sexual orientation, age, disability, religion, HIV status, conscience, belief, political opinion, culture, language or birth.'

10 P Lenta P 'Muslim Headscarves in the Workplace and Schools' *South African Law Journal* (2007) SALJ 301.

11 A Krishnaswami *Study of Discrimination in the Matter of Religious Rights and Practices* (1960) 20.

12 Constitution of the Republic of South Africa, 1996 sections 9(3) and 9(4).

> marital status, ethnic or social origin, colour, sexual orientation, age, disability, religion, conscience, belief, culture, language and birth.

Section 9 also makes provision for section 9(4):

> (4) No person may unfairly discriminate directly or indirectly against anyone on one or more grounds in terms of subsection (3). National legislation must be enacted to prevent or prohibit unfair discrimination.

Here it becomes a bit more complicated since churches and other religious organisations also have other fundamental rights that protect them, like the right to freedom of association and the right to freedom of religion, two equally important fundamental rights, not applicable to the state. It has therefore become necessary to appropriately balance the different rights entrenched in the Bill of Rights and to engage in a process of balancing competing rights. This balancing exercise often requires the balancing of two distinct sets of rights. On the one hand are the fundamental rights of equality, dignity and non-discrimination, and on the other hand we find the so-called community or associative rights, including the right to freedom of association, the right to freedom of religion, and the right to associate in cultural, religious and linguistic communities. The case of Johan Strydom[13] is probably the first case where the court had to deal with issues of religious freedom, equality, non-discrimination and homosexuality. It did not involve a minister or a religious leader, but a music teacher. Strydom worked as an independent contractor in the so-called 'kunste-akademie' (arts academy) of the church, teaching music to students. He was dismissed from his post in July 2005 because he became involved in a same-sex relationship with another man. Mr Strydom challenged his dismissal before the Equality Court and instituted proceedings under the Promotion of Equality and Prevention of Unfair Discrimination Act 4 of 2000 (PEPUDA). He argued that the church had infringed his constitutionally protected right to equality, dignity, privacy and freedom to work in the profession of his choice, on the grounds of his homosexual orientation. The court found that the Dutch Reformed Church unfairly discriminated against Mr Strydom because the church could not prove that he was involved in religious instruction. His contract was terminated on the basis that he was involved in a homosexual relationship. The decision was criticised in that religious freedom did not enjoy priority above the individual's right to equality. The church had strong views on the meaning of a 'spiritual leader'. According to the church:

> Just as the respondent would not allow its ministers, officials, spiritual leaders and lecturers to be alcoholics or to have active extra-marital affairs, it could not allow them to be involved in active homosexual practices.

13 *Strydom v Nederduitse Gereformeerde Gemeente Moreleta Park* 2009 4 SA 510 (T). For a more detailed discussion of this case, see also EH van Coller 'Religious Institutions and Fundamental Rights: Applicability, Interaction and Limitations' in C Cianitto (eds) *Law, Religion, Constitution* (2013) 209–226.

The Equality Court had to decide if the church unfairly discriminated against Strydom on the grounds of sexual orientation, and if a religious institution could be exempt from the provisions of PEPUDA dealing with discrimination based on sexual orientation in the workplace in relation to a music teacher. The court also had to decide whether a religious institution is allowed to discriminate beyond their spiritual leaders, to include a music teacher not involved in religious instruction. The court found that the church unfairly discriminated against Johan Strydom. The court based its decision mainly on the fact that Mr Strydom served as an independent contractor, was in no way involved in the spiritual activities of the Church and that he was also not a member of the Dutch Reformed Church. The church was ordered to pay Strydom damages and to apologise unconditionally for its conduct. The court was of the opinion that the church had not proved that Strydom's job entailed religious instruction or that the discrimination against him had been fair or justified. In the words of Justice Basson: 'I am not convinced on the evidence presented by the church that on the facts of the matter at hand the complainant was in such a position of spiritual leadership.'

The court in Strydom referred to an important and interesting American case of *Corporation of the Presiding Bishop of the Church of Jesus Christ of Latter-day Saints v Amos.*[14] In *Amos* certain provisions of the Civil Rights Act[15] were at stake in terms of which religions institutions were allowed to discriminate on grounds of religion in their employment and labour relations, irrespective of whether an employee was in fact performing a religious function or not.[16] This extended definition was challenged on the basis of the 'establishment clause' and the court affirms that the exception applies to all non-profit activities of the organisation and emphasises the fact that 'it is a significant burden on a religious organization to require it, on pain of substantial liability, to predict which of its activities a secular court will consider religious'.[17] It is not that easy however to draw the line between 'religious' and 'secular' and it would be understandable that religious institutions '[would] be concerned that a judge would not understand its religious

14 *Corporation of the Presiding Bishop of the Church of Jesus Christ of Latter-day Saints v Amos* 483 U.S. 327 (1987).

15 Chapter VII of the Civil Rights Act of 1964, 42 USC 2000e, makes it unlawful for an employer to appoint or fire an individual or to otherwise discriminate against any person on the basis of remuneration, conditions of employment or any benefit based on race, ethnicity, religion or sexuality. It includes dismissals, promotion or any other conduct in the workplace. Section 702 creates and exception and reads as follow APPLICABILITY TO FOREIGN AND RELIGIOUS EMPLOYMENT SEC. 2000e-1. *[Section 702]*
(a) Inapplicability of subchapter to certain aliens and employees of religious entities
This subchapter shall not apply to an employer with respect to the employment of aliens outside any State, or to a religious corporation, association, educational institution, or society with respect to the employment of individuals of a particular religion to perform work connected with the carrying on by such corporation, association, educational institution, or society of its activities

16 This exception only applies in respect of religion and not in the case of discrimination based on race, gender or sexuality.

17 *Corporation of the Presiding Bishop* 336.

tenets and sense of mission' and possible liability 'might affect the way an organization carried out what it understood to be its religious mission'.[18] Lenta[19] is however of the opinion that it does not mean that 'religious associations should not be required to demonstrate to the court that the position related to the unfair discrimination is sufficiently closely connected to the doctrinal core of the church', which the church had not sufficiently proved in the view of the court in *Strydom*. He is further of the view that religious institutions should not be allowed to discriminate 'unless the job in question is sufficiently closely connected to the doctrinal core of the religion'. He therefore supports the view that the court's decision in *Amos* was incorrect. This approach by the courts 'to delve (carefully) into questions of core tenets of belief – and decide which beliefs are trumped and which beliefs are not' is however not shared by Woolman[20] who rather supports the view of Brennan J in *Amos* that 'religious organizations have an interest in autonomy in ordering their religious affairs'.[21] Brennan J upholds the constitutionality of section 702 'covering all types of church employee, no matter what the job, appropriately balances the right of employees to religious liberty and the autonomy of religious organizations'.[22]

If Strydom had been in a position of spiritual leadership or even the minister of the congregation, it seems that the court would have decided differently and may have found the discrimination to be fair. This approach is also voiced by constitutional law expert Pierre de Vos who is of the opinion that it would constitute a violation of the right to freedom of religion of:

> churches, mosques or synagogues to force them to employ a gay dominee, imam, rabbi or priest or to force the Catholic Church to ordain woman priests. The same would be true for forcing them to employ someone giving religious instruction at that institution.[23]

However, this approach, according to him, does not apply to an individual in a non-religious capacity and he argues that the approach adopted by the court in relation to Mr Strydom was a sensible compromise and that '[t]o have held otherwise would have … created a situation in which religious institutions are in effect above the law…'.[24]

It is submitted that such an approach is not in line with the essence of the right to freedom of religion, which guarantees religious autonomy in so far as 'each religious denomination should be respected when it says what its ethos

18 *Corporation of the Presiding Bishop* 336.
19 Lenta 2009 *SALJ* 843.
20 S Woolman S 'On the Fragility of Associational Life: A Constitutional Liberal's Response to Patrick Lenta' *SAJHR* (2009) 25(2) 298.
21 *Amos v Corporation of the Presiding Bishop* 483 US 327, 340 (1987).
22 Lenta 2009 *SALJ* 843.
23 P de Vos 'On Freedom of Religion and the Gay Music Teacher' *Constitutionally Speaking Blog* (3 September 2008) 655.
24 De Vos *Constitutionally Speaking Blog* 655.

is'.[25] As pointed out earlier, a court is hardly in a position to determine and interpret religious doctrines and to give content to something essentially religious in nature. Therefore, when a religious organisation is of the view that, from a religious point of view, certain functions are of a religious nature, or as in this case, that a music teacher acts in the capacity of spiritual leader within the church, courts need to show deference and respect the religious autonomy of the organisation. However, religious organisations must be in a position to defend any exclusionary or discriminatory practices. The onus rests on them to convince the court of the religious nature of the function, which onus the church did not discharge according to the court in *Strydom*. Woolman[26] is of the view that the court came to the correct conclusion and submits that the court would have found in favour of the church, had they presented a well-structured argument based on article 15 (freedom of religion), article 18 (freedom of association) and article 31 (right to associate in religious communities) of the Constitution. In support of the decision in *Amos* and the view of Woolman for instance, courts should display utmost restraint when deciding religious matters. This view, however, is not supported by Bilchitz[27] who rather supports a 'presumption of equality' approach, by stating:

> Courts thus are required to decide upon whose side they should intervene. Both the presumption of equality and the harmful nature of discrimination … require the state to favour the group against which discrimination is being perpetrated.[28]

Such a view does not give the necessary recognition to the right to freedom of religion and the right to freedom of association in a pluralistic society and further ignores the *sui generis* nature of religious organisations. Woolman[29] correctly summarises the *sui generis* character of religious institutions as follows:

> Like it or not, religion is different. Time – sacred time – for religion is circular, not linear. Linear time – human time – is profane. Religion returns through holiday and ritual to the beginning: when God – of one stripe or another – made the world and laid down the law. Others – non-members – may find the religious beliefs and practices of a faith perverse. But rational distinctions – or the absence of rational distinctions – is hardly the point when an organised faith is put in the position of defending God's law – not their own. It is God's law that provides the setting for meaningful action for the members of the Nederduits Gereformeerde Gemeente Moreletta Park.

25 P Colton 'Religious Entities as Legal Persons – Ireland' in L Friedner *Churches and Other Religious Organisations as Legal Persons* (2007) 128.
26 Woolman 2009 *SAJHR* 283.
27 D Bilchitz 'Should Religious Associations Be Entitled to Discriminate?' *South African Journal of Human Rights* (2011) 27(2) 219.
28 Bilchitz 2011 *SAJHR* 230–231.
29 Woolman 2009 *SAJHR* 294.

> The notion that they could alter God's law is akin to idolatry. It confuses the sacred and the profane.

Although the court in *Strydom* gave recognition to the importance of the right to freedom of religion by referring to the view of the Constitutional Court in *Prince v President, Cape Law Society and Others*,[30] Basson J went further to state that the right to equality 'is viewed as foundational to our constitutional order'. With reference to *Minister of Education & Another v Syfrets Trust Ltd NO & Another*,[31] the court was of the view that 'equality is not merely a fundamental right; it is a core value of the Constitution. This is borne out by various provisions in the Constitution itself, which articulate the ideal of equality'.[32] Lenta[33] submits that the court in *Strydom* is creating the impression that the right to equality is a more fundamental right than the right to freedom of association and the right to freedom of religion. Such an approach and accompanying view are accordingly false and he is of the view that the right to freedom of religion is one of the most fundamental rights and that 'it would not be a huge exaggeration to suggest that this freedom is the grain of sand in the oyster of politics around which the pearl of liberalism gradually form'.[34] I support the view of Benson,[35] who correctly points out that 'equality is not more important than freedom of religion'. This view does not support the 'egalitarian form of liberalism' approach taken by Bilchitz[36] that requires 'a strong presumption in favour of equality and mitigates against effectively exempting religious associations from the provisions of the Constitution and PEPUDA relating to non-discrimination'.[37] In a report compiled by experts in the field of voluntary associations, this view is also rejected in favour of an approach that requires a 'more nuanced balancing of rights' and that:

> a mere conflict between an associational right and the right to equality cannot always result, irrespective of circumstances, in the predominance of the right to equality. The consequence of this interpretation would be to emasculate associational rights and severely restrict cultural liberties.[38]

30 *Prince v President, Cape Law Society and Others* 2002 (2) SA 794 (CC) in *Strydom* para 9.
31 *Minister of Education & Another v Syfrets Trust Ltd NO & Another* 2006 (4) SA 25 (CC) in *Strydom* para 10.
32 *Strydom* para 10.
33 Lenta 2009 *SALJ* 834–836.
34 Lenta 2009 *SALJ* 836 and the view of K Hasson 'Religious Liberty and Human Dignity: A Tale of Two Declarations' *Harvard Journal of Law & Public Policy* (2003) 27: 88–89.
35 I Benson 'The Freedom of Conscience and Religion in Canada: Challenges and Opportunities' *Emory International Law Review* (2007) 21(2) 148.
36 Bilchitz 2011 *SAJHR* 22.
37 See further the views of S de Freitas 'Freedom of Association as a Foundational Right: Religious Associations and *Strydom v Nederduitse Gereformeerde Gemeente, Moreleta Park*' *South African Journal on Human Rights* (2012) 28(2) 258–272.
38 Human Rights Commission 2006 *Exclusionary Policies* 18.

However, no rights are absolute; including the rights entrenched in sections 15, 18 and 31 of the Constitution. Section 31(2) makes it clear that any exclusionary policies, actions or procedures by voluntary associations, including religious entities, would not be allowed unconditionally and can be limited but only in accordance with the requirements of the limitation clause and the test for proportionality. It is therefore not necessary to presume beforehand that any associational rights are subordinate and of lesser value than the right of equality and dignity. Most recently, in the case of *Gaum and Others v Van Rensburg NO and Others*,[39] the court suggested that in relation to the appointment of religious ministers, and in the terms of the Constitution, religious institutions and churches may be prohibited from unfairly discriminating against gays and lesbians. The case concerned a decision taken by the Dutch Reformed Church (DRC), and will be discussed in more detail in Chapter 10. The next section will focus on the limitation of rights in accordance with section 36 of the Constitution.

Limitation of rights

Constitutional limitation

In accordance with the requirement set out in section 36 of the Constitution (the limitation clause), the freedom to manifest a belief can be curtailed legitimately for certain purposes. As pointed out by Krishnaswami:[40]

> However, there are certain manifestations which are so obviously contrary to morality, public order, or the general welfare that public authorities are always entitled to limit them, or even to prohibit them altogether. Into this category fall such practices as the sacrifice of human beings, self-immolation, mutilation of the self or others, and reduction into slavery or prostitution, if carried out in the service of, or under the pretext of promoting, a religion or belief.

Section 31 permits exclusionary policies, rules and conduct provided that they are not constitutionally offensive. The issue is to determine when exclusionary policies, rules and conduct are inconsistent with any provision of the Bill of Rights. In order to demonstrate inconsistency for the purposes of section 31(2), it must be established that the exclusionary practices infringe a provision of the Bill of Rights and that such infringement is not reasonable and justifiable in an open and democratic society, as required by section 36 of the Constitution. As pointed out by the Constitutional Court in *Ferreira v Levin*,[41] the onus of proving an infringement of a provision of the Bill of Rights will be on the person making such an

39 *Gaum and Others v Van Rensburg NO and Others* (40819/17) [2019] ZAGPPHC 52 (8 March 2019).
40 Krishnaswami *Study of Discrimination* 29.
41 *Ferreira v Levin NO* 1996 (1) SA 984 (CC) para 44.

assertion, and the responsibility of establishing the requirements of section 36 will be on the religious organisation.

As pointed out earlier, section 31(2) of the Constitution was intended to ensure that practices offensive to the Bill of Rights, such as offensive group practices, were not shielded by the protection afforded by section 31(1). A 'constitutionally offensive group practice' has been described as an exclusionary policy, rule or conduct adopted by an association that are not permitted by the Constitution. In deciding whether or not these policies, rules or conduct are permitted by the Constitution, the limitation clause and the test for proportionality is extremely important. Of particular importance is the fact that such an enquiry does 'not start from the premise that associational rights are presumptively inferior and of less weight than the rights to equality and dignity'.[42]

Most of the complaints against voluntary associations require a balancing of rights between natural and juristic persons. This would require a court to assess whether, in a particular case, there had been a constitutional limitation of the right of the complainant. In order to achieve this, a court would have to consider the purpose of the limitation and all the other factors referred to in section 36 of the Constitution, which include:

- The nature of the right being limited and its importance to an open and democratic society.
- The nature and extent of the limitation, which would require an assessment of the extent to which the right is infringed.
- The relationship between the limitation and its purpose. This would require an assessment of the link between the limitation or discriminatory practice and the objectives and goals of the organisation.
- Less restrictive means to achieve the purpose.

The court followed this approach in the case of *Taylor v Kurtstag* NO.[43] In *Taylor*, the applicant sought to set aside a *Cherem*, issued by a Jewish ecclesiastical court, which had the effect of excommunicating him from the Jewish society for failing to comply with its decision. The applicant approached the court in order to prevent the publication of the *Cherem*. He argued that it violated his individual right to freedom of religion. The court held that adherents to Jewish Orthodoxy have the right to practise their religion in association with others and that freedom of religion also includes freedom of autonomy in setting requirements for the admission of their members. The court had to balance the individual right of the applicant against the association's rights of the community and whether the limitation of the applicant's rights could be justified. The court concluded that in the circumstances the limitation on the applicant's rights was reasonable and justifiable and that the associational rights of the religious organisation took precedence over the personal rights of the individual. The court did a comprehensive balancing

42 Human Rights Commission 2006 *Exclusionary Policies* 19.
43 See earlier discussion in Chapter 3.

exercise by assessing the full extent of the limitation on the rights of the applicant and weighed this against the associational rights of the organisation. In conclusion the court was of the view that it was reasonable and justifiable to limit the applicant's rights.

Another example is found in the case of *Christian Education*, which involved a challenge to section 10 of the South African Schools Act, which prohibited corporal punishment in any school. The court strived for balance under section 36 of the Constitution and held that the purpose of the ban on corporal punishment would be undermined if an exemption was allowed for the applicants. The Constitutional Court was of the view that section 10 of the Schools Act imposed a constitutionally acceptable limitation in terms of section 36 of the Constitution on parents' free exercise of their religious beliefs. After carefully analysing the limitation clause, the court concluded that the prohibition on corporal punishment in the Schools Act, although limiting the right to freedom of religion of Christian parents, was reasonable and justifiable. According to the court:

> On the basis of these assumptions made for the purposes of argument, I proceed to examine whether, under section 36, the negative impact which the Schools Act has on the practice of corporal correction in the schools of the appellant's religious community, is to be regarded as reasonable and justifiable in an open and democratic society based on human dignity, freedom and equality. If, even applying the approach most favourable to the appellant, the answer is yes, then it will not be necessary to consider alternative interpretations which would be less supportive of appellant's position.[44]

In relation to limiting the right to freedom of religion, it has been suggested that the principle of 'harm' must be used to determine degrees of protection and that only religious practices that cause harm should be limited.[45] Difficulties with an analysis under the limitation clause have also been raised:

> first because of the problems of weighing considerations of faith against those of reason, and secondly because of the problems of separating out what aspects of an activity are religious and protected by the Bill of Rights and what are secular and open to regulation in the ordinary way.[46]

However, it is important to note that even religious practices can be limited and that there is no automatic right to be exempted from the ordinary laws of the land and other regulations on the grounds of belief. Religious practices are particularly susceptible to limitation and the state must therefore prohibit practices that can cause harm to persons. An example is the judgment in the *Prince* case.

44 *Christian Education South Africa* para 28.
45 I Currie and J De Waal *The Bill of Rights Handbook* 6 ed (2013) 322, with reference to Denise Meyerson *Rights Limited* (1997) part 1.
46 Currie & De Waal *Bill of Rights Handbook* 322.

Mr Gareth Prince used dagga for religious purposes as an integral part of practising his religion as Rastafarian. When he wanted to register his contract of articles with the Cape Law Society, the Society refused to register his contract because they were not satisfied that he was a 'fit and proper person' as required by the Attorney's Act 53 of 1979, especially since he declared his intention to continue using dagga for religious purposes. Mr Prince argued that his possession and use of dagga was protected under the Constitution as part of his right to exercise his religion. He unsuccessfully challenged the society's decision in the Cape High Court[47] and the Supreme Court of Appeal.[48] He then lodged an appeal with the Constitutional Court,[49] where a divided court eventually dismissed the appeal with a 5–4 majority, but before doing so handed down a significant interim judgment, in which both sides were given the opportunity to gather and adduce the additional evidence required for the court to make an informed decision. Since this was only done in rare circumstances, the Constitutional Court made an attempt to accommodate the concerns of the religious minority and explained its decision as follows:

> [T]he appellant belongs to a minority group. The constitutional right asserted by the appellant goes beyond his own interest – it affects the Rastafari community. The Rastafari community is not a powerful one. It is a vulnerable group. It deserves the protection of the law precisely because it is a vulnerable minority. The very fact that Rastafari use cannabis exposes them to social stigmatisation… Our Constitution recognises that minority groups may hold their own religious views and enjoins us to tolerate and protect such views. However, the right to freedom of religion is not absolute. While members of a religious community may not determine for themselves which laws they will obey and which they will not, the state should, where it is reasonably possible, seek to avoid putting the believers to a choice between their faith and respect for the law.[50]

The Constitutional Court acknowledged the fact that Rastafari is a religion, that Mr Prince was a genuine follower of that religion and that the use of cannabis is central to the Rastafari religion.[51] The court unanimously held that the statutory prohibition on the use or possession of dagga was a limitation on the rights of the Rastafari to practise their religion.[52] The court then had to consider whether this limitation was justifiable in terms of section 36 of the Constitution. The court was divided on this point, particularly in relation to the existence of the less restrictive means to achieve the purpose of controlling the use and possession of dagga. The minority emphasised religious diversity and was of the view that:

47 *Prince v President of the Law Society, Cape of Good Hope* 1998 (8) BCLR 976 (C).
48 *Prince v President, Cape Law Society* 2000 (3) SA 845 (SCA).
49 *Prince v President, Cape Law Society and Others* 2002 (2) SA 794 (CC).
50 *Prince* CC para 26.
51 *Prince* CC para 40.
52 *Prince* CC para 44.

> In a constitutional democracy like ours that recognises and tolerates diverse religious faiths, tolerance of diversity must be demonstrated by accommodating the practices of all faiths, if this can be done without undermining the legitimate government interest.[53]

Although they accepted that the goal of preventing the abuse of drugs was a legitimate goal, the minority was of the view that it was unreasonable because they were overbroad:

> They are ostensibly aimed at the use of dependence-producing drugs that are inherently harmful and trafficking in those drugs. But they are unreasonable in that they also target uses that have not been shown to pose a risk of harm or to be incapable of being subjected to strict regulation and control.[54]

The majority was concerned about the state's ability to enforce its drug legislation, should an exemption in general terms for the possession and use of harmful drugs by persons who do so for religious purposes were to be permitted.[55] They also had some concerns about the practical difficulties in enforcing a permit system, as was suggested by Mr Prince, such as 'the financial and administrative problems associated with setting up and implementing any such system, and the difficulties in policing that would follow if permits were issued sanctioning the possession of cannabis for religious purposes'.[56] The Constitutional Court accordingly endorsed the decision of the Supreme Court of Appeal and dismissed the appeal.

The South African context in which the section 36 balancing exercise must be undertaken is of the utmost importance, and was highlighted by the court in both the *Christian Education* and the *Prince* case. In *Christian Education*, the court confirmed that the limitation clause provides for a 'nuanced and context-sensitive form of balancing'.[57] This approach requires an overall assessment, which may vary from case to case and there can be no absolute standard. According to the court:

> In essence, the Court must engage in a balancing exercise and arrive at a global judgment on proportionality and not adhere mechanically to a sequential check-list. As a general rule, the more serious the impact of the measure on the right, the more persuasive or compelling the justification must be. Ultimately, the question is one of degree to be assessed in the concrete legislative and social setting of the measure, paying due regard to the means which are realistically available in our country at this stage, but without losing sight of the ultimate values to be protected.[58]

53 *Prince* CC para 79.
54 *Prince* CC para 81.
55 *Prince* CC para 132.
56 *Prince* CC para 134.
57 *Prince* CC para 30.
58 *Prince* CC para 31

A similar approach was followed by the Constitutional Court in *Prince*, and Sachs J emphasised the importance of contextualising the balancing exercise, with reference to 'the context of a lived and experienced historical, sociological and imaginative reality'[59] and further 'to begin with, the very problem that is under consideration has to be located in the vast experiential dimensions of faith'. As this court has stated:

> The right to believe or not to believe, and to act or not to act according to his or her beliefs or non-beliefs, is one of the key ingredients of any person's dignity. Yet freedom of religion goes beyond protecting the inviolability of the individual conscience. For many believers, their relationship with God or creation is central to all their activities. It concerns their capacity to relate in an intensely meaningful fashion to their sense of themselves, their community and their universe. For millions in all walks of life, religion provides support and nurture and a framework for individual and social stability and growth. Religious belief has the capacity to awake concepts of self-worth and human dignity which form the cornerstone of human rights. It affects the believer's view of society and founds the distinction between right and wrong. It expresses itself in the affirmation and continuity of powerful traditions that frequently have an ancient character transcending historical epochs and national boundaries.[60]

Example

As outlined in Chapter 4, religious autonomy means that there rests a duty on the state to respect the religious rights of religious institutions and to create the space for them to enjoy these rights, free from state interference. Where the state seeks to regulate religious practices, it effectively means that these rights are limited and such limitation must be justified in terms of section 36 of the Constitution. An example of where proposed legislation in order to regulate religious institutions may be unconstitutional is the recent report and accompanying proposals for new legislation published by the CRL Rights Commission.

In April 2017 the CRL Rights Commission published its final Report on the *Commercialisation of Religion and Abuse of People's Belief Systems.* According to the Report, the proposals made by the Commission originated from various newspaper reports and complaints to the Commission, and the subsequent investigation by the Commission into abuses taking place in certain religious institutions. In its report, the Commission proposed the broad-scale regulation of religion in South Africa. In order to achieve that, they proposed that existing legislation should be amended to compel all religious institutions to register, or by creating new legislation that would establish statutory regulatory bodies

59 *Prince* CC para 151.
60 *Prince* CC para 151

responsible for regulating religious institutions and practitioners through registering and licencing.

Freedom of Religion South Africa (FOR SA) and the South African Council for the Protection and Promotion of Religious Rights and Freedoms, representing a large number (including many of the major) churches, denominations and faith groups in South Africa, endorsed a document in which they commented on this Report. They argue that the CRL Rights Commission's proposals for regulation fails the section 36 analysis and, should it be implemented, may be unconstitutional.

If one looks at the proposals outlined in the Commission's final report, there is no question that religious institutions' right to freedom of religion will be limited. Some of the main proposals include, for instance, the compulsory registration, licencing and accreditation of all religions.[61] Religious bodies will have to be recognised and monitored by regulatory bodies, in the form of peer review councils.[62] One of the proposals by the Commission relates to the fact that 'the traditional structured religions along with religious institutions that have structured systems in place should be able to articulate them and thus be accredited to act as 'umbrella organizations' or associations'.[63] This may discriminate against less 'traditional' religious institutions in violation of the institutional right to freedom of religion. As argued correctly by FOR SA and the South African Council for the Protection and Promotion of Religious Rights and Freedoms,[64] favouring some religious institutions to the exclusion of others can constitute unfair discrimination on the basis of one's religion or religious affiliation. The principle of neutrality in relation to religious beliefs is crucial, as expressed by the European Court of Human Rights: 'in exercising its regulatory power … in its relations with the various religions, denominations and beliefs, the State has a duty to remain neutral and impartial'.[65] It will also place a limitation on the right to form new religious communities. The state must be able to justify all of these limitations against the criteria of section 36 of the Constitution, otherwise any proposal or any legislation that provides for these limitations may be unconstitutional. In relation to what is required in terms of section 36, there is no doubt about the importance of the right to freedom of religion in a democratic and pluralistic society like South Africa. The importance of both the individual, and in particular the collective aspect of the right, has been discussed in detail in the previous chapters.

61 Final Report on 'The Commercialisation of Religion and Abuse of People's Belief Systems' by the Commission for the Promotion and Protections of the Rights of Cultural Religious and Linguistic Communities (CRL Rights Commission) (April 2017) 32–33.

62 *Commercialisation Report* 34.

63 *Commercialisation Report* 31.

64 Comments on the CRL Rights Commission's Report on the 'Commercialisation' of Religion, submitted by Freedom of Religion South Africa (FOR SA) and the South African Council for the Protection and Promotion of Religious Rights and Freedoms (28 February 2017) 56.

65 *Metropolitan Church of Bessarabia v Moldova*, § 116 (ECtHR 2001).

In relation to the importance of the purpose of the limitation, the limitation must be lawful and legitimate. The CRL Rights Commission explained the purpose of their recommendation in their report as the responsibility to guard against the undermining and abuse of religious freedom and therefore to protect individuals from abusive practices by religious leaders and institutions. No doubt this is a legitimate and lawful purpose for the limitation. As the court pointed out in the case of *MEC for Education: KwaZulu-Natal and Others v Pillay*,[66] even the 'most vital practice of a religion or culture can be limited for the greater good. No belief is absolute, but those that are closer to the core of an individual's identity require a greater justification to limit'.

In relation to the nature and extent of the limitation, it has been highlighted above that the extent of the regulation (in the form of the various requirements) limits both the individual as well as the collective right to freedom of religion. Thus, various components of the right to freedom of religion will be limited. In relation to the link between the limitation and its purpose, the question is whether the severity of the limitation on religious institutions outweighs the importance and purpose of the limitation. In order for it to be reasonable and justifiable in an open and democratic society, it must be proportionate to the benefit. FOR SA and the South African Council for the Protection and Promotion of Religious Rights and Freedoms are of the view that the proposed recommendations 'will limit various critical aspects of freedom of religion to such an extent that there will be no rational relationship between the limitation and its purpose'.[67] There is also no way of knowing whether any legislative changes or regulative requirements will in fact limit religious abuses and provide for the required protection of individuals from religious malpractices. Accordingly, the view is that 'when it is uncertain whether a limitation will indeed achieve the purpose, there is also not a rational relationship between the limitation and its purpose'.[68]

The last requirement considers whether there are less restrictive means or alternative methods that can be used to achieve the same purpose. The far-reaching proposals for regulation and creating new legislation will not necessarily solve the problem and may not be the less restrictive means of achieving the purpose, as required. An alternative method is exactly what the CRL Rights Commission has proposed in its report, where they have acknowledged the fact that many of the abuses that took place related to non-compliance with existing legislation. In fact, one of their recommendations was that the Commission itself 'should provide essential assistance in helping organizations to get their house in order and to ensure compliance with existing legislation ...'[69] This finds support in the comments submitted in that 'it is quite possible that less restrictive means are available in the form of the effective enforcement of existing legislation to achieve the same

66 *MEC for Education: KwaZulu-Natal and Others v Pillay* 2008 (1) SA 474 (CC) para 95.
67 *Comments Commercialisation of Religion* 60.
68 *Comments Commercialisation of Religion* 60
69 *Commercialisation Report* 29.

purpose'.[70] Legislation to deal with most of the highlighted issues in the report do in fact exist, and can be better enforced with the help of existing enforcement agencies, individuals, the CRL Rights Commission and religious institutions, by reporting abuses to the appropriate bodies.

Based on the above analysis in accordance with section 36, it is clear that the CRL Rights Commission's proposed regulation of the religious sector in the form of new legislation, once enacted, will not pass constitutional muster. Not only will it impact severely on the institutional autonomy of religious institutions, it has also been shown that alternative methods are available that are not as restrictive as the recommendations proposed.[71]

Conclusion

This chapter has illustrated that states are obliged to respect and to ensure to all individuals subject to their jurisdiction the right to freedom of religion or belief without distinction of any kind, such as race, colour, sex, language, religion or belief or other status. The Religious Charter emphasises the right of every person and religious institution to the impartiality and protection of the state in respect of religion.[72] The state must further create a positive and safe environment for the exercise of religious freedom, but may not promote, favour or prejudice a particular faith, religion or conviction, and may not indoctrinate anyone in respect of religion.[73] No person may be unfairly discriminated against on the grounds of their faith, religion or religious affiliation.[74]

On a national level, legislation should be reviewed to assure that any differentiations among religions are justified and that they are not used as a justification for discrimination. Religious institutions should regularly evaluate their exclusionary policies, rules and conduct in accordance with the requirements set out in the Constitution. Religious institutions, whose objectives are to achieve constitutionally legitimate goals, must be allowed to adopt exclusionary rules and policies in order to afford appropriate weight to associational rights aimed at developing and protecting religious liberties.

Any limitation to religious freedom rights should be legitimate and lawful, and less restrictive means to achieve the purpose should always be considered. As pointed out in this chapter, and as required by the section 36 analysis to make use of less restrictive means to limit abusive religious practices, some of the existing laws are much less restrictive than the far-reaching and oppressive regulation of religion proposed by the CRL Rights Commission in its report on the

70 *Comments Commercialisation of Religion* 60.
71 For a more detailed account of the constitutionality of the regulation of religion, see G du Plessis 'The Constitutionality of the Regulation of Religion in South Africa – Untoward Restrictions of the Right to Religious Freedom?' *South African Law Journal* forthcoming.
72 Religious Charter section 3.
73 Religious Charter sub-section 3.1
74 Religious Charter sub-section 3.2

commercialisation of religion. Any limitation to the right to freedom of religion, in order to constitute a reasonable and legitimate limitation that passes constitutional muster, must be found to be justified in relation to the purpose, importance and effect of the provision which resulted in its limitation. It is important that the availability of less restrictive means to achieve this purpose must be taken into account. The standard required by section 36 that needs to be applied is the 'nuanced and contextual one' and not the 'rigid one of strict scrutiny' test. As pointed out by the court:

> Limitations analysis under our Constitution is based not on formal or categorical reasoning but on processes of balancing and proportionality as required by section 36… What it requires is the maximum harmonisation of all the competing considerations, on a principled yet nuanced and flexible case-by-case basis, located in South African reality yet guided by international experience, articulated with appropriate candour and accomplished without losing sight of the ultimate values highlighted by our Constitution.[75]

Our courts have acknowledged the fact that, when engaging in such a balancing exercise, religious and secular activities are not that easy to separate, and often overlap.

With this in mind, the next part of the book, through the various chapters, will discuss in more detail the rights, responsibilities and freedoms associated with religious institutions in particular, within some specific spheres of society where government regulation of religion has occurred or are necessary or has proved to be problematic. Aspects that will be addressed through the various discussions and case examples include aspects of religious education; religious rituals, rites and practices; religious marriages; aspects of financial regulation; hate speech and blasphemy; and other religious exemptions. Through the regulation of these religious practices, a balance often needs to be struck between religious beliefs and practices on the one hand, and the reasonable and legitimate regulation of these practices by the state through legislation and other means, on the other.

Bibliography

Benson I 'The Freedom of Conscience and Religion in Canada: Challenges and Opportunities' *Emory International Law Review* (2007) 21(2) 111–166.

Bilchitz D 'Should Religious Associations Be Entitled to Discriminate?' *South African Journal of Human Rights* (2011) 27(2) 219–248.

Colton P 'Religious Entities as Legal Persons – Ireland' in L Friedner (ed) *Churches and Other Religious Organisations as Legal Persons* (2007) 125–138Leuven: Peeters.

Comments on the CRL Rights Commission's Report on the 'Commercialisation' of Religion, submitted by Freedom of Religion South Africa (FOR SA) and the South African

75 *Prince* CC para 155.

Council for the Protection and Promotion of Religious Rights and Freedoms (28 February 2017). Online at: https://forsa.org.za.

Currie I and J de Waal *The Bill of Rights Handbook* 6 ed (2013) Cape Town: Juta.

De Freitas S 'Freedom of Association as a Foundational Right: Religious Associations and *Strydom v Nederduitse Gereformeerde Gemeente, Moreleta Park*' *South African Journal on Human Rights* (2012) 28(2) 258–272.

De Vos P 'On Freedom of Religion and the Gay Music Teacher' Constitutionally Speaking Blog (3 September 2008).

Du Plessis G 'The Constitutionality of the Regulation of Religion in South Africa – Untoward Restrictions of the Right to Religious Freedom?' *South African Law Journal* forthcoming.

Final Report on 'The Commercialisation of Religion and Abuse of People's Belief Systems' by the Commission for the Promotion and Protections of the Rights of Cultural Religious and Linguistic Communities (CRL Rights Commission) (April 2017). Online at: www.crlcommission.org.za.

Hasson K 'Religious Liberty and Human Dignity: A Tale of Two Declarations' *Harvard Journal of Law & Public Policy* (2003) 27(1) 81–92.

Krishnaswami A *Study of Discrimination in the Matter of Religious Rights and Practices* (1960) New York: United Nations Publication.

Lenta P 'Muslim Headscarves in the Workplace and Schools' *South African Law Journal* (2007) 124(2) 296–316.

Pienaar G 'Konstitusionele Voorskrifte rakende Regspersone' *Tydskrif vir Hedendaagse Romeins-Hollandse Reg* (1997) 60564–588.

South African Human Rights Commission (SAHRC) *Report Public Inquiry Exclusionary Policies of Voluntary Associations: Constitutional Considerations* (2006). Online at: www.sahrc.org.za.

Van Coller EH 'Religious Institutions and Fundamental Rights: Applicability, Interaction and Limitations' in C Cianitto, W Cole Durham Jr, S Ferrari and D Thayer *Law, Religion, Constitution* (2013) 209–226Farnham, UK: Ashgate.

Van der Vyver J 'Equality and Sovereignty of Religious Institutions: A South African Perspective' *Santa Clara Journal of International Law* (2012) 10(1) 147–169.

Woolman S 'On the Fragility of Associational Life: A Constitutional Liberal's Response to Patrick Lenta' *South African Journal on Human Rights* (2009) 25(2) 280–305.

Part 2

5 The right to worship in community with others

Introduction

As discussed earlier, the right to worship is an important part of the collective right to freedom of religion and normally takes place in community with others and may even take place in public. The Krishnaswami Report[1] highlighted the importance of the collective aspects of the right to freedom of religion, particularly as part of the right to manifests one's religion. However, most countries are moving towards limiting or even prohibiting the right to worship in public. Countries with a state religion or established church often recognise the right to worship in public only for their own followers, and members of other faiths are denied this right. Unreasonable government regulation can also affect a community's right to worship. This is expressed as:

> Licences for the opening of places of worship may be arbitrarily withheld, or permits for the assembling of a group of worshippers arbitrarily refused. Or, if the licence or permit is not withheld or refused, it may be granted on terms which are onerous or difficult to comply with, and which may in effect negate — or at least seriously curtail — the right to worship in common.[2]

Communities perform rituals for various purposes. These rituals are extraordinary practices performed by the living for the spiritual world, and include special gatherings of the clans aimed at communal religious practices, like the rites of passage and sometimes:

> special rituals as requested by ancestors, like the bringing back of the spirit of some family member who died far away from home. In these religious gatherings the community acts out its various forms of worship. Through these rituals, unity and healing are achieved.[3]

1 A Report commissioned by the sub-commission on the Prevention of Discrimination and Protection of Minorities in 1956.
2 A Krishnaswami *Study of Discrimination in the Matter of Religious Rights and Practices* (1960) 31.
3 N Mndende 'Law and Religion in South Africa: An African Traditional Perspective' *NGTT* (2013) 54(4) 78. For further readings on this topic, see N Mndende *African*

In the early 1960s, Krishnaswami, Special Rapporteur to the United Nations on the Prevention of Discrimination and Protection of Minorities, highlighted the importance of religious rituals and practices. With reference to a 1955 Supreme Court of India case, he observed:

> A religion may not only lay down a code of ethical rules for its followers to accept; it might prescribe rituals and observances, ceremonies and modes of worship which are regarded as integral parts of religion, and these forms and observances might extend even to matters of food and dress.[4]

Section 15 of the Constitution provides for very wide protection of religious freedom. The right to believe always goes hand in hand with the right to manifest and practise those beliefs, which means that one has the right to the private or public, and the individual or joint, observance and exercise of one's religious or other convictions. Religious activities such as the slaughtering of animals are ways in which believers manifest and practise their beliefs. These practices form part of the right to freedom of religion, protected under section 15 of the Constitution, read together with section 31, which guarantees the right to persons belonging to religious communities to enjoy and practise their religion with other members of that community. This is further entrenched in section 4 of the South African Charter of Religious Rights and Freedoms (SACRRF). This section states:

> every person has the right to the private or public, and individual or joint, observance or exercise of their convictions, which may include but are not limited to reading and discussion of sacred texts, confession, proclamation, worship, prayer, witness, arrangements, attire, appearance, diet, customs, rituals and pilgrimages, and the observance of religious and other sacred days of rest, festivals and ceremonies.

As correctly pointed out by Krishnaswami,[5] the collective aspect of the right to manifest religion or believe is extremely important 'since intervention by the State to regulate or to limit manifestations of a religion or belief are more frequent when these manifestations are performed "in community with others" than when they are performed "alone"'. Religious institutions have the right to uphold community life. This flows from the important right to manifest religion as part of the right to freedom of religion (as outlined in sections 15 and 31 of the Constitution) and the right of freedom of association (section 18). The right to uphold community life and to worship in community with others seeks to protect different aspects of the religious practice of members of religious institutions. This

Spiritual Journey: Rites of Passage among the Xhosa Speaking of South Africa (2006) Cape Town: Icamagu Institute; N Mndende *Tears of Distress: Voices of a Denied Spirituality in a Democratic South Africa* (2009) Idutywa: Icamagu Institute; JS Mbiti *Introduction to African Religion* 2 ed (2015) Long Grove, IL: Waveland.

4 Krishnaswami *Study of Discrimination* 19.

5 Krishnaswami *Study of Discrimination* 21.

chapter discusses a number of these practices and also illustrates through case examples and relevant legislative provisions that any limitations of the right to uphold religious community life must be prescribed by law and regulated through legislation, and limited only in terms of the Constitution. The practices include burial rights; circumcision and rites of passage; aspects of witchcraft; religious slaughter and dietary practice; equipment and various religious symbols; and religious holidays.

Burial rights

Introduction

Cultural and religious communities are often deeply connected to certain places in the natural world. These religious or sacred sites often carry with them 'a whole range of rules and regulations regarding people's behaviour in relation to a set of beliefs to do with the spirits of the ancestors, as well as of more remote and powerful gods or spirits'.[6] Issues relating to land and property have become much contested in South Africa lately. Add religion to the mix and the words of the American religious liberty scholar, Douglas Laycock, comes to mind when he stated in the late 1990s that 'land use regulation has become the most widespread obstacle to the free exercise of religion'.[7] Burial rights relates to the whole range of death and burial practices in respect of the deceased, including aspects such as places of worship, disposal of the dead, burial grounds, crematoria and religious sites. Over the years, cultural communities all over the world have experienced constant threats to their sacred sites, and religious and cultural communities in South Africa have experienced the same. Religious heritage sites and religious traditions play a significant role in educating future generations and creating a sense of belonging in communities. Among many cultures, a cemetery or burial site is often much more than just a place of final rest for the dead, but also a place of spiritual and cultural reference. In some cultures, particularly in African cultures, it is a place of connecting with ancestral spirits and for ancestral veneration.

Legislative protection

Apart from the constitutional provisions protecting religious rights, some of the other legal mechanisms in place to protect and promote communities' religious rights and heritage in terms of burial rights and relevant to this discussion include the Religious Charter, the National Heritage Resources Act 25 of 1999 ('Heritage Act') and various international instruments. The Religious Charter makes provision for the right of every person to have access to sacred places and burial sites

6 MM Ratipa 'Just Piles of Rock to Developers but Places of Worship to Native Americans' – Exploring the Significance of Earth Jurisprudence for South African Cultural Communities' *Potchefstroom Electronic Law Journal* (2015) 18(1) 3198–3199.
7 R Adhar and I Leigh *Religious Freedom in the Liberal State* 2 ed (2013) 346.

relevant to their convictions. Such access and the preservation of such places and sites must be regulated within the law and with due regard for property rights. According to the Charter:

> 4 Subject to the duty of reasonable accommodation and the need to provide essential services, every person has the right to the private or public, and individual or joint, observance or exercise of their convictions, which may include but are not limited to reading and discussion of sacred texts, confession, proclamation, worship, prayer, witness, arrangements, attire, appearance, diet, customs, rituals and pilgrimages, and the observance of religious and other sacred days of rest, festivals and ceremonies.
>
> 4.1 Every person has the right to private access to sacred places and burial sites relevant to their convictions. Such access, and then preservation of such places and sites, must be regulated within the law and with due regard for property rights.

In accordance with section 4 of the Charter, anyone is entitled to visit sacred places and burial sites, as long as property rights and other legal considerations are observed. Importantly, any visit to sites on private land must be arranged with the landowner, and may not put an unreasonable burden on the landowner or cause damage of any kind to the property. Emphasis is placed on mutual respect and consideration.[8] When interpreting the Bill of Rights, a court must also promote the values that underlie an open and democratic society based on human dignity, equality and freedom and must consider international law.[9] In this regard, the International Labour Organization (ILO) Convention 169 is relevant. Although South Africa is not a signatory to this Convention, it provides relevant guidelines and has persuasive value when a dispute of this nature must be resolved by the courts. ILO Convention 169 is the Indigenous and Tribal Peoples Convention of 1989 (ITP Convention).[10] The ITP Convention is based on respect for the cultures and ways of life of indigenous and tribal peoples. It aims at overcoming discriminatory practices affecting these peoples and enabling them to participate in decision-making that affects their lives.

The ITP Convention acknowledges the fact that in many parts of the world indigenous people are unable to enjoy their fundamental human rights to the same degree as the rest of the population of the states within which they live, and that their laws, values, customs and perspectives have often been eroded. The Preamble specifically recognises 'the aspirations of these peoples to exercise control over their own institutions, ways of life and economic development and to maintain and develop their identities, languages and religions, within the

8 See Religious Charter 29.

9 Constitution of the Republic of South Africa, 1996, section 39(1).

10 International Labour Organization *Indigenous and Tribal Peoples Convention, 1989 (No. 169)*. Convention concerning Indigenous and Tribal Peoples in Independent Countries (Entry into force: 05 Sep 1991) Adoption: Geneva, 76th ILC session (27 June 1989).

framework of the States in which they live'. Article 14.2 of the Convention gives due and full recognition to 'the right of the [indigenous] people to use lands not exclusively occupied by them, but to which they have traditionally had access for their subsistence and traditional activities'. Similar sentiments are echoed in Article 26[11] of the United Nations Declaration on the Rights of Indigenous Peoples (UNDRIP). UNDRIP was adopted through resolution 61/295 of the General Assembly. While as a General Assembly declaration UNDRIP is not a legally binding instrument under international law, it 'represents a commitment on the part of the United Nations and Member States to its provisions, within the framework of the obligations established by the Charter of the United Nations'.[12] UNDRIP elaborates on existing human rights standards by attempting 'to bestow indigenous peoples with a set of special or new human rights, but rather provides a contextualized elaboration of general human rights principles and rights as they relate to the specific historical, cultural and social circumstances of indigenous peoples'.[13] UNDRIP contains further provisions that traditional communities can refer to in their mission to protect their cultural sites. Article 25 emphasises the rights of indigenous peoples to 'maintain and strengthen their distinctive spiritual and material relationships with the lands they have traditionally owned or otherwise occupied or used, and to uphold their responsibilities to future generations'. Article 29 further provides for the right to the conservation and protection of the environment and the productive capacity of their lands or territories and resources. Re-enforcing the values expressed in the Heritage Act, it provides for private access to religious and cultural sites[14] and the right to maintain, control, protect and develop their cultural heritage.[15]

On a national level in terms of legislation, the Heritage Act is important in relation to the protection of religious and cultural heritage. The South African Heritage Resources Agency (SAHRA) is the national administrative body responsible for the protection of South Africa's cultural heritage. It was established through the Heritage Act. The legislation aims to promote good management of the national estate,[16] and to enable and encourage communities to nurture and conserve their legacy so that it may be bequeathed to future generations.

11 Section 26 provides that 'Indigenous peoples have the right to own, develop, control and use the lands and territories, including the total environment of the lands … which they have traditionally owned or otherwise occupied or used. This includes the right to the full recognition of their laws, traditions and customs, land tenure systems and institutions for the development and management of resources, and the right to effective measures by States to prevent any interference with, alienation of or encroachment upon these rights'.

12 *The United Nations Declaration on the Rights of Indigenous Peoples: A Manual for National Human Rights Institutions(UNDRIP)*, the Office of the United Nations High Commissioner for Human Rights, August 2013, 37. Online at: www.ohchr.org/Documents/Issues/IPeoples/ UNDRIPManualForNHRIs.pdf.

13 *Ibid.*

14 UNDRIP article 12.

15 UNDRIP article 31(1).

16 Section 3(1) of the Act states that those heritage resources of South Africa that are of cultural significance or other special value for the present community and for future

In terms of the Act, 'heritage resource' means any place or object of cultural significance. 'Cultural significance' includes reference to spiritual value and, according to section 3(1), they are considered part of the national estate. The national estate also includes graves and burial grounds, including ancestral graves.[17] A place or object will also be considered part of the national estate if it has cultural significance or other special value because of its strong or special association with a particular community or cultural group for social, cultural or spiritual reasons.[18] In addition to the formal protection of culturally significant graves, all graves older than 60 years and not in a cemetery (such as ancestral graves in rural areas) are protected. The legislation protects the interests of communities which have an interest in the graves and require that they must be contacted and consulted before any disturbance can take place. Agreements must also be made with such communities and individuals regarding the future of such grave or burial ground. In this regard, section 5 of the Act emphasises the fact that heritage resources form an important part of the history and beliefs of communities and must be managed in a way that acknowledges the right of affected communities to be consulted and to participate in their management. Despite numerous provisions in legislation protecting burial rights, religious communities still face various challenges, particularly in relation to the reuse and relocation of graves and access to sacred places and burial sites on public and private land. The next section will highlight a few of these challenges.

Challenges

Reuse of graves

In terms of the Constitution, municipalities have the right to administer any matter assigned to them by national or provincial legislation and may make and administer bylaws for the effective administration of the matters that they have the right to administer. Part B of schedule 5 specifically provides for cemeteries, funeral parlours and crematoria. According to eThekwini cemetery bylaws, the city may reuse graves which are more than 10 years old, where leases have not been renewed, after advertising its intention to allow interested lessees to apply for renewals. In September 2015, the eThekwini Municipality called on the public to claim all unclaimed family graves, by renewing grave leases to ensure graves more than 10 years old were legally leased. Religious and traditional leaders were shocked at the call to claim graves for recycling, since various religions and cultures do not allow the practice. In relation to the Zulu culture, the chairman of the KZN House of Traditional Leaders stated that they respect graves and that

generations must be considered part of the national estate and fall within the sphere of operations of heritage resources authorities. Section 2 includes a list of such resources, including graves and burial sites.

17 NHRA section 3(2)(g).

18 NHRA section 3(3)(g).

'once a person has passed away, we respect that person and we can't do anything to remove the grave except to discuss with the family'.[19]

After receiving a number of complaints from the public in relation to the reuse of graves, the CRL Rights Commission, during an investigation into religious and cultural leaders and practices, also investigated the policy and practices of the eThekwini Municipality in relation to the reuse of graves and issued a report.[20] The Commission was informed that local governments' disregard for the principles regarding religious and cultural rights of most communities have led them to feel that the practice of reuse of graves without their consent is a violation of their religious and cultural rights.[21]

Some of the solutions and alternatives to conventional burial proposed by the South African Local Government Association (SALGA) include the use of eco-cemetery concepts, intensive recycling of graves, a multiple-use approach to cemeteries and the employing of a variety of cost-effective methods as alternatives to traditional/in-ground burial, including cremations.[22] However, communities are still not in favour of these methods. In African religious belief systems, it is important to have access to graves as it is custom to visit the sites and perform rituals when people face problems.[23] Many traditional religious communities in South Africa see the world of the ancestors as 'analogous' and 'contiguous' to the world of the living.[24] They also believe that the improper care of the dead has more sinister and far-reaching consequences for the community at large.[25]

Many of the problems that communities have experienced seems to be traced back to poor communication, lack of consultation with communities and various stakeholders, and poor implementation of the Heritage Act and other relevant legislation.[26] A lack of communication and proper consultation was a repeated

19 L Comins 'Durban's Plan to Recycle Graves' (14 September 2015) Online at: www.iol.co.za/news/south-africa/kwazulu-natal/durbans-plan-to-recycle-graves-1915860.

20 See the CRL Rights Commission *Report 'Reuse of Graves by Local Governments: A Solution or Violation of Cultural and Religious Rights of Communities'*. Report compiled by the Commission for the Promotion and Protection of the Cultural, Religious and Linguistic Communities 18. Online at: http://crlcommission.org.za/docs/reuse-report.pdf.

21 *Reuse of Graves Report* 3.

22 *Reuse of Graves Report* 19.

23 According to Mndende 2013 *NGTT* 75, African tradition religion means the 'indigenous religion of the Africans. It is the religion that has been handed down from generation to generation by the forebears of the present generation of Africans. It is not a fossil religion (a thing of the past) but a religion that Africans today have made theirs by living it and practicing it'. See further PA Dopamu 'Towards Understanding African Traditional Religion' in EM Uka (ed) *Readings in African Traditional Religion* (1991) 19–37 New York: Peter Lang.

24 See further H Ngubane 'Some Notions of '"Purity" and "Impurity" Amongst the Zulu' *African Journal of the International African Institute* (1976) 46(3) 274–284.

25 B Saccaggi and A Esterhuysen 'Sekuruwe Grave relocation: A Lesson in Process and Practice' *The South African Archaeological Bulletin* (2014) 69(200) 176.

26 For a discussion of some of the challenges faced by SAHRA, see A Esterhuysen 'Undermining Heritage' *The South African Archaeological Bulletin* (2009) 64(189) 1;

theme in many of these cases and often communities are not aware of or not informed about the legislation.

Access to sacred places and burial sites

In relation to access to sacred places and burial sites, a conflict between the right to freedom of religion and property rights is inevitable. The right to bury on farmland has been particularly problematic. On the one hand, landowners feel that they have a right to enjoy undisturbed use and ownership of their land. On the other hand, occupiers feel that as occupiers of land they have a right of security of tenure including the right to bury their deceased family members on land where they reside. In South Africa, both the land owners and occupiers are protected by section 25 of the Constitution and the Extension of Security of Tenure Act 62 of 1997 (ESTA), which gives effect to section 25.

An interesting case came before the Supreme Court of Appeal in *Nkosi and Another v Bührmann*,[27] where the appellant, Grace Nkosi, wished to have the body of her late son, Petros Nkosi, buried on a farm in the Ermelo district where she resided as an occupier. She relied heavily on section 5(d) of ESTA, which provides that an occupier shall have the right to freedom of religion, belief and opinion and of expression. This case raised a sensitive and emotionally contentious question involving, on the one hand, the right to religious freedom, and particularly the right to practise one's religion, and, on the other hand, the right not to be deprived of one's land except by law. The respondent, who is the owner of the farm, refused consent for the burial. The main question that they had to address in relation to the right to freedom of religion was whether the right to freedom of religion entitled the appellant by law to take some of the respondent's land for a grave. The court acknowledged that funeral and graveside rites, rituals and ceremonies are very much part of religious beliefs and practice[28] and that it is the right of all citizens to observe and carry out their religious practices when burying their dead.[29] The court highlighted the fact that a burial not only requires a piece of ground to be available, but also the necessary permission or consent of the land owner, whether the state, a juristic person or an individual.[30] The court came to the conclusion that the right to freedom of religion and religious practice has internal limits and that it 'does not confer unfettered liberty to choose a grave site nor does it include the right to take a grave site without the consent of the owner

and further EH van Coller 'Burials Rights: Protecting the Religious and Cultural Heritage of Communities in South Africa' in M Christian Green et al (eds) *Religious Pluralism, Heritage and Social Development in Africa* (2017) 333–351; D Skosana 'Protecting the Dead: The South African National Heritage Resources Act in Context' in M Christian Green et al (eds) *Religious Pluralism, Heritage and Social Development in Africa* (2017) 315–331.

27 *Nkosi and Another v Bührmann* 2002 1 SA 372 (SCA).

28 *Nkosi* para 46.

29 *Nkosi* para 47.

30 *Nkosi* para 47.

of the land concerned'.[31] The court subsequently dismissed the appeal. As a result of this judgment, the legislature amended the provisions of ESTA and enacted section 6(2)(dA).[32] Section 6(2)(dA) of ESTA allowed occupiers to assert a right of familial burial as against landowners, provided certain conditions were met. In order to enjoy this protection, the occupier must thus establish on the balance of probabilities that he or she is an 'occupier' on the farm where he or she intends burying the deceased; the deceased was a member of his or her family; the burial sought would be in accordance with his or her religious and/or cultural beliefs; the deceased was residing on land which the occupier resided at the time of death of the deceased; and an established practice on land exists to bury deceased family members.

Just over a year after it came into force, section 6(2)(dA) was challenged in the case of *Nhlabathi*,[33] where the Nhlabathi family approached the Land Claims Court (LCC) for an order permitting the deceased's burial on the farm of the respondent. When the family requested permission for the remains to be buried on the farm, the owner rejected the request and they decided to approach the LCC and relied on section 6(2)(dA) of ESTA. The application to bury in *Nhlabathi* was successful[34] and the court was happy to conclude that at the time of his death, the deceased was residing on the farm and that nothing was put before them to substantiate a submission that the proprietary rights of the owner in this case might outbalance the burial rights of the first applicant. In the court's view, there existed an established practice to permit the burial of deceased occupiers and members of their families on the farm. The applicants belonged to the Christian Church in Zion and the burial would be conducted in accordance with the rites of that church, just as the burials of their two children. In a later case of *Dlamini and Another v Joosten And Others*,[35] the court, with reference to section 6(2)(dA), confirmed that once a burial practice has been established, the landowner may not subsequently withdraw consent. The Dlamini family has resided and worked on the farm for generations, and over the years they had buried their deceased on the farm in accordance with their religion and cultural belief with the consent of the landowners. However, in 2002 the owners withdrew the permission, and when the Dlaminis sought permission from them to bury the deceased, this was refused. The Dlaminis submitted that it is a religious or cultural belief that deceased members of their family must be buried close to their homestead so that the spirits of their ancestors might be close to them. They argued successfully that once a practice of allowing burials had been established on the farm, as it had been in the

31 *Nkosi* para 49.

32 Without prejudice to the generality of the provisions of section 5 and subsection (1), and balanced with the rights of the owner or person in charge, an occupier shall have the right to bury a deceased member of his or her family who, at the time of that person's death, was residing on the land on which the occupier is residing, in accordance with their religion or cultural belief, if an established practice in respect of the land exists.

33 *Nhlabathi and Others v Fick* [2003] 2 All SA 323 (LCC) para 36.

34 *Nhlabathi* para 44.

35 *Dlamini and Another v Joosten And Others* 2006 (3) SA 342 (SCA).

case of the deceased, it could not be withdrawn unilaterally. The Supreme Court of Appeal upheld the appeal.

In 2014, the Land Claims Court was confronted with an urgent application by Mr Selomo in *Selomo v Doman*,[36] in terms of 6(2)(dA) of ESTA to bury his deceased daughter at the family gravesite on a farm where he had previously resided. The court had to decide whether Mr Selomo was an occupier in terms of ESTA and whether he and his daughter were still residing on the farm at the time of her death, as required by 6(2)(dA) of ESTA. The court referred to numerous cases and legislative provisions in order to substantiate the conclusion that a burial should be allowed. Of importance is the fact that the court recognised that dignity, religion and culture should not overshadow real rights.[37] The court relied heavily on the fact that the burial would cause very limited prejudice for the respondent, as opposed to the considerable prejudice suffered by the applicant.[38] Parker and Zaal argue that the court could have strengthened its argument by, for instance, relying on the right to freedom of religion in section 15 of the Constitution.[39] They are further of the view that although the decision can be criticised as bad in law and despite numerous technical flaws, the court appreciated that 'for those holding traditional indigenous beliefs appropriate familial burials are a crucial matter of dignity and respect'. Based on this view, the judgment 'extended the law governing indigenous burial practices'.[40]

Pilgrimages

A pilgrimage to a holy place is seen as a way for people to reconcile themselves with God[41] and is often associated with sacred places. Pilgrimages are also associated with religious tourism and in South Africa we find various pilgrimages. The Cape Camino, for instance, advertises itself in the following manner:

> The sense of being on a spiritual journey, and the sense of peace, as well as the knowledge that we can do extraordinary things by placing one foot in front of the other for a million steps.[42]

The Heritage Act aims to promote good management of the national estate,[43] and to enable and encourage communities to nurture and conserve

36 2014 JDR 0780 (LCC).
37 *Selomo v Doman* para 43.
38 *Selomo v Doman* paras 41–43.
39 For a more detailed discussion of the relevant cases, particularly the *Seloma* decision, see J Parker and FN Zaal 'Extending Recognition of Indigenous Burial Practices in *Selomo v Doman* 2014 JDR 0780 (LCC)' *Potchefstroom Electronic Law Journal* (2016) *19* 19.
40 Parker & Zaal 2016 *Potchefstroom Electronic Law Journal* 3.
41 See https://www.scross.co.za/2009/12/sa_pilgrimages/
42 See https://capecamino.co.za/
43 Section 3(1) of the Act states that those heritage resources of South Africa that are of cultural significance or other special value for the present community and for future generations must be considered part of the national estate and fall within the sphere

their legacy so that it may be bequeathed to future generations. According to the preamble:

> Our heritage is unique and precious and it cannot be renewed. It helps us to define our cultural identity and therefore lies at the heart of our spiritual well-being and has the power to build our nation. It has the potential to affirm our diverse cultures, and in so doing shape our national character. Our heritage celebrates our achievements and contributes to redressing past inequities. It educates, it deepens our understanding of society and encourages us to empathise with the experience of others. It facilitates healing and material and symbolic restitution and it promotes new and previously neglected research into our rich oral traditions and customs.

This quotation from the Heritage Act encapsulates the spirit of the SAHRA. Heritage resources contribute significantly to research, education and tourism and according to the World Tourism Organization (UNWTO), the United Nations agency responsible for the promotion of responsible, sustainable and universally accessible tourism, approximately 300 to 330 million tourists visit the world's key religious sites every year, including burial sites.[44] UNWTO Secretary-General, Teleb Rifai, views religious tourism as crucial in building cultural dialogue and peace. According to Rifai, 'Religious tourism can also be a powerful instrument for raising awareness regarding the importance of safeguarding one's heritage and that of humanity, and help preserve these important sites for future generations'.[45]

South Africa has many sacred sites, as many as there are cultures and beliefs, ranging from sacred hills, valleys and lakes to mosques, kramats – the holy shrines of Islam – and Hindu temples. There are more than 20 recognised kramats in the Cape Peninsula area, with one of the oldest known gravesites in Constantia.[46] These kramats mark the graves of Holy Men of the Muslim faith who have died at the Cape. Some of the top religious sites in South Africa, according to the travel website Trip Advisor, are the Hare Krishna Temple of Understanding in Durban, St George's Cathedral in Cape Town Central, the Dutch Reformed Church in Stellenbosch, Regina Mundi in Soweto, Nizamiye Mosque in Midrand and the Cathedral of St Michael and St George in Grahamstown.[47] On the Free State–Lesotho Border, pilgrims have started to re-occupy certain highland caves in the

of operations of heritage resources authorities. Section 2 includes a list of such resources, including graves and burial sites.

44 World Tourism Organization 'Tourism Can Protect and Promote Religious Heritage. Press Release 14083' (10 December 2014). Online at: http://media.unwto.org/press-release/2014-12-10/tourism-can-protect-and-promote-religious-heritage.

45 *Ibid.*

46 L Collingridge 'The Cape's Kramats: A Unique Religious and Cultural heritage' (8 September 2015). Online at: www.southafrica.net/blog/en/posts/entry/the-capes-kramats-a-unique-religious-and-cultural-heritage.

47 Trip advisor 'Religious Sites in South Africa/ (November 2016). Online at: hwww.tripadvisor.co.za/Attractions-g293740-Activities-c47-t10 South_Africa.html.

area because they are seen as 'sacred to the ancestors'. According to Coplan,[48] these pilgrims to the sacred caves 'practice every form of African religion from pre-Christian Basotho ritual and medicine to independent Apostolic to established mission church Christianity'. It seems that attempts by the local white farmers to expel the pilgrims have been unsuccessful 'as the state is no longer willing to place the sanctity of private property above popular rights of access to religious and heritage sites'.[49]

Since the Religious Charter provides for the right of communities to access sacred places and burial sites relevant to their convictions, they have to make sure that those involved clearly understand their religious views and convictions. Churches and religious institutions can play a role in supporting their communities in preserving and protecting their heritage. Religion is a vital aspect of cultural heritage in South Africa for many individuals and groups. According to the National Heritage Council, 'it is imperative that religious organisations (whether churches or traditional religious groups) as part of their obligations, position themselves as positive custodians of social and cultural values of the communities they serve'.[50]

Conclusion

The Canadian Courts affirmed that 'a place of worship is necessary to the practice of a religion'.[51] As further observed by Adhar and Leigh, 'A state that denies a religious community the very opportunity to establish and operate a place of worship is surely under a severe burden to justify it'.[52] Religious heritage sites provide important meeting grounds for both visitors and communities. They can drive economic growth and international tourism, but more importantly they contribute and develop tolerance, respect and mutual understanding between different cultures and religions. As suggested by Coplan:[53]

> Land can be expropriated, but not cultural memory, further vivified by a more recent pan-African nationalist consciousness … the solution lies in coexistence, in black and white sharing such sites and putting them to their different – indeed complementary – uses together. This notion, made thinkable by the democratic transformation of 1994, is indeed a new frontier in South African race relations; one that its pioneers, both black and white, may commend with cogency to the rest of South Africa.

48 DB Coplan 'Land from the Ancestors: Popular Religious Pilgrimage along the South Africa-Lesotho Border' *Journal of Southern African Studies* (2003) 29(4) 976.

49 *Ibid.*

50 S Mancotywa 'Critical Conversations about Heritage' *Popularising Contemporary Heritage Issues* National Heritage Council of South Africa (2014) 10. Online at: www.nhc.org.za/a-book-that-sparks-debate-about-contemporary-heritage-issues-launched/.

51 Adhar & Leigh *Religious Freedom in the Liberal State* 347.

52 *Ibid.*

53 Coplan 2003 *Journal of Southern African Studies* 993.

Heritage resources have the capacity to promote reconciliation, understanding and respect, and contribute to the development of a unifying South African identity. They provide evidence of the origins of South Africa and must be carefully managed. Often there is a lack of understanding on the part of the courts, especially in relation to different, minority and traditional religions, and it has been stated that '[m]uch of the jurisprudence appears to be grounded in a worldview that separates land from religion, history from spirituality, and belief from practice'.[54] Reliance on legislation assisted communities in asserting their burial rights. Religious communities have a duty to educate and inform the court of their specific religious views or practices, although regulation by the state through various means is not excluded. As stated by Krishnaswami:

> Regulation by public authorities of these grounds and of the burial, cremation, or other methods for the disposal of the dead is legitimate and unavoidable in the interests of morality, public order and the general welfare — including, of course, considerations of public health.[55]

Circumcision and rites of passage

Male circumcision in South Africa is a rite of passage from adolescence to adulthood. It is seen, particularly by the Xhosa people, as a life cycle that marks the transition from boyhood to manhood and celebrates a change in status. The Xhosa, Sotho, Pedi, Venda and the Tsonga tribes commonly practise this custom and it has been reported that, particularly among the Xhosa speakers, information about the circumcision ritual is traditionally only known and shared by men and not to women, children or any outsiders 'as it is believed that this upsets the ancestors, which can result in misfortune'.[56] It is generally passed from generation to generation clandestinely. With reference to Van Gennep,[57] the concept of rites of passage is further seen as a set of symbolic actions, either in ritual or ceremony, as a process intended to mark a transition in the human life cycle of the individual and the community. The community holds these rituals in high esteem and they play significant roles in how communities define themselves and their values. Van Gennep is further of the view that rites of passage are also rituals and ceremonies that are celebrated surrounding events such as childbirth, puberty, initiation, circumcision, menopause, ageing and death.[58]

54 Ratiba 2015 *Potchefstroom Electronic Law Journal* 3226.
55 Krishnaswami *Study of Discrimination* 34.
56 T Mavundla 'Rationalization of Indigenous Male Circumcision as a Sacred Religious Custom. Health Beliefs of Xhosa Men in South Africa' *Journal of Transcultural Nursing* (2009) 20(4) 396.
57 A van Gennep *The Rites of Passage* (1960).
58 As referred to in the 'Report on Some Challenges that Lead to Deaths and Injuries at Initiation Schools in South Africa' *CRL Rights Commission* (2017) 23.

In a study under Xhosa men, it became clear that the traditional circumcisions is also viewed as a 'sacred' or 'holy' religious custom and according to this study, it was found that 'engaging in cultural circumcision is equal to a religious belief'.[59] In some communities, such rituals are religious and are conducted for religious purposes, as is the case in almost all religious faiths in South Africa. In others, they are traditional and cultural with a strong element of spirituality.[60] The CRL Rights Commission is of the view that the practice of initiation as a rite of passage is often viewed 'too simply and superficially' and that they equate initiation solely with circumcision. According to the Commission, this view is inaccurate and probably based on the fact that many male initiation rites must be performed with the traditional ritual of circumcision in order to be seen as complete and affirming the male's passage to manhood.[61]

The Commission, in its executive summary of the Report on Public Hearings on Initiation Schools in South Africa,[62] describes the initiation practices as rites of passage common to many cultures. It is seen as both a personal experience as well as a manifestation of community values, aspirations and heritages. The Commission describes the institution of initiation as a 'community's cultural, spiritual and religious right'.[63] Serious problems associated with the practice of this rite have been reported in recent years, particularly in relation to practices at initiation schools.

As a result of this, various provinces and municipalities have drafted legislation and bylaws. They are however piecemeal and address different aspects in different pieces of legislation. Some legislation addresses the medical, environmental and governance aspects of initiation, while others focus again on other aspects, such as traditional leadership and tradition healers. The laws and policies applied in various provinces regarding initiation and initiation schools also differ. The CRL Rights Commission, in its report, tried to address some of these problems and reach some solutions with communities. The Commission made numerous recommendations in its executive report.[64] Following further hearings, the Commission published a further report in 2017 on some challenges that led to deaths and injuries at initiation schools in South Africa.[65] Section 12(8) of the Children's Act 38 of 2005 makes it clear that circumcision of male children under the age of 16 is prohibited, except when circumcision is performed for religious purposes in accordance with the practices of the religion concerned and in the manner prescribed; or performed for medical reasons on the recommendation of a medical practitioner. An increase in initiation schools and reports of injuries, illnesses and

59 Mavundla 2009 *Journal of Transcultural Nursing* 399.
60 *Initiation Report* 23.
61 *Ibid.*
62 Executive Summary 'Report on Public Hearings on Initiation Schools in South Africa' *CRL Rights Commission* (June 2014).
63 Executive Summary 8.
64 See *Initiation Report* 13. An in-depth discussion of the report falls outside the scope of this discussion.
65 See further *Initiation Report.*

deaths that has occurred because of these practices at initiation schools made it clear that there is a lack of engagement with communities in order to make sure that they act within the ambit of the various laws. According to the Commission, it is clear that initiation schools' legislation have so far not been effectively implemented. To that effect, the Minister of Cooperative Governance and Traditional Affairs introduced the Customary Initiation Bill that seeks to introduce, for the whole of South Africa, the conceptual framework of initiation as a cultural practice; health, security, space and infrastructural issues; justice and governance issues; monitoring and quality assurance. Parliament is currently conducting public hearings on the Customary Initiation Bill.

During a public lecture on women's parental rights in *ulwaluko* (circumcision), Judge of Appeal Nambitha Dambuza said that the recently tabled Customary Initiation Bill is an attempt to regulate initiation schools and to give women a more active role in the custom. The Bill proposes that the National and Provincial Initiation Committees play a compliance enforcement role once the Bill has been passed into law. The Provincial Committee in particular will be tasked with coordinating and monitoring the activities and practices taking place at initiation schools, as well as keeping track of provincial initiation schools and their initiates. The Provincial Committee will also have the responsibility of investigating alleged abuse cases made against initiation practices and schools. The Bill prescribes that no boy under the age of 16 can undergo initiation and also provides for sanctions in instances where there is non-compliance. Dambuza argues that to retain the custom of *ulwaluko*, changes that are in line with the principles of the Constitution need to be made. According to her, 'the custom is not static, it must change, and that change will not happen if women take a backseat'.[66]

Witchcraft

Meaning

Beliefs and practices associated with magic and the supernatural have existed in African societies for generations. In biblical texts, magic is often associated with witchcraft, sorcery, spells, divination and with evil and demons.[67] South African legislation, including the Witchcraft Suppression Act 3 of 1957, does not provide a definition of 'witch' or 'witchcraft' and in the absence of clearly defined definitions, communities have had to use their own definitions based on their understanding of witchcraft. The Draft Mpumalanga Witchcraft Bill 2007 (which was never published or officially distributed) defined witchcraft as 'the secret use of muti, zombies,

66 Judge of Appeal Nambitha Dambuza 'Women's Parental Rights Concerning Ulwaluko Rites' Public Lecture, Rhodes University Faculty of Law (24 April 2018).

67 D Wallace 'Rethinking Religion, Magic and Witchcraft in South Africa: From Colonial Coherence to Postcolonial Conundrum' *Journal for the Study of Religion* (2015) 28(1) 26.

spells, spirits, magic powders, water, mixtures, etc, by any person with the purpose of causing harm, damage, sickness to others or their property'.

Tebbe[68] further describes witchcraft as 'the practice of using supernatural power of evil, in order to harm others or to help oneself at the expense of others'. Self-defined witches, as represented by The South African Pagan Rights Alliance (SAPRA), defines witchcraft as 'an ancient religio-magical technique and modern Pagan spirituality that employs the use of divination, sympathetic magic and Pagan ritual practices'.[69] SAPRA expressed its dissatisfaction with the Draft Mpumalanga Witchcraft Bill and viewed it as discriminatory against self-defined witches. Maybe a better-balanced definition of witchcraft was provided by Prof Theodore Petrus in response to SAPRA's comments:

> [T]he term 'witchcraft' means different things to different people. Differences in the perception of witchcraft are largely based on differences in context. In the context of Wicca, witchcraft is viewed as something positive as witches are practitioners of 'white' or good magic … [However], in the African context, witchcraft is viewed negatively as witches are seen as practitioners of 'black' or evil magic…[70]

Consequently, the Commission recognised that it was necessary to separate the practice of Pagan witchcraft from practices associated with harmful witchcraft in formulating a definition.[71] The Commission opted for a route distinguishing between 'witchcraft' and 'harmful witchcraft', with a focus on harmful witchcraft for purposes of future regulation. The Commission therefore recommended that only harmful practices associated with witchcraft should be regulated. The Commission then proposed the following definition:

> 'Harmful witchcraft' means the intentional or purported use of non-natural or supernatural means (whether that involves the use of physical elements or not) to threaten, or to cause,
>
> (i) Death or injury to or disease or disability to any person; or
>
> (ii) Destruction or loss of or damage to property of any description; or
>
> (iii) Utilises belief and particular practices associated with harmful witchcraft to instil psychological distress or terror.[72]

The Commission recommended that the crimes or harmful practices to be subjected to regulation are: witchcraft accusations, witch findings, crimes associated with harmful witchcraft practice and muti killings.[73]

68 N Tebbe 'Witchcraft and the Constitution' in T Bennet (ed) *Traditional African Religions in South Africa* (2011) 160–161.
69 Discussion Paper 139 'The Review of the Witchcraft Suppression Act 3 of 1957' *South Africa Law Reform Commission* Project 135 (2016) 13.
70 *Witchcraft Discussion Paper* 33.
71 *Witchcraft Discussion Paper* 42.
72 *Witchcraft Discussion Paper* 43.
73 *Witchcraft Discussion Paper* 44.

Legislative framework

Following a request from the South African Pagan Council (SAPC) in 2008, to conduct an investigation into the constitutionality of the Witchcraft Suppression Act, the South African Law Reform Commission published an issue paper[74] with some preliminary proposals for law reform in relation to the 'Review of the Witchcraft Suppression Act 3 of 1957'. A further discussion paper[75] was published for comment. This paper includes recommendations on the proposed review of the Witchcraft Suppression Act and outlines some preliminary conclusions reached and solutions identified by the Commission. Section 1 of the Witchcraft Suppression Act contains categories of conduct and sets out certain offences relating to the practice of witchcraft that is prohibited in terms of the Act. In its issue paper,[76] the Law Reform Commission submitted that the practice of witchcraft is not *per se* prohibited, but rather conduct that leads to harm as a result of advice given by people who claim to have knowledge of witchcraft or the use of supernatural powers. Later, the provincial legislature proposed the Mpumalanga Witchcraft Suppression Bill of 2007, which was aimed at criminalising both witch hunts and the act of accusing someone of witchcraft as well as pretending to practise witchcraft. Organisations such as SAPRA and the Traditional Healers Organisation opposed the Bill on various grounds and the Bill was abandoned and never passed into law by the provincial government.

The main issue in the LRC issue paper was not to determine whether the practice of witchcraft or a belief in it exists, but rather the question as to whether there is a need for regulation. According to the Ralushai Report,[77] the practice of witchcraft was regulated by traditional courts before it was regulated through the Witchcraft Suppression Act in terms of which cases involving witchcraft were adjudicated by the courts.

Pagans see witchcraft as an expression of their religion. According to O'Brien, the President of the Board of Directors of a U.S. Pagan seminary:

> My religion is not a faith, as other religious persons define this term. It is experiential. In the world of interfaith relations in which I am active, we distinguish between revealed Abrahamic religions and experiential religions of the Pagan religious movement. In the context of interfaith, I call myself a Pagan. In the academic field of religious studies, Paganism is considered a new religious movement (NRM), meaning that it is fewer than 200 years old. We share this NRM category with Latter Day Saints, Baha'i, Scientology and others.[78]

74 Issue Paper 29 'Review of the Witchcraft Suppression Act 3 of 1957' *South Africa Law Reform Commission* Project 135 (2014).

75 *Witchcraft Discussion Paper*.

76 *Witchcraft Issue Paper* 24.

77 Ralushai Commission of Inquiry (Chairperson Professor NV Ralushai) 'Report of the Commission of Inquiry into Witchcraft Violence and Ritual Murders in the Northern Province of the Republic of South Africa' (1996).

78 D Leff 'Witchcraft is a Religion!' (16 April 2012). Online at: https://www.news24.com/MyNews24/Witchcraft-is-a-religion-20120414.

According to SAPC, since witchcraft is an expression of their religion, the suppression thereof and the prohibition of the practice of witchcraft contradicts for instance their right to religious freedom under section 15 of the Constitution.[79] They argue that the Constitution requires all religions to be treated equally and that subsections (d) and (f) of the Act that prohibits magic and the use of charms is in fact also practised by various other religions, including but not limited to Hinduism.[80] However, at the World Parliament of Religions held in Cape Town in 1999, the Anglican Archbishop objected to the participation of Pagans at the Parliament and viewed their practice of magic not as 'religious'.[81] SAPRA further define their religion as a 'nature-venerating religion that believes that the Earth and its creatures are sacred' and submit that they must be recognised as a religious minority.[82] There are various recognised denominations within the Pagan religion, including 'Witchcraft, Wicca, Stregharia, Druidry and Shamanism'.[83] SAPC was the first Pagan organisation to be listed as an official Pagan Church in Africa. It is a Registered Religious Organisation, in terms of section 5(1) and (2) of the Civil Union Act 17 of 2006 and a recognised not-for-profit community based organisation (CBO).

After publication of the SALRC issue paper in 2015, the SALRC received various submissions from interested stakeholders in response to the issues that it had identified in the issue paper. The discussion paper outlines recommendations on the proposed review of the Witchcraft Suppression Act and some preliminary conclusions reached and solutions identified by the Commission. The SAPC re-emphasised their previous submission that there should be no regulation of witchcraft and that perpetrators should be dealt with in terms of existing laws.[84] They further submit that traditional courts should not handle cases dealing with harmful practices and that 'crimes associated with witchcraft should be investigated by appropriate authorities and dealt with in terms of the law of the country'.[85]

The Commission for Gender Equality (the CGE) also made some submissions and suggested that traditional healers should be regulated to control the use of human tissue and other poisons used in traditional medicines.[86] As a result, the Commission recommended that the current Act, which fails to adequately make these distinctions, should be repealed. The Commission recommended that the repealed Act should be replaced with 'a modern law that concerns itself with

79 *Witchcraft Discussion Paper* 2.
80 *Witchcraft Discussion Paper* 5.
81 Wallace 2015 *Journal for the Study of Religion* 39. According to the Archbishop 'I don't think that's a religion. As we understand it here and if we put it in the South African context, people will say it's not on'. See further D Wallace 'The Modern Pagan Witch: Negotiating a Contested Religious Identity in Post-apartheid South Africa' in D Brown (ed) *Religion and Spirituality in South Africa: New Perspectives* (2009) 124–144.
82 *Witchcraft Issue Paper* 39.
83 *Ibid.*
84 *Witchcraft Discussion Paper* 9.
85 *Witchcraft Discussion Paper* 10.
86 *Witchcraft Discussion Paper* 13.

prohibiting conduct that is harmful to society'.[87] They acknowledged the fact that existing laws can be used to deal with harmful practices, but is of the view that these laws have not been of much assistance. They are in support of a single law that will deal with harmful practices associated with witchcraft practice and proposed a law to be called the Prohibition of Witchcraft Practices Associated with Witchcraft Beliefs Act, which will deal with issues such as witchcraft accusations, witch findings, crimes associated with or motivated by the belief in witchcraft, and muti killings.[88]

The current Act prohibits the practice of witchcraft for all practitioners, including Wiccans. The proposed new law should penalise those who practise 'harmful witchcraft' or instil fear in others that they will be bewitched, while not restricting harmless practices associated with Wicca or traditional healing. A series of witchcraft related incidents[89] led to stricter regulation by government and in accordance with section 51 of the Criminal Law Amendment Act 105 of 1997,[90] stricter punishments have been laid down for witchcraft-related murders or any activity relating to the removal of a body part.[91] The Witchcraft Suppression Act also does not does not deal with muti killings, which is partially dealt with by the Sentencing Act, although the provision in the Sentencing Act is not linked to killings associated with witchcraft. The SALRC in its discussion paper regarded killings committed in order to remove body parts to make muti 'as a serious societal concern'.[92] Muti is traditional medicine created by 'an expert who possesses esoteric knowledge and deploys secret methods'.[93] It is further seen as a supernatural remedy.[94] The SALRC is of the view that proposed legislation should focus on 'the perpetrators of the violence (those who do the actual killing of victims),

87 *Witchcraft Discussion Paper* 85.

88 *Ibid.*

89 See for instance A Waywell 'Elderly Women Targeted in E Cape Village over Witchcraft Claims' *eNCA News* (15 January 2017). Online at: www.enca.com/south-africa/elderly-women-terrorised-in-ecape-village-over-witchcraft-claims; C Bailey 'Muti Killings is a Way of Life in Rural Areas' *IOL News* (16 January 2010). Online at: www.iol.co.za/news/south-africa/muti-killings-is-a-way-of-life-in-rural-areas-470603.

90 Read with Schedule 2, Part I (e)-(f), as amended by section 5 of the Criminal Law (Sentencing) Amendment Act 38 of 2007.

91 5. Schedule 2 to the Criminal Law Amendment Act, 1997, is amended—
(a) by the addition in Part I after paragraph (d) of the paragraphs setting out the categories of 'murder', of the following paragraphs:
'(e) the victim was killed in order to unlawfully remove any body part of the victim, or as a result of such unlawful removal of a body part of the victim;
(f) the death of the victim resulted from, or is directly related to, any offence contemplated in section 1(a) to (e) of the Witchcraft Suppression Act, 1957 (Act No. 3 of 1957).'

92 *Witchcraft Discussion Paper* 90.

93 Tebbe *Witchcraft and the Constitution* 165.

94 According to the Draft Mpumalanga Witchcraft Bill 2007, 'Muti means any mixture of herbs, water, wollen cufs etc, used by wizards, igedla, inyanga, African Churches, Foreign traditional Healers, etc for the purposes of curing deseases, helping others who come to consult to them for whatever purposes and including causing harm to others or their properties.'

traditional healers who contract others to commit murders to get body parts for them, and the end users of such muti' and that all the role players should be punished.[95] However, the SAPRA firmly believes that muti murders have nothing to do with witchcraft, 'because actual witches are not the perpetrators of such crimes'.[96] They reiterate the view that it should be enforced under the Human Tissues Act 65 of 1983, which was passed specifically to prevent such crimes. However, this Act has been repealed by the National Health Act 61 of 2003, which came into force on 2 May 2005.

It has been suggested that the regulation of witchcraft in the form of new legislation is not necessary, since alternatives already exist, such as the common law, existing laws dealing with murder and assault in cases of witchcraft violence, defamation laws against people who accuse others of witchcraft, and mediation options to resolve disputes relating to witchcraft.[97] Other proposals include the drafting of a Code of Conduct for traditional healers, 'to encourage responsible action and accountability' and other non-legal interventions such as educational programmes aimed at informing the general public about witchcraft. Well-known religious cases such as *Christian Education South Africa*;[98] *Prince v President, Cape Law Society*;[99] and *MEC for Education: KwaZulu-Natal and Others v Pillay*[100] confirmed the court's protective stance in relation to religious minorities. It is important to balance the interests of the individuals whose rights are affected and to accommodate religious minorities in the constitutional discourse. The SALRC discussion paper confirmed the view that 'calls by people who claim that the practice of witchcraft is part of their religious expression should be taken into account when determining whether witchcraft practice must be outlawed'.[101]

Example

An interesting case came before the National Bargaining Council for the Sugar Manufacturing and Refining Industry in *National Sugar Refining and Allied Industries Union obo Mngomezulu v Tongaat Hulett Sugar Ltd (Darnall)*.[102] A former employee of Tongaat Sugar, Mr Mngomezulu, was dismissed for misconduct after he was accused of using witchcraft to intimidate another employee, Ms Nxele. Ms Nxele found a substance on the door handle of her car. She

95 *Witchcraft Discussion Paper* 90–91.
96 TP Ward 'South Africa's Witchcraft Suppression Act Ruled Unconstitutional' *The Wild Hunt Modern Pagan News & Commentary* (27 January 2016). Online at: https://wildhunt.org/tag/south-african-pagan-rights-alliance.
97 *Witchcraft Issue Paper* 50.
98 *Christian Education South Africa v Minister of Education* 2000 (4) SA 757 (CC).
99 *Prince v President, Cape Law Society and Others* 2002 (2) SA 794 (CC).
100 *MEC for Education: KwaZulu-Natal and Others v Pillay and Others* (1) SA 474 (CC).
101 *Witchcraft Discussion Paper* 46.
102 *National Sugar Refining and Allied Industries Union obo Mngomezulu v Tongaat Hulett Sugar Ltd (Darnall)* [2016] 11 BALR 1172 (NBCSMRI).

subsequently experienced some distress and consulted a traditional healer who believed that the substance was muti, intended to cause harm to Ms Nxele. She accused Mr Mngomezulu of using witchcraft against her with the intent to cause her spiritual, mental or physical harm. In its decision, the Commissioner referred to the Supreme Court of Appeal's judgment in *Kievits Kroon Country Estate (Pty) Ltd v Mmoledi*.[103] According to Cachalia JA:

> Our courts are familiar with and equipped to deal with disputes arising from conventional medicine, which are governed by objective standards, whereas questions regarding religious doctrine or cultural practice are not. Courts are therefore unable and not permitted to evaluate the acceptability, logic, consistency or comprehensibility of the belief. They are concerned only with the sincerity of the adherent's belief, and whether it is being invoked for an ulterior purpose. This of necessity involves an investigation of the grounds advanced to demonstrate that the belief exists.[104]

The Commissioner referred to section 1(a) of the Witchcraft Suppression Act 3 of 1957,[105] which declared the use of witchcraft to be an offence. The Commissioner then focused on Ms Nxele's perception of the substance rather that its nature and the fact that the use of the muti intimidated her. According to the Commissioner:

> The act of witchcraft does not have to achieve its purpose (because only the perpetrator and the Sangoma will know the exact effect he desired) for it to become an act of misconduct. I agree with Lawrence [attorney for the respondent] that the mere use of muti or traditional preparations to intimidate, scare or threaten another person is sufficient.[106]

Consequently, Mr Mngomezulu was charged with breaching the relationship of trust and good faith between him and his employer and was dismissed.

To conclude, the SALRC discussion paper has emphasised the fact that the practice of witchcraft can no longer be seen only through the lens of indigenous communities, where it is necessarily associated with evil. The practice of witchcraft should also be seen as an exercise of the right to religion, practised by other sections of the community.[107] In the light of the constitutional protection of the rights of religious minorities, the religious rights of these groups cannot be ignored.

103 *Kievits Kroon Country Estate (Pty) Ltd v Mmoledi* 2014 (1) SA 585 (SCA).
104 *Kievits Kroon* para 27.
105 Any person who (a) imputes to any other person the causing, by supernatural means, of any disease in or injury or damage to any person or thing, or who names or indicates any other person as a wizard; shall be guilty of an offence.
106 M Labuschagne 'Witchcraft as Misconduct' *De Rebus* (May 2017) 51. Online at: www.derebus.org.za/witchcraft-as-misconduct/.
107 See *Witchcraft Discussion Paper* 84.

Religious slaughter and dietary practice[108]

Introduction

The slaughter of animals as part of cultural and religious practices is a global phenomenon and highlights the difficult boundaries to be drawn between the rights to freedom of religion on the one hand and other rights, such as animal rights, on the other. In accordance with various religious practices, the animal must be conscious when killed, to conform to the specific prescripts, such as to be considered kosher under Jewish law or halal under Islamic law. However, legislation in various other countries requires animals to be stunned before they are slaughtered, particularly in Europe. It is important for religious communities to be able to enjoy and practise their religion, subject to the rights of others. The CRL Rights Commission recommended that municipalities should look at amending bylaws to allow communities to slaughter for religious and cultural reasons, but at the same time, they must ensure the welfare of the animals.

What is religious slaughter?

Two prominent religions, particularly in Europe, where religious slaughter is of great importance, are Judaism and Islam. In Judaism, the practice of religious slaughter is known as *shechita* and in Islam as *dhabiha*. Meat that conforms to the Jewish dietary laws is referred to as *kosher* and *halal* in accordance with Islamic requirements. For animal slaughter to be lawful under Jewish and Shariah law, certain conditions have to be met before an animal is cut and bled. In both religions, the animal must be alive when these procedures are carried out and animals may not be stunned before they are slaughtered. The ritual must be carried out by a certified practitioner and the animal must bleed to death.[109] The welfare of animals is very important in both religions. Animals should not experience any pain or be subjected to unnecessary suffering. However, there is no uniform approach of what is acceptable or not within these religions and in some countries, the stunning of animals prior to the killing of the animal is the norm for many religious groups.

In Africa, particularly South Africa, the African Traditional Religions are very prominent. There is no universally agreed definition of African Traditional Religion (ATR), although authors agree on certain shared features, such as 'the belief in a supreme being, divinities, spirits, ancestors, and the practice of magic and

108 This section is based on a Conference paper 'Burial Rights – Protecting the Religious Rights and Heritage of Communities' delivered at the fourth ACLARS (African Consortium for Law and Religion Studies) Conference 'Religious Pluralism, Heritage, and Social Development in Africa' at the Faculty of Law, University of Addis Ababa, Ethiopia 22–24 May 2016.

109 See further G van der Schyff 'Ritual Slaughter and Religious Freedom in a Multilevel Europe' *Oxford Journal of Law and Religion* (2014) 3(1) 78.

medicine'.[110] According to Mbiti, ATR was for the believers 'the normal way of looking at the world and experiencing life itself'.[111] Emphasis is placed on the daily experience of the person in such a manner that the African spiritual experience is described as on in which the 'divine … interpenetrates into the daily experience of the human person so much that religion, culture, and society are imperatively interrelated'.[112] For the purposes of this discussion, important aspects of ATR include the belief in ancestral spirits according to certain set rituals and practices. An important feature of indigenous African beliefs is 'the correct observance of these rituals'. In ATR the focus is also much more on the communal nature of the practice, and in the traditional African society 'religious beliefs stand at the centre of life'.[113] During ritual performances, the members come together and perform the ritual as a collective.[114] An interesting example of a ritual bull killing came before the courts in *Smit v King Goodwill Zwelithini.*[115] In *Smit*, the Zulu King, Goodwill Zwelithini, decided to revive the First Fruits Festival (also called the *Umkhosi Ukweshwama*) with the ritual of bull slaughtering. Animal activists were outraged and the Animals Rights Africa Trust approached the court for an interdict to try and prevent the slaughtering of the bull. The ceremony has been described as 'an annual event that takes place at around the same time each year for significant religious and cultural reasons'.[116] For purposes of the right to freedom of religion in section 15 of the Constitution, and for constitutional protection, it is important to determine whether the ritual bull slaughter can indeed be classified as religion. By applying some of the characteristics of ATR outlined above, it would be difficult not to classify this Zulu tradition as religious in nature. According to Rautenbach 'there is enough empirical evidence to prove that Zulus believe their traditions, including the Festival, to be religious'. And further:

> The primary phenomenon of religion is ritual. Ritual is religion in action…Belief, although its recitation may be part of the ritual, or a ritual in its own rights, serves to explain, to rationalize, to interpret and direct the energy of the ritual performance…It is ritual which accomplishes what religion sets out to do.[117]

110 NM Nyaundi 'African Traditional Religion in Pluralistic Africa: A Case of Relevance, Resilience and Pragmatism' in Bennet T (ed) *Traditional African Religions in South Africa* (2011) 6.
111 JS Mbiti *Introduction to African Religion* (1975) 12; 17.
112 S Masonda 'The Practice of African Traditional Religion in Contemporary South Africa' in Bennet T (ed) *Traditional African Religions in South Africa* (2011) 20.
113 Masonda *The Practice of African Traditional Religion* 20.
114 Mndende 2013 *NGTT* 78.
115 *Smit NO and Others v King Goodwill Zwelithini Kabhekuzulu and Others* (10237/2009) [2009] ZAKZPHC 75 (4 December 2009).
116 *Smit* v *King Goodwill Zwelithini* para 9.
117 C Rautenbach 'Umkhosi Ukweshwama: Revival of a Zulu Festival in Celebration of the Universe's Rites of Passage' in Bennet T (ed) *Traditional African Religions in South Africa* (2011) 75.

It can thus be argued that the Zulu tradition was indeed a religious ritual, which should qualify for constitutional protection. The court in *Smit* found the facts presented by the two parties to be in dispute based on different versions of the slaughter practice presented to the court. Due to the factual dispute between the parties, the court dismissed the application. The *Ukweshwama* ceremony was allowed to go ahead. The court was also of the view that:

> The slaughter of the bull and the manner in which it is done, is to approach the relevant authorities with the view of resolving the conflict between the Applicant and the representatives of the ZULU nation. Hopefully Parliament would intervene with a view to put this issue to rest.

The court declined to resolve or discuss the religious debate further. It is important to note that the court relied on Parliament to intervene and resolve the issue of religious slaughter. In this regard, the legislative framework applicable to religious slaughter and the ways in which legislation can reasonably regulate the practice is important.

Legislative framework

The limitation and regulation of religious slaughter practices may be necessary in order to preserve peace and tranquillity, particularly in localities where people of different faiths reside. The justifiable regulation of the practice through legislation and municipal bylaws can be a reasonable and justifiable way of limiting the practice of religious slaughter as a manifestation of the right to freedom of religion, in terms of law of general application and in accordance with section 36 of the Constitution. Rautenbach is of the view that:

> Although a court is not empowered to pronounce upon the truth or credibility of religion, constitutional limitations aimed at the achievement of a desirable social result may be placed on religious rituals. It is not desirability of the ritual that is evaluated but the desirability of its effect, and one has to agree that it is the responsibility of government to give direction in the form of policy and legislation when dealing with these issues.[118]

Section 2 of the Animals Protection Act 71 of 1962 highlights the various offences in respect of animals, including offences such as neglect, torture or any other action by a person that causes unnecessary suffering to an animal. A person found guilty of any such an offence can be liable on conviction to a fine or to imprisonment in accordance with the provisions of the Act. In terms of section 8 of the Act, inspectors of the Society for the Prevention of Cruelty to Animals (SPCA) may enter the premises of a person or owner with the person or owner's permission, to examine the conditions under which the animals are kept. When the

118 Rautenbach *Umkhosi Ukweshwama* 86.

owner refuses to give the inspector permission to enter, the inspector has to obtain a warrant from a magistrate to enter the premises. Members of the public, who suspect that animals are mistreated, should approach their local SPCA and lay a complaint. However, there are many towns and places in South Africa with no SPCA or animal welfare society. Animal cruelty is a criminal offence, and it is important that members of the public report instances of animal cruelty or animal abuse to the South African Police Service (SAPS), who should investigate any such complaint. Here local government authorities can play an important role through the enactment of various bylaws aimed at regulating slaughter practices.

In terms of the Constitution, municipalities have legislative authority in relation to matters set out in Part B of schedule 5, which includes municipal abattoirs. The slaughtering of animals is thus typically a matter over which a municipality will have the power to make bylaws. The CRL Rights Commission has thus recommended that municipalities look at amending their bylaws to allow communities to slaughter animals for religious and cultural reasons. An example of a municipal regulation on religious slaughter is the Ekurhuleni Metropolitan Municipality Public Health Bylaw.[119] The bylaw allows the slaughtering of animals, subject to the requirements of the regulation. According to the Municipality:

> Ekurhuleni is not opposed to the private slaughtering of animals for ritual purposes. To do that would be an infringement on the rights of people as enshrined in the Constitution of the Republic of South Africa under the Bill of Rights. However, the exercising of these rights must be done in a way that is respectful of other people's rights as well.[120]

The regulations stipulate that any person who intends to slaughter an animal in any place other than an abattoir, must notify the relevant Municipal Council in writing, at least 14 days prior to the event. A person must also obtain the written permission from the relevant landowner and may not slaughter the animal in a position where the slaughtering can be observed by any person on neighbouring premises or any member of the public.[121]. According to the South African Local Government Organisation (SALGA), municipalities accept and acknowledge the practice of ritual slaughter and according to them it is necessary for municipalities 'to review by-laws where the practice is not permitted, and where it does not exist it should be developed to accommodate the practice'.[122] The CLR Rights Commission recommended that individuals or communities who take part in ritual slaughter practices should always obtain the necessary permission from their local authority for the planned slaughter. Municipalities should monitor that the meat was handled in a hygienic manner and that animals are at all times treated in a

119 Ekurhuleni Metropolitan Municipality 'Public Health Bylaws' [Council Resolution: AET (012009) dated 23 September 2009].

120 Sapa 'Correct Procedures must be Followed when Slaughtering Animals' *South African Government News Agency* (23 September 2009).

121 See section 125 of the regulations.

122 Sapa 'By-laws Need to Accommodate Slaughter' *News24* (29 March 2019).

humane manner. However, in practice, there are often very poor or a total a lack of communication and engagement on the part of local government with communities. Communities are also ignorant of the laws, procedures and practices that are available to them in order to assert their religious rights. Local governments should appropriately and effectively engage in discussions with all affected communities before making laws or regulations, particularly in relation to slaughtering practices.

Unfortunately, animals are often transported for thousands of kilometres for ritual and informal slaughter. They are transported in unsuitable vehicles and abused by immobilising them with cruel severing methods. The slaughter practices are not monitored and those performing the slaughter practices often have no or very little experience. The welfare and humane treatment of animals therefore remains a priority. Apart from regulating slaughter practices through the Animals Protection Act and the various municipal bylaws, the provisions of the Meat Safety Act 40 of 2000 is also important. The legislation and applicable regulations aim to prevent cruelty to animals and sets national standards in relation to abattoirs, although it creates an exception in relation to the slaughter of animals for religious purposes. However, these provisions can provide guidance in relation to the humane treatment of animals.

In accordance with the provision of the Meat Safety Act, the term 'slaughter' means the killing of an animal in order to obtain meat and animal products therefrom. Section 7 of the Act prohibits the slaughter of animals at any place other than in an abattoir, but creates a special exemption in subsection 2(a) with reference to slaughter for own consumption or for cultural or religious purposes. The Red Meat Regulations promulgated in accordance with the Meat Safety Act, provides in Part V for the humane treatment of animals and the slaughter process, including regulations applicable to the methods of stunning, bleeding and bleeding times. In order to be permitted to perform a ritual slaughter of animals in an abattoir, the person performing the slaughter must have the written authorisation of the abattoir owner and the relevant religious community must nominate him.[123] The same requirements apply for the humane execution of the slaughter. All animals slaughtered at an abattoir must be rendered unconscious by a method of stunning in accordance with section 73 of the regulations, before doing the bleeding incision. Methods of stunning include the captive bolt method, electrical method or any other method approved by the provincial executive officer.

Part XI of the regulations focus specifically on the slaughter of animals for own consumption and for religious and cultural purposes. Section 129 of the regulations focuses on the slaughter of animals outside of an abattoir, for indigenous religious or cultural purposes. It is a requirement to obtain written permission from the local authority or a landowner of the area where such slaughtering will take place. The regulations provide further that the slaughter must be executed in a humane manner. Especially in relation to the various provisions of the Meat Safety Act, communities are not aware of the relevant provisions, or they do not

123 See section 130 of the regulations.

follow the relevant procedures outlined in the regulations, particularly in relation to slaughter practices outside of an abattoir. It is also difficult for local authorities to enforce and regulate these activities, unless formal complaints have been lodged by members of the public.

Conclusion

From this section it is clear that religious slaughter is an important component of the right to freedom of religion, although it is not always easy to strike a balance between competing rights and interests. The practice of ritual slaughter can be justifiably limited and regulated through legislation and municipal bylaws as an alternative method to a total ban of the practice. A total ban on ritual slaughter would not pass constitutional muster, since section 36 specifically requires that less restrictive means or alternative methods (in the form of regulation) should be considered, in order to achieve the purpose. Support for this is also found on an European front, where the view has been expressed that:

> A categorical denial of the right to ritual slaughter can be said to be too severe an interference with the scope of protection as it does not even allow the possibility that slaughter can be conducted in a way compatible with both religious requirements and the need to ensure that animals do not suffer more than had they been stunned.[124]

Legislation and regulations seek to strike a balance between the humane slaughtering of animals on the one hand, and the protection of religious beliefs on the other, and 'between societies' right to a healthy environment and a religious community's right to perform ritual slaughtering'.[125] The religious rules applicable to food and the accompanying slaughter rituals are seen as 'deeply symbolic' and an expression of a relationship between the believer and God. Complying with these rules is a way in which 'the faithful are reminded of the presence of the significant in the common place' and it 'affects the moral and spiritual character of the individual, which ultimately determines his wellbeing and salvation'.[126] To confirm the view of Krishnaswami:[127]

> Although it would not seem possible to impose upon the public authorities a duty of securing by positive measures the observance of dietary practices of all faiths in all circumstances, the general rule should be that no one should be prevented from observing the dietary practices prescribed by his religion or belief.

124 Van der Schyff 2014 *Oxford Journal of Law and Religion* 97.
125 Rautenbach *Umkhosi Ukweshwama* 88.
126 IJ Kroeze 'How to Eat: Vegetarianism, Religion and Law' *The Journal for Transdisciplinary Research in Southern Africa* (2012) 8(1) 5.
127 Krishnaswami *Study of Discrimination* 36.

This applies equally to the practice of ritual laughter, in order for religious believers to be able to conform to the required dietary laws of their respective religion.

However, in adhering to these religious practices, communities must also make sure to comply with the relevant laws and regulations. In the informal meat sector, and in many rural areas, meat is not inspected and distributed to consumers with little regulation. Ritual and religious slaughter practices are carried out in accordance with local customs, often without the necessary inspection by qualified veterinary officers. Not only does the improper handling of meat cause health risks, it is often done in an inhumane manner, contrary to municipal bylaws and legislation advocating for the humane treatment of animals. Apart from the humane treatment of animals, human health is of the utmost importance in relation to the sale and slaughter of animals, especially where meat is handled improperly and can cause contamination, causing health hazards. Although the Meat Safety Act makes provision for exemptions to slaughter for own consumption or for cultural or religious purposes, they are still conditional, and subject to municipal bylaws and regulations. The meat obtained from religious or ritual slaughter may not be sold to any person. All stakeholders need to join forces in order to create awareness under the public, particularly in rural areas, of the laws and regulations applicable to the sale and slaughtering of animals, and why these laws are important.

Equipment and symbols

Introduction

It has been argued that when public authorities 'prohibit or limit the wearing of certain apparel, the use of bells or musical accompaniments, or the display of symbols associated with a religion or belief', such a prohibition may in fact 'prevent the observance or exercise of an essential and often obligatory part of a religious practice, or at least an established custom'.[128] Religious dress and symbols play an important role in cultural and religious practices. Many examples of cases dealing with religious dress and symbols (including hairstyles and the wear of headscarves) happened in the context of education and will be discussed in more detail in the next section on Religion in Education. This section will thus only briefly give some examples of religious dress outside of the school environment and then focus on the ringing of bells as an important religious practice.

Religious dress

The wearing of a headscarf is a clear manifestation of religion that would be protected by religious freedom.[129] The obligation to wear a headscarf in Islam can be

128 Krishnaswami *Study of Discrimination* 33.

129 The headscarf ban debate has become an increasingly contentious issue worldwide, particularly in European countries. The European Court of Justice also ruled on

traced back to the *Qur'an*.[130] It is argued that while the *Qur'an* does not explicitly refer to a headscarf, they are 'generally interpreted to require Muslim women who have reached puberty to wear a headscarf when in public'.[131] There also seems to be consensus among Muslim scholars that the headscarf is obligatory in Islam.[132] In 2006, Fairouz Adams, a Muslim prison official, was dismissed by her employer for wearing a headscarf to work and for violating the corporate identity of the Department of Correctional Services.[133] A settlement was reached out of court between the department and the Muslim Judicial Council (MJC) and she was reinstated. In relation to state employees, like Fairouz in the example above, there is an argument that if the state permits employees to wear religious symbols, such as headscarves, it poses the risk of bias on the part of state employees.[134] Lenta disagrees with this view in that just because the state allows individuals to wear religious symbols, it does not mean that the state endorses the religion. According to him the state:

> condones those beliefs only to the extent that it permits the religious to engage in a religiously mandated practice; the accommodation respects individuals' right to freedom of religion. The state does not thereby support the religions of the individuals to whom exemptions are granted.[135]

Not to allow for an exemption to permit Muslim women employees and learners to wear a headscarf is grounds for unfair discrimination, especially where it leads to a dismissal or suspension. It addition to a finding of discrimination, a refusal to grant an exemption is an infringement of the individual's right to freedom of religion.

The Supreme Court of Appeal in *Department of Correctional Services v Popcru and Others*[136] was faced with another difficult issue of whether the dismissal of Rastafari and Xhosa respondents for refusing to cut their dreadlocks worn in observance of sincerely held religious and cultural beliefs were discriminatory and automatically unfair on grounds of religion, culture and gender. The respondents were all correctional officers of the Department of Correctional Services. All of them wore dreadlocks and refused to cut their hair. The

numerous issues involving religious dress. A discussion on the position in other countries, particularly in Europe, falls outside the scope of this book. However, for some comparative views, see F Osman 'Legislative Prohibitions on Wearing a Headscarf: Are they Justified?' *Potchefstroom Electronic Law Journal* (2014) 17(4) 1318–1349; P Lenta 'Muslim Headscarves in the Workplace and Schools' *South African Law Journal* (2007) 296–319.

130 Osman 2014 *Potchefstroom Electronic Law Journal* 1320.

131 Osman 2014 *Potchefstroom Electronic Law Journal* 1319.

132 Osman 2014 *Potchefstroom Electronic Law Journal* 1320.

133 'Prison Official Sacked for Headscarf to Sue' *IOL News* (3 May 2006).

134 See Lenta 2007 *South African Law Journal*.

135 Lenta 2007 *South African Law Journal* 310.

136 *Department of Correctional Services and Another v Police and Prisons Civil Rights Union (POPCRU) and Others* 2013 (4) SA 176 (SCA).

departmental dress code prohibits the wearing of dreadlocks by male correctional officers and the Department argued that their choice to wear dreadlocks could have resulted in a reduction of discipline and failure to rehabilitate inmates. The Department dismissed the correctional officers, who then approached the Labour Court for relief. Both the Labour Court and the Labour Appeal Court found that their dismissals were automatically unfair as contemplated in section 187(1)(f) of the Labour Relations Act 66 of 1995 (the LRA). The reasons put forward by the respondents for their refusal to cut their hair, included 'an outward manifestation of the religion'; cultural reasons and in order to 'obey his ancestors' call, given through dreams, to become a "sangoma" or traditional healer in accordance with his Xhosa culture'.[137] The Labour Court found and accepted that the respondents were dismissed because 'they wore dreadlocks and disobeyed the commissioner's instruction to cut them; that they wore the dreadlocks in pursuance of sincerely held religious or cultural beliefs and that their female counterparts were not prohibited from wearing dreadlocks'. According to the court it was 'beyond doubt that the impact of the instruction would have a devastating impact on their beliefs and faith'.[138] With reference to the case of *Prince v President, Cape Law Society*,[139] the Supreme Court of Appeal (SCA) held that:

> a policy that effectively punishes the practice of a religion and culture degrades and devalues the followers of that religion and culture in society; it is a palpable invasion of their dignity which says their religion or culture is not worthy of protection and the impact of the limitation is profound.[140]

The court concluded that a policy that restricts the practice of a religious or cultural belief, where it does not affect an employee's ability to perform his duties, cause undue hardship or jeopardise the safety of the public or other employees, is not justified. The court dismissed the appeal. An argument in support of prohibiting a headscarf is often the need to maintain a uniform dress code. An exemption for the headscarf can be easily administered without undermining the objectives of a uniform dress code. According to Osman:[141]

> Schools and employers can easily prescribe the colour and type of headscarf and the manner in which it is worn. This could very easily accommodate the religious beliefs of Muslim females and maintain the neatness and uniformity of a dress code without placing an undue burden on the institution.

137 *POPCRU* para 6.
138 *POPCRU* para 15.
139 *Prince v President, Cape Law Society* 2002 (2) SA 794 (CC) para 51.
140 *POPCRU* para 22.
141 Osman 2014 *Potchefstroom Electronic Law Journal* 1340.

Ringing of bells[142]

As a general principle of law, a property owner has the right to freedom to enjoy his property free from a noise nuisance. However, there also rests a duty on an owner to exercise his powers within the normal and acceptable limits of reasonableness and not to infringe on other owners' right of enjoyment of their property. Where any landowner exceeds this reasonable exercise of ownership rights, the conduct creates a nuisance to his neighbour that is actionable in accordance with the principles of neighbour law. Nuisance laws form part of our neighbour law that provides for the rules and regulations on how property owners should use their properties. Neighbour law exists as a mechanism to balance the rights of neighbours, particularly where competing interests exist. Any sound that impairs or may impair the convenience or peace of a reasonable person, like church bells or the sound of musical instruments or sound amplifiers, qualifies as a noise nuisance that can be regulated on a national, provincial or local level through appropriate noise control regulations and bylaws. In relation to liturgical bell ringing or a call to prayer, a clear conflict of rights arises. Residents are entitled to use and enjoy their property free from a noise nuisance. At the same time, churches and religious institutions, through their members, are entitled to exercise their religious convictions, even in the public sphere. The regulation of certain practices is often a way of finding a balance between conflicting rights, which is clearly the case here. As stated by Krishnaswami:[143]

> Regulation by public authorities of the use of symbols, bells, musical accompaniments and amplifiers associated with a religion or belief may be necessary in order to preserve peace and tranquillity, particularly in localities where people of different faiths reside.

In January 1992, the Minister of Environment Affairs promulgated the Noise Control Regulations under section 25 of the Environment Conservation Act 73 of 1989. Since 1996, in terms of Schedule 5 of the Constitution, the individual provinces have been responsible for administering these regulations and have enacted their own noise control regulations. In terms of the Constitution, municipalities further have legislative authority in relation to matters set out in Part B of Schedule 5, which include public nuisance and noise pollution. The Constitution envisages that municipalities will administer noise nuisance with support and oversight from the provincial government. Various municipalities have enacted noise and nuisance bylaws. Most regulations, including the Western Cape Noise Control Regulations, distinguish between a disturbing noise and a noise nuisance. A disturbing noise is an objective and scientifically measurable noise level compared to

142 For a more detailed discussion on this issue, see a recent article published by the author EH van Coller 'Laat die Klokke Lui …! Is die Lui van Klokke 'n Geraasoorlas of Bloot die Billike Uiting van Geloofsoortuigings?' *LitNet Akademies* (2018) 15(3) 769–787.

143 Krishnaswami *Study of Discrimination* 33.

the existing ambient noise level. A noise nuisance is a subjective measure and means any sound that impairs or may impair the convenience or peace of a reasonable person. The various noise control regulations prohibit both forms of noise. Section 3 of the Western Cape Noise Control Regulations prohibits any person from operating or playing a musical instrument, sound amplifier or loudspeaker that can cause a noise nuisance. The section further prohibits any person to emit a sound by means of a bell, alarm, whistle, loudspeaker or similar device that can cause a noise nuisance. However, liturgical bell ringing of churches in the traditional sense is part of the legitimate exercising of a religious conviction and a way in which believers may manifest their beliefs. The regular ringing of bells for these purposes should not be seen as constituting a substantial burden to the public, but rather as a socially acceptable activity. This is confirmed by the City of Tshwane Noise Management Policy.[144] According to this policy, there are some activities in any normal and well-functioning community that, from a noise perspective, may sometimes be found to be intrusive and disturbing to some individuals or groups living close to the source of the noise. However, the policy suggested that these activities should be approached from a different angle. Religious activities such as church bells on Sunday mornings, a muezzin calling from a mosque:

> are such activities which must be accepted by all as a healthy aspect of our urban community life, albeit as diverse groups and individuals within a community, but with the proviso that such activities are undertaken at reasonable times and are not excessively disruptive to other essential/normal activities or to the point of being a health hazard.[145]

Since the right to believe always goes hand in hand with the right to manifest and practise those beliefs, it is important to emphasise again the right to the private or public, and the individual or joint, observance and exercise of one's religious or other convictions. Religious activities such as the ringing of church bells on Sunday mornings and a muezzin calling from a mosque are ways in which believers manifest and practise their beliefs. These practices form part of the right to freedom of religion, protected under section 15 of the Constitution, read together with section 31, which guarantees the right to persons belonging to religious communities to enjoy and practise their religion together with other members of that community. In relation to the ringing of church bells to indicate the time of the day, it may be argued that this kind of ringing must be somewhat less loud, since it is not for a religious, but rather some social purpose. This type of practice may constitute a noise nuisance that is subject to regulation through the various noise control regulations and bylaws. However, no fundamental right is absolute and even the right to freedom of religion can be justifiably limited in accordance with the Constitution to the extent that the limitation is reasonable and justifiable in an open and democratic society based on human dignity, equality and freedom.

144 City of Tshwane Noise Management Policy (June 2004) 33.
145 City of Tshwane Noise Management Policy 33.

The limitation and regulation of these practices may be necessary in order to preserve peace and tranquillity, particularly in localities where people of different faiths reside. In an interesting case before the Western Cape High Court, *Garden Cities Incorporated Association Not For Gain v Northpine Islamic Society*,[146] a developer of townships in the Cape Peninsula sold a property to the Islamic Society who intended to erect a mosque on it. They concluded an agreement to the effect that the Islamic Society would not conduct any activities that would cause a nuisance or disturbance. According to the agreement:

> No amplified sound:
> (a) The purchaser will conduct no activities on this erf which will, in the opinion of Garden Cities, be a source of nuisance or disturbance to other owners of erven in the township and, in particular, no sound amplification equipment will be used on or in the buildings and/or structures to be erected on this erf.
> (b) No 'call to prayer' will be made from the buildings and/or structures and the purchaser undertakes to install a light at the top of the minaret which will be switched on at the hour of prayer. The light to be installed will be used in such a way as not to be a nuisance or disturbance to other owners of erven in the township.[147]

However, the Islamic Society installed a sound amplifier, which resulted in numerous complaints from residents. The residents' association then approached the court for an interdict to prohibit the Islamic Society from using the amplification equipment. The Islamic Society argued that the prohibition on the call to prayer infringed on their right to freedom of religion. The court was of the view that the prohibition regulated only a particular ritual practised at a particular place and that the regulation was in the interests of other members of the community. The court interdicted the Islamic Society from using any sound amplification equipment on the property and ordered them to remove all loudspeakers and sound amplification equipment installed on the property.

What was clear from the discussion was the fact that the use of religious symbols, church bells or even musical accompaniments and amplifiers associated with a religion or belief must be enjoyed with due consideration of the rights of others. Liturgical bell ringing, or the call to prayer as a form of religious manifestation, is not exempt from noise control regulations and bylaws, but these laws and their application must also take into account the religious needs of the community. This equally applies to the wearing of religious dress and the display of religious symbols, particularly in the workplace and public places.

146 *Garden Cities Incorporated Association Not For Gain v Northpine Islamic Society* 1999 2 SA 268 (C).

147 *Garden Cities Incorporated* 270 C-E.

Religious holidays

Sunday observance

The observance of religious and other sacred days of rest, festivals and ceremonies forms an important part of the right of believers to practice and manifest their beliefs. Earlier legislation in the 1600s aimed at protecting certain religious tenets often dealt with issues relating to aspects of Sunday observance. In a judgment by the Natal Provincial Division in 1923 in *Hennessey v Durban Town Council*,[148] a ratepayer of Durban applied for a motion to restrain the Durban Town Council, in respect of the municipal orchestra, from holding Sunday concerts and other forms of entertainments. The applicants submitted that these concerts as well as the sale of programmes on Sunday is contrary to section 1 of the Sunday Observance Act 24 of 1878. The court relied on various municipal bylaws and found that the respondents were in fact authorised by the provisions of Ordinance 14 of 1916 and 11 of 1918 'to give municipal concerts conjointly with non-musical performances'.[149] The court further held that the sale of programmes on Sunday is not a commodity and therefore not contrary to the Sunday Observance Law.

The importance of observance of Sundays and religious holidays diminished with the new constitutional dispensation and replaced much of the Christian ethos underlying Sundays and (religious) public holidays. In the case of *S v Lawrence; S v Negal; S v Solberg*[150] the Constitutional Court had to deal with the constitutionality of selling liquor on Sundays. Lawrence, Negal and Solberg were all employees of the Seven Eleven supermarket chain, and were all charged and convicted for contraventions of the Liquor Act 27 of 1989. They claimed that their convictions were unlawful because the prohibition on such sales infringed the right to freely engage in economic activity in terms of section 26 of the interim Constitution and, in addition, that the Act's prohibition on the sale of alcohol on 'closed days' (defined as Sundays, Good Friday and Christmas Day), violated the right to freedom of religion. The court was divided on the issue of freedom of religion and by a vote of six to three, and for different reasons, the sale of liquor by Seven Eleven on Sundays was upheld by the Constitutional Court. Chaskalson P (Langa DP, Ackermann J and Kriegler J concurring) held that Sundays have acquired a secular as well as a religious character and held that there was no violation of the right to freedom of religion.[151] O'Regan J, in a minority judgment (Goldstone J and Madala J concurring) held that the Act did infringe the right but that the offending provision could be severed from the Act.[152] Sachs J (Mokgoro J concurring) was of the view that the identification of Sundays, Good Friday and Christmas Day as closed days for purposes of selling liquor does involve an

148 *Hennessey v Durban Town Council* 1923 NPD 317.
149 *Hennessey* 317.
150 *S v Lawrence; S v Negal; S v Solberg* 1997 10 BCLR 1348 (CC); 1997 2 SACR 540 (CC).
151 *S v Lawrence* para 95.
152 *S v Lawrence* para 133.

endorsement by the state of the Christian religion in a manner that is problematic and that it infringed the constitutional principle of freedom religion, belief and opinion.[153] He held that the infringement was nevertheless a justifiable limitation and therefore not unconstitutional and concurred in the order proposed by Chaskalson P. The court therefore dismissed the appeals, upholding the sections of the Liquor Act, which prohibit the sale of wine on Sundays.[154]

Numerous statutes still contain references to Sundays. The Prohibition of the Exhibition of Films on Sundays and Public Holidays Act 16 of 1977 is one example. Based on the Constitutional Court arguments in *S v Lawrence; S v Negal; S v Solberg*, Carnelley[155] submits that 'it could be argued that the legislation is either unconstitutional or has fallen into disuse'. In relation to trading hours, various statutes and bylaws regulate business hours on certain days, selling of liquor or gambling activities. Where provisions explicitly promote the precepts of only one religion, such as Christianity, by recognising these days worthy of special treatment, it can be argued that it is unconstitutional for violating the right of freedom of religion of other religions. If legislation regulates trading hours on a Sunday and it is for other legitimate purposes as found by the Constitutional Court in *S v Lawrence; S v Negal; S v Solberg*, these provisions can be constitutional and enforceable. However, each case should be assessed on its own facts.

In a more recent case in the Labour Court in *SACTWU v Berg River Textiles*,[156] a lay preacher challenged his work requirement of work on Sundays because of a modification in the shift arrangement implemented at his place of work. During the first Sunday on which he was required to work, he failed to report for duty. During a disciplinary hearing, the claimant pleaded not guilty on the basis that he was entitled, by virtue of his right to freedom of religion, to refuse to work on the Sunday. He was nevertheless found guilty and dismissed. He approached the Labour Court to challenge his dismissal. The court held that his Sunday work prohibition was considered to be a central tenet of his beliefs, which were also acknowledged by his workplace management. He had often turned down promotions and overtime to go to church and not work on Sundays. Despite this, his employer alleged that working on Sunday was an inherent requirement of his job and that they could not accommodate him. The court saw no reason why the employer could not accommodate their employee. Explaining the sincere belief held by the employee, Steenkamp J held:

153 *S v Lawrence* para 160.

154 In *Gold Circle (Pty) Ltd v Premier, KwaZulu-Natal* 2005 4 SA 402 (D), the court applied the provisions of the 1996 Constitution and declared certain provisions of the Regulation of Racing and Betting Ordinance 28 of 1957 (KZN) unconstitutional 'as it promoted the precepts of Christianity and unjustifiably discriminated against non-Christians by prohibiting horseracing on closed days (Sundays, Good Friday, Ascension Day and Christmas Day). As such, it did not provide equal protection or benefits as is required by the Constitution'. See M Carnelley 'Sundays and Public Holidays' in WA Joubert and M Kuhne (eds) *LAWSA* (2017) 23 para 257.

155 Carnelley 2017 *LAWSA* para 261.

156 *SACTWU v Berg River Textiles* [2012] JOL 28114 (LC).

> The point is simply this: Williams was the only employee who chose to register a complaint premised on his religious beliefs. It is clear that the respondent's management knew of Williams's religious convictions and had known for some time. More particularly, the respondent knew that the Sunday work prohibition was a central tenet of his beliefs – so much so that he had in the past turned down promotions and lucrative overtime work in order to go to church, preach and not work on Sundays.[157]

The court was happy to conclude that the claimant established a *prima facie* case of discrimination against his religious beliefs, which resulted in his dismissal. According to the court, it constituted an automatically unfair dismissal for the purposes of the Labour Relations Act.[158] According to the court:

> The dismissal of Williams was automatically unfair. The real or proximate cause for his dismissal was his religious beliefs; had he been willing to work on Sundays, he would not have been dismissed. The respondent did not make any effort, or at least not a sufficient effort, to accommodate him by exploring alternatives to Sunday work for him.[159]

The court ordered his employer to reinstate him retrospectively into the same position that he occupied prior to his dismissal, provided that he may not be compelled to work on Sundays [160]

Religious and public holidays

In relation to public holidays, the Public Holidays Act 36 of 1994 is important. Section 2A empowers the President to declare additional holidays. Since 1994, various additional holidays were included in the national calendar. For instance, Ascension Day was already removed as a religious public holiday and Easter Monday was changed to Family Day. Currently there are 12 public holidays on the calendar, of which only two are Christian holidays, namely Good Friday and Christmas day. The other ten public holidays on the national calendar, are all secular holidays. After some complaints by minority groups in relation to unfair discrimination concerning public holidays, the CRL Rights Commission held public hearings in 2012, and published a report with recommendations in 2013.[161] The main argument put forward in the report was that the Public Holidays Act, in so far as it only recognises Christian holidays, is biased and

157 *SACTWU* paras 39–40.
158 *SACTWU* para 43.
159 *SACTWU* para 49.
160 *SACTWU* para 53.
161 An in-depth discussion of this report and all the recommendations fall outside the scope of this book. The full report 'CRL Commission, Public Holidays vs Religious/Cultural Holidays. In Pursuit of Equality Among Religious and Cultural Groups'. Online at: www.crlcommission.org.za/docs/public-holidays-report.pdf.

discriminatory against the religious rights of other religious groups. The findings by the CRL Rights Commission included that there is 'mischief' in the Public Holidays Act, because it endorses Christianity and excludes other religions. The Basic Conditions of Employment Act also does not regulate leave for religious holidays.[162] The Commission recommended that the Department of Home Affairs and the Presidency should restructure and cluster some of the existing public holidays. Other recommendations included the removing of some holidays, declaring some as half days where people can be released early on those days and by adding religious holidays for some of the other religions. A recommendation is also to capture important holidays of religious groups on the calendar, not as public holidays, but for the public to be aware of those days.[163]

According to FOR SA, 'there is a direct correlation between the majority religion of the country and the religious days that are set apart as public holidays in that country. Of the 12 public holidays in South Africa, only two are Christian'. They feel strongly that in the absence of 'proof of the discriminatory impact that Christian public holidays have on others, it is hard to accept that these holidays serve to "deepen religious divides"'.[164] This is supported by Krishnaswami,[165] who took the view that 'official holidays and days of rest in many countries correspond to a large extent to the religious holidays and days of rest of the predominant group'. The Public Holidays Act provides that any public holiday may be exchangeable for any other day, which is fixed by agreement or agreed to between an employer and employee. FOR SA is of the view that non-Christian employees therefore have the right to request paid leave on another day, such as Diwali or Ramadan, instead of Good Friday or Christmas day. Employers in South Africa generally show tolerance towards people of different religions in the workplace.[166]

Subsequent to the publication of the CRL Rights Commission report on public holidays, SALRC published a discussion document on legislation administered by the Department of Home Affairs in 2015.[167] With reference to the Public Holidays Act, the Commission was of the view that:

> there is an element of prejudicial treatment in that the two main Christian holidays are declared as paid public holidays and adherents of other religions who celebrate other faith based holidays are disadvantaged in that their holidays are not declared public holidays and they do not have an automatic benefit of pay on those days.

162 See *Public Holidays Report* 30.
163 *Public Holidays Report* 31.
164 FOR SA 'Good Friday and Christmas Under Threat' (27 February 2015). Online at: https://forsa.org.za/good-friday-and-christmas-under-threat/.
165 Krishnaswami *Study of Discrimination* 48.
166 See *Good Friday and Christmas Under Threat.*
167 Discussion Paper 133 'Statutory Law Revision: Legislation Administered by the Department of Home Affairs' *South Africa Law Reform Commission* Project 25: 56.

They recommended that the section should be reviewed and suggested that either these holidays be reviewed or that equal weight be given to holidays of other faiths.[168]

In conclusion, it can be said that in a multi-religious society, problems will always arise in connection with the observance of religious and public holidays. As a general rule, subject to interest of the general society as a whole, 'the prescriptions of each religion or belief relating to holidays and days of rest should be taken into account'.[169] Religious holidays play an important part in the life of believers and members of every religion. The reality is also that different religions attach differing degrees of importance to religious holidays and days of rest; while for some, 'strict observance of such days is a categorical imperative, for others it involves only a limited prohibition of certain activities or a prescription to attend services or to perform certain ceremonies'.[170]

Conclusion

Through the discussion and various examples, this chapter has illustrated the importance of the right, as part of the right to believe, to be able to manifest and practise those beliefs by members of religious communities. Not only does the Constitution and other legislation guarantee this aspect of the right to religious freedom, it also protects the right to the private or public, and the individual or joint, observance and exercise of one's religious or other convictions. Legislation also seeks to regulate religious practices in a reasonable and justifiable manner in order to strike a balance between competing rights, provided that these laws, procedures and administrative practices are clear and generally available to those affected thereby. The reasonable regulation of religious practices through legislation is a justifiable way of limiting the practices in terms of law of general application. As pointed out as follows:

> Thus while public authorities may legitimately regulate the exercise of the right to freedom of worship 'in community with others' and 'in public' in the general interest, taking account of rival demands, it must be affirmed that as a general rule everyone should be free to worship in accordance with the prescriptions of his religion or belief, either alone or in community with others, and in public or in private; and that equal protection should be accorded to all forms of worship, places of worship, and objects necessary for the performance of rites.[171]

Religion is not static and rituals and practices must also adapt to changing circumstances. It is no easy task to strike a balance between the right to freedom of

168 *Statutory Law Revision Report* 56.
169 Krishnaswami *Study of Discrimination* 36.
170 Krishnaswami *Study of Discrimination* 35.
171 Krishnaswami *Study of Discrimination* 31–32.

religion and the manifestation of those rights on the one hand, and inclusivity and the regulation of those practices through legislation on the other hand. The government has to find an adequate balance of all needs concerned. The preamble of the South African Charter of Religious Rights and Freedoms emphasises and recognises the fact that rights also impose the corresponding duty on everyone in society to respect the rights of others. In exercising our various rights, whether the right to freedom of religion or the right to manifest those rights in different circumstances, everyone should aim to act lawfully and ethically in accordance with the principles of tolerance, fairness, openness and accountability.

Bibliography

Adhar R and I Leigh *Religious Freedom in the Liberal State*2 ed (2013) Oxford: Oxford University Press.

Bailey C 'Muti Killings is a Way of Life in Rural Areas' *IOL News* (16 January 2010). Online at: www.iol.co.za/news/south-africa/muti-killings-is-a-way-of-life-in-rural-areas-470603.

Carnelley M 'Sundays and Public Holidays' in WA Joubert and M Kuhne (eds) *The Law of South Africa*3 ed (2017) 23 para 257, South Africa: LexisNexis.

Collingridge L 'The Cape's Kramats: A Unique Religious and Cultural heritage' (8 September 2015). Online at: www.southafrica.net/blog/en/posts/entry/the-capes-kramats-a-unique-religious-and-cultural-heritage.

Comins L 'Durban's Plan to Recycle Graves' (14 September 2015). Online at: www.iol.co.za/news/south-africa/kwazulu-natal/durbans-plan-to-recycle-graves- 1915860.

Convention concerning Indigenous and Tribal Peoples in Independent Countries (Entry into force: 05 Sep 1991) Adoption: Geneva, 76th ILC session (27 June 1989). Online at: https://www.ilo.org.

Coplan DB 'Land from the Ancestors: Popular Religious Pilgrimage along the South Africa-Lesotho Border' *Journal of Southern African Studies* (2003) 29(4) 976.

CRL Rights Commission 'Public Holidays vs Religious/Cultural Holidays. In Pursuit of Equality Among Religious and Cultural Groups'. Holidays Report – April 2013. Online at: www.crlcommission.org.za/docs/public-holidays-report.pdf.

CRL Rights Commission Report 'Reuse of Graves by Local Governments: A Solution or Violation of Cultural and Religious Rights of Communities'. Reuse of Graves Report – May 2015. Online at: http://crlcommission.org.za/docs/reuse-report.pdf.

CRL Rights Commission Executive Summary 'Report on Public Hearings on Initiation Schools in South Africa' (June 2014).

CRL Rights Commission 'Report on Some Challenges that Lead to Deaths and Injuries at Initiation Schools in South Africa' (2017).

Dambuza (Judge of Appeal) 'Women's Parental Rights Concerning Ulwaluko Rites' Public Lecture, Rhodes University Faculty of Law (24 April 2018).

Dopamu PA 'Towards Understanding African Traditional Religion' in EM Uka (ed) Readings in African Traditional Religion (1991) 19–37New York: Peter Lang.

Ekurhuleni Metropolitan Municipality 'Public Health Bylaws' [Council Resolution: AET (012009) dated 23 September 2009].

Esterhuysen A 'Undermining Heritage' *South African Archaeological Bulletin* (2009) 64 (189) 1–3.

FOR SA 'Good Friday and Christmas Under Threat' (27 February 2015). Online at: https://forsa.org.za/good-friday-and-christmas-under-threat.

International Labour Organization *Indigenous and Tribal Peoples Convention, 1989 (No. 169)* (Entry into force: 05 Sep 1991) Adoption: Geneva, 76th ILC session (27 June 1989). Online at: www.ilo.org/dyn/normlex/en/f?p=NORMLEXPUB:12100:0::NO::P12100_ILO_CODE:C169.

Krishnaswami A *Study of Discrimination in the Matter of Religious Rights and Practices* (1960) New York: United Nations Publication.

Kroeze IJ 'How to Eat: Vegetarianism, Religion and Law' *The Journal for Transdisciplinary Research in Southern Africa* (2012) 8(1) 1–16.

Labuschagne M 'Witchcraft as Misconduct' *De Rebus* (2017) May (573) DR 51. Online at: www.derebus.org.za/witchcraft-as-misconduct.

Leff D 'Witchcraft is a Religion!' *News24* (16 April 2012). Online at: www.news24.com/MyNews24/Witchcraft-is-a-religion-20120414.

Lenta P 'Muslim Headscarves in the Workplace and Schools' *South African Law Journal* (2007) *124(2)*296–319.

Mancotywa S *Critical Conversations about Heritage: Popularising Contemporary Heritage Issues* (2014) *Pretoria*:National Heritage Council of South Africa.

Masonda S 'The Practice of African Traditional Religion in Contemporary South Africa' in Bennet T (ed) *Traditional African Religions in South Africa* (2011) 19–35Cape Town: UCT Press.

Mavundla T, F Netswera, B Bottoman and F Toth'Rationalization of Indigenous Male Circumcision as a Sacred Religious Custom: Health Beliefs of Xhosa Men in South Africa' *Journal of Transcultural Nursing* (2009) 20(4) 395–404.

Mbiti JS *Introduction to African Religion* (1975) London: Heinemann Educational Publishers.

Mbiti JS *Introduction to African Religion* 2 ed (2015) Long Grove, IL: Waveland.

Mndende N *African Spiritual Journey: Rites of Passage among the Xhosa speaking of South Africa* (2006) Cape Town: Icamagu Institute.

Mndende N *Tears of Distress: Voices of a denied spirituality in a democratic South Africa* (2009) Idutywa: Icamagu Institute.

Mndende N 'Law and Religion in South Africa: An African Traditional Perspective' *NGTT* (2013) 54(4) 74–82.

Ngubane H 'Some Notions of "Purity" and "Impurity" Amongst the Zulu' *African Journal of the International African Institute* (1976) 46(3) 274–284.

Nyaundi NM 'African Traditional Religion in Pluralistic Africa: A Case of Relevance, Resilience and Pragmatism' in Bennet T (ed) *Traditional African Religions in South Africa* (2011) 1–18Cape Town: UCT Press.

Osman F 'Legislative Prohibitions on Wearing a Headscarf: Are they Justified?' *Potchefstroom Electronic Law Journal* (2014) 17(4) 1318–1349.

Parker J and FN Zaal 'Extending Recognition of Indigenous Burial Practices in *Selomo v Doman* 2014 JDR 0780 (LCC)' *Potchefstroom Electronic Law Journal* (2016) 191–28.

'Prison Official Sacked for Headscarf to Sue' *IOL News* (3 May 2006). Online at: www.iol.co.za.

Ralushai Commission of Inquiry (Chairperson Professor NV Ralushai) *Report of the Commission of Inquiry into Witchcraft Violence and Ritual Murders in the Northern Province of the Republic of South Africa*. Report Commissioned by the Premier of the Northern Province. The Commission, National Government Publication (1996).

Ratipa MM 'Just Piles of Rock to Developers but Places of Worship to Native Americans' – Exploring the Significance of Earth Jurisprudence for South African Cultural Communities' *Potchefstroom Electronic Law Journal* (2015) 18(1) 3197–3236.

Rautenbach C 'Umkhosi Ukweshwama: Revival of a Zulu Festival in Celebration of the Universe's Rites of Passage' in Bennet T (ed) *Traditional African Religions in South Africa* (2011) 63–89Cape Town: UCT Press.

Saccaggi B and A Esterhuysen 'Sekuruwe Grave relocation: A Lesson in Process and Practice' *The South African Archaeological Bulletin* (2014) 69(200) 173–181.

SAPA 'By-laws Need to Accommodate Slaughter' *News24* (29 March 2019). Online at: www.news24.com/southafrica/news/by-laws-need-to-accommodate-slaughter-20110329.

SAPA 'Correct Procedures must be Followed when Slaughtering Animals' *South African Government News Agency* (23 September 2009). Online at: www.sanews.gov.za/features/correct-procedures-must-be-followed-when-slaughtering-animals.

Skosana D 'Protecting the Dead: The South African National Heritage Resources Act in Context' in M Christian Greenet al (eds) *Religious Pluralism, Heritage and Social Development in Africa* (2017) 315–331 Stellenbosch South Africa: SUN Media.

Leff D 'South African Law Reform Commission finds Witchcraft Suppression Act unconstitutional' *PENTON* (20 January 2016). Online at: www.penton.co.za/sa-law-reform-commission-finds-witchcraft-suppression-act-unconstitutional.

South Africa Law Reform Commission *Statutory Law Revision: Legislation Administered by the Department of Home Affairs. Discussion Paper 133. Project 25.*

South Africa Law Reform Commission *The Review of the Witchcraft Suppression Act 3 of 1957. Discussion Paper 139. Project 135* (2016). Online at: www.justice.gov.za/salrc/dpapers/dp139-WitchcraftSuppression.pdf.

South Africa Law Reform Commission *Review of the Witchcraft Suppression Act 3 of 1957. Issue Paper 29. Project 135* (2014).

Tebbe N 'Witchcraft and the Constitution' in T Bennet (ed) *Traditional African Religions in South Africa* (2011) 156–181Cape Town: UCT Press.

Trip advisor 'Religious Sites in South Africa' (November 2016). Online at: www.tripadvisor.co.uk/Attractions-g293740-Activities-c47-t10-South_Africa.html.

United Nations Declaration on the Rights of Indigenous Peoples: A Manual for National Human Rights Institutions (2013) Geneva: Asia Pacific Forum of National Human Rights Institutions and the Office of the United Nations High Commissioner for Human Rights. Online at: www.ohchr.org/Documents/Issues/IPeoples/ UNDRIPManualForNHRIs.pdf.

Van Coller EH 'Burial Rights: Protecting the Religious and Cultural Heritage of Communities in South Africa' in M Christian Greenet al (eds) *Religious Pluralism, Heritage and Social Development in Africa* (2017) 333–351 Stellenbosch: African Sun Media.

Van Coller EH 'Laat die Klokke Lui …! Is die Lui van Klokke 'n Geraasoorlas of Bloot die Billike Uiting van Geloofsoortuigings?' *LitNet Akademies* (2018) 15(3) 769–787.

Van der Schyff G 'Ritual Slaughter and Religious Freedom in a Multilevel Europe' *Oxford Journal of Law and Religion* (2014) 3(1) 76–102.

Van Gennep A *The Rites of Passage* (1960) Chicago, IL: University of Chicago Press.

Wallace D 'Rethinking Religion, Magic and Witchcraft in South Africa: From Colonial Coherence to Postcolonial Conundrum' *Journal for the Study of Religion* (2015) 28(1) 23–51.

Wallace D 'The Modern Pagan Witch: Negotiating a Contested Religious Identity in Post-apartheid South Africa' in D Brown (ed) *Religion and Spirituality in South Africa: New*

Perspectives (2009) 124–144Scottsville Pietermaritzburg: University of KwaZulu-Natal Press.

Ward TP 'South Africa's Witchcraft Suppression Act Ruled Unconstitutional' *The Wild Hunt Modern Pagan News & Commentary* (27 January 2016). Online at: https://wildhunt.org/tag/south-african-pagan-rights-alliance.

Waywell A 'Elderly Women Targeted in E Cape Village over Witchcraft Claims' *eNCA News* (15 January 2017). Online at: www.enca.com/south-africa/elderly-women-terrorised-in-ecape-village-over-witchcraft-claims.

World Tourism Organization 'Tourism Can Protect and Promote Religious Heritage. Press Release 14083' (10 December 2014). Online at: http://media.unwto.org/press-release/2014-12-10/tourism-can-protect-and-promote-religious-heritage.

6 Religion in education

Introduction

The accommodation of religion in the public sphere is particularly prominent in relation to religious observance in the school context. Religious observances in South African state and state-aided institutions are permissible under the Constitution as long as they comply with the requirements of the Constitution and the South African Schools Act 84 of 1996 and do not infringe on any of the rights or freedoms in the Constitution. Religious observance inevitably has the potential to create conflict between different rights and perspectives. Often a conflict arises between a schools' legitimate exercise of their constitutionally guaranteed right to religion and the limiting effect that it might have on an individual learner's right to be free to choose and practise their own religion or abstain from religious observances at all.

Apart from the Constitution, the Schools Act is also relevant as far as it makes specific provision for school governing bodies to make rules relating to religious observances. A further important document is the National Policy on Religion and Education which was published in 2003 with the express purpose of regulating the manner in which religious observances are conducted at public schools. There are also a number of international law instruments that relate to the right to religious freedom and religious observances, although the emphasis in this section will be specifically on the South African context.[1]

Religious observances, in both public and independent schools in South Africa, are regulated within a very particular constitutional, legislative and policy framework. This chapter will provide an overview of the constitutional, legislative and policy framework that regulates religious observances in the educational context, specifically in schools.

1 For a valuable and interesting comparative contribution on Religion in Public Education in various European Countries, see 'Religion in Public Education' by Gerhard Robbers (ed), 2011, proceedings of the 22nd annual conference of the European Consortium for Church and State Research took place from 11–14 November 2010 in Trier, Germany.

Legislative framework

The Constitution of the Republic of South Africa, 1996

Relevant constitutional provisions include sections 15, 29 and 31 of the Constitution. Section 15(2) makes it clear that religious observances may be conducted at state or state-aided institutions, provided that (a) those observances follow the rules made by the appropriate public authorities; (b) they are conducted on an equitable basis; and (c) attendance is free and voluntary. In *Wittman v Deutscher Schülverein*, the court held that a 'religious observance' was an act of a religious character, a rite. The observance must be religious in that it must form part of a particular system of faith and worship. It includes observances such as the daily opening of a school by prayer, reading of the scripture and possibly a sermon or religious message, and benediction.

In relation to the meaning of 'state-aided', the court in *Wittman* followed a very narrow approach. According to the court these institutions were a very specific category of schools, institutions and colleges in respect of which grants-in-aid are made or a loan was granted. They are not necessarily a public school that is state funded or a private school, but lie somewhere in between. They are funded by the state and therefore also subject to state regulation. The court examined the interpretation to be given to the phrase 'state-aided' and held that the German School was indeed registered as a private school in terms of Act 104 of 1986. The court held further that the German School was accordingly not an executive organ of state and not subject to the provisions of s 14 of the interim Constitution.[2] Currie and De Waal support the court's definition, although they caution that the decision was taken under the Interim Constitution and that section 15(2) of the current Constituent applies to state and state-aided schools and they support restricting the application of section 15(2) to the so-called 'government schools'.[3] It also does not apply to religious education. Section 29 of the Constitution further provides for the right to basic education and the right to establish and maintain independent educational institutions. Section 31 is also important, since it guarantees the right to form, join and maintain cultural, religious and linguistic associations and other organs of civil society, which can include educational institutions.

The 1996 Schools Act

In the context of the public school system, section 7 of the Schools Act gives effect to section 15(2) of the Constitution and is an almost identical reflection of the wording of section 15(2). Due to the principle of subsidiarity, should any challenge be brought against the religious policy of a public school, reliance would first have to be placed on section 7 of the Schools Act, before relying directly on

2 See *Wittman v Deutscher Schülverein, Pretoria* 1998 (4) SA 423 (T) 452F-G; 454E-F.
3 I Currie and J De Waal *The Bill of Rights Handbook* 6 ed (2013) 331.

the constitutional provisions, unless the Schools Act is challenged for not giving effect to the provisions in the Constitution. The South African Schools Act was enacted to provide for a uniform system for the organisation, governance and funding of schools. In relation to religion, the South African Schools Act protects 'freedom of conscience and religion at public schools' by providing that religious observances may be conducted at public schools. It indicates that this must be done in accordance with rules issued by a school governing body, on an equitable basis, and where attendance by 'learners and members of staff is free and voluntary'. It also reminds us that these observances are subject to the requirements of provincial laws and the Constitution.[4]

Section 57[5] of the Schools Act further provides for 'Public Schools on Private Property' owned by religious organisations. They have the right to specify a religious ethos and character, subject to an agreement with the provincial authorities. In both such institutions the National Policy on Religion in Education would not prescribe requirements for religious instruction and religious observances by this policy. However, in maintaining the curriculum standards with respect to religion education, both independent schools and public schools on private property with a recognised religious character are required to achieve the minimum outcomes for religion education.

The Schools Act delegates the power to make rules regarding religious observances in schools, to the school governing body. Section 8 of the Act provides that a governing body of a public school must adopt a code of conduct for their learners, after consultation with the learners, parents and educators. The code of conduct must aim at establishing a disciplined and purposeful environment to facilitate effective education and learning in schools. The national Department of Education published *The Guidelines for Consideration of Governing Bodies in Adopting Code of Conduct for Learners*. These guidelines indicate that they are subject to the Constitution, and 'must reflect' constitutional democracy, human rights and transparency. Under section 4 of the code, it sets out the values and principles applicable to the rights of learners. It endorses the principles of non-discrimination and equality.[6] It also provides for mutual respect for another's convictions and cultural traditions. With reference to the right of freedom of expression, the policy highlights that the freedom of expression is also extended to forms of outward expression as seen in clothing selection and hairstyles.[7] However, the policy emphasises that learners' rights to enjoy freedom of expression are not absolute. Section 11 of the guidelines sets out certain offences that may lead

4 Section 7.

5 Section 57. If the owner of the private property referred to in section 56 is a religious organisation, such owner may require that the agreement contemplated in section 14 must recognise, in an appropriate manner consistent with this Act, the distinctive religious character of the school.

6 See section 4.2 No person may unfairly discriminate against a learner. All learners shall enjoy equal treatment before the law and shall receive equal protection and benefits of the law.

7 See section 4.5.1.

to suspension, including repeated violations of school rules or the code of conduct. However, provincial regulations must also be consulted in the compilation of a list of offences that may lead to suspension of a learner. Particularly in relation to offences that relate to uniform and hairstyle violations that are motivated by religious and cultural practices, schools and school governing bodies must read and interpret the guidelines generously and as a whole. They must take cognisance of the various rights and values in drafting a code of conduct.

The 2003 National Policy on Religion and Education

The Department of Education adopted the National Policy on Religion in Education in 2003 in order to give full expression to the invocation of religion in the Constitution and the principles governing religious freedom. The policy proposes that the interaction between religion and public education must be based on the cooperative model of religion–state interaction. In the foreword to the policy, the diversity of the South African population is stressed, by making sure that, particularly in public schools, no particular religious ethos should be dominant over, and suppress, others. It further aims to protect the equal rights of all students to be at school, and appreciates their right to have their religious views recognised and respected. The policy, which applies to all public schools in the country, distinguishes between three different ways in which religion could be relevant in schools: 'religious education', 'religious instruction' and 'religious observances'. Each will be discussed in the next section, with the emphasis on religious observance as a manifestation of the right to freedom of religion.

The 2005 Draft National Guidelines on School Uniforms

In 2006, the Department of Basic Education produced the National Guidelines on School Uniform, in order to give guidance to school governing bodies in developing their school uniform policies. The purpose of these guidelines is to ensure that practices related to school uniform do not impede access to education in any manner and do not infringe any constitutional rights of persons. Section 15 of the guidelines states that a refusal to wear the approved school uniform may be treated as a disciplinary matter in terms of the code of conduct. The guidelines emphasise the fact that School Governing Bodies (SGBs) should take account of the circumstances of the school community, and be sensitive to them when designing a new school uniform.[8] The school uniform guidelines speak directly to the issue of religious and cultural diversity and protect learners' rights to religious and cultural dress and hairstyles.[9] The Religion in Education Policy, in its

8 Section 19.

9 Section 29 – Religious and Cultural Diversity.

(1) A school uniform policy or dress code should take into account religious and cultural diversity within the community served by the school. Measures should be included to accommodate learners whose religious beliefs are compromised by a uniform requirement.

definition of religious observance, includes reference to religious dress as part of those activities and behaviours, which recognise and express the views, beliefs and commitments of a particular religion. Jewellery, clothes and hairstyles often play an important role in cultural and religious practices. Many schools have strict rules in their various codes of conduct about what is allowed or not.

Religious Charter

Section 7 of the Religious Charter is relevant in so far as it guarantees every person the right to be educated or to educate their children, or have them educated, in accordance with their religious or philosophical convictions. Subsection 7.1 provides that 'the state, including any public school, has the duty to respect this right and to inform and consult with parents on these matters. Parents may withdraw their children from school activities or programs inconsistent with their religious or philosophical convictions'. Subsection 7.2 further provides that 'every educational institution may adopt a particular religious or other ethos, as long as it is observed in an equitable, free, voluntary and non-discriminatory way, and with due regard to the rights of minorities'. Subsection 7.3 provides for private education institutions, established on the basis of a particular religion, philosophy or faith. Section 8 provides for the right to receive and provide religious education, training and instruction and that the state may subsidise such education, training and instruction. Subsection 7.2 has been described as a provision that:

> follows logically from the right to conduct religious observances in a public school. There is no institution without any ethos (even so-called neutrality is an ethos), and if there is a particular majority religion in a school, that school will in all probability naturally adopt and reflect that ethos. The Bill of Rights, in particular section 15(2), acknowledges this. I am confident that the Charter reflects the proper, constitutional approach to religion in public schools, and will go a long way in regulating this issue equitably.[10]

Subsection 4.4 of the Charter further provides:

> Every person has the right to conduct single-faith religious observances, expression and activities in state or state-aided institutions, as long as such observances, expression and activities follow rules made by the appropriate

(2) If wearing a particular attire, such as yarmulkes and headscarves, is part of the religious practice of learners or an obligation, schools should not, in terms of the Constitution, prohibit the wearing of such items. Male learners requesting to keep a beard as part of a religious practice may be required by the school to produce a letter from their religious teacher or organisation substantiating the validity of the request. The same substantiation is applicable to those who wish to wear a particular attire.

10 R Malherbe 'Religion in School' *NGTT* (2013) 54 (4) 9.

> public authorities, are conducted on an equitable basis, and attendance at them is free and voluntary.[11]

The issue of a particular religious ethos has been challenged in a recent High Court decision in *Organisasie vir Godsdienste-Onderrig en Demokrasie v Laerskool Randhart and Others*,[12] and will be discussed in more detail in the next section. In the light of this decision, section 4.4 of the Charter may also be open to some challenges.

Religious ethos

As pointed out earlier, the National Policy on Religion in Education distinguishes between three different ways in which religion could be relevant in schools: 'religious education', 'religious instruction' and 'religious observances'. Each will be discussed briefly, although the emphasis in this section will be on religious observance, which include aspects of religious convictions important to followers of a particular religion, such as prayer, singing, ceremonies, dress, dietary requirements and religious symbols.

Religious education

In terms of the policy, religious education is the study of religion and thus education about different religions in South Africa and the rest of the world. It is a formal curricular programme aimed at creating an understanding of diverse religions and tolerance for these religions, and promoting social justice and human rights. The policy further draw a distinction between a single-faith approach to religious education, which provides religious instruction in one religion, and a multiple single-faith approach, which provides parallel programmes in religious instruction for an approved set of religions. The policy supports a multi-tradition approach to the study of religion education that does not promote any particular religion. The curriculum standards for religion education will also apply to both independent and public schools, and both must attain the minimum outcomes for religion education, should they offer it as part of their curriculum.

Religious instruction

Religious instruction is also sometimes referred to as religious education, which is not the general study of religion, but the kind of education that teaches about a particular religion. According to the policy, religious instruction is understood to

11 For further criticism, see F Settler 'Legal and Civic Contestations over Tolerance in South Africa's National Policy on Religion and Education' *Alternation Special Edition* Special Edition 10(2013) 21.

12 *Organisasie vir Godsdienste-Onderrig en Demokrasie v Laerskool Randhart and Others* 2017 (6) SA 129 (GJ). Discussed in more detail under the section on religious ethos.

include instruction in a particular faith or belief, with a view to the inculcation of adherence to that faith or belief. Religious instruction cannot be part of the national curriculum or be taught in public schools, and should primarily be the responsibility of the home, the family and religious communities. However, schools are encouraged to allow the use of their facilities for such programmes in a manner that does not interrupt or detract from the core educational purposes of the school. This could include voluntary gatherings and meetings of religious associations during break times. The policy does not apply to independent schools. Various independent schools are set up by religious communities, where it is expected that these schools will provide religious instruction for learners from their particular religious community.

In the case of *Wittman*, for instance, 12-year-old Tanja Wittman was forced by the school to attend Lutheran-based religious education classes. While religious observance was described by the court as an act of a religious character, religious education was not. The court highlighted that 'whereas the interim Constitution and Constitution both provide for religious observances, both are silent about religious instruction in State and State-aided institutions. A Bible period is not forbidden and neither is the study of the Koran'.[13] However, the court recognised the fact that the right of freedom of religion (in the case of religious minorities) and the right to freedom of thought, belief and opinion (in the case of atheists and agnostics) entails that attendance may not be enforced. The court thus drew a distinction between religious observance and religious instruction. In relation to the requirement in *Wittman* that Tanja had to attend morning prayer as well as religious instructions, the school board was of the view that:

> We are not forcing anybody into Christianity; but it belongs to the understanding of the subject religious instructions as an educational subject, to work on our cultural background and to provide the pupils with knowledge, with which they can decide on in religious questions.[14]

According to the German School, the religious instruction taught at the school was taught 'supra-denominationally' and 'lessons were not related to a Church but imparted to pupils as general knowledge of various faiths. Knowledge of the cultural background inclusive of religion was vital for the comprehension of the German language, literature and history'.[15] The policy makes it clear that confessional or sectarian forms of religious instruction in public schools are inappropriate for a religiously diverse and democratic society. Although religious education can be of a confessional nature or of an informative general nature, neither can be religious observance.

13 *Wittman v Deutscher Schülverein* 449 E.
14 *Wittman v Deutscher Schülverein* 431 I.
15 *Wittman v Deutscher Schülverein* 432 E-F.

Religious observance

In relation to religious observance, the policy does not explain every form of religious observance but rather sets out guidelines. Different types of religious observance are mentioned, including voluntary public occasions, which make use of school facilities, for a religious service on a day of worship or rest; voluntary occasions when the school community (teachers and pupils) gather for a religious observance; observances held in a voluntary gathering of pupils and/or teachers during a school break; and an observance that may be ongoing, and entail other dimensions such as dress, prayer times and diets, which must be respected and accommodated in a manner agreed upon by the school and the relevant faith authorities.[16]

The foreword to the policy specifically states that no particular religious ethos should be dominant over and suppress others, and that everyone's right to have their religious views must be recognised and respected. In relation to religious observance, the policy requires that it must be free and voluntary, and provided for on an equitable basis.[17] In relation to the requirement of 'free and voluntary', van Schalkwyk[18] argues that for section 15(2) to be a functional part of the Constitution, 'a certain measure of indirect coercion will be inevitable as religious observances can never be conducted to completely eliminate all forms of coercion'. To subject a learner to a compulsory religious activity will infringe the right to freedom of religion. As stated by Chaskalson P in the Constitutional Court judgment in *S v Lawrence, S v Negal, S v Solberg*:

> Compulsory attendance at school prayers would infringe freedom of religion. In the context of a school community and the pervasive peer pressure that is often present in such communities, voluntary school prayer could also amount to the coercion of pupils to participate in the prayers of the favoured religion … section 14(2) makes clear that there should be no such coercion. It is in this context that it requires the regulation of school prayers to be carried out on an equitable basis. I doubt whether this means that a school must make provision for prayers for as many denominations as there may be within the pupil body; rather it seems to me to require education authorities to allow schools to offer the prayers that may be most appropriate for a particular school, to have that decision taken in an equitable manner applicable to all schools, and to oblige them to do so in a way which does not give rise to indirect coercion of the 'non-believers'.[19]

16 See section 59.

17 Section 58. See further R Malherbe 'The Constitutionality of Government Policy Relating to the Conduct of Religious Observances in Public Schools' *Tydskrif vir Suid-Afrikaanse Reg (TSAR)* (2002) 391–418; R Malherbe 'The Right to Freedom of Religion in South African Schools: Recent Disturbing Developments' *International Journal for Education Law and Policy* (2004) 248–257.

18 C van Schalkwyk *The Constitutionality of Religious Observances in South African Public School* (LLM Thesis, University of Stellenbosch, 2016) 138.

19 *S v Lawrence; S v Negal; S v Solberg* 1997 10 BCLR 1348 (CC); 1997 2 SACR 540 (CC) para 103.

The impact of coercion can be mitigated by, for instance, choosing a time and place for religious observances in such a way as to ensure that learners experience the least amount of pressure.[20] Keeping the effect of indirect coercion to a minimum will require sensitivity on the part of the teachers, learners, parents and school community. There is an obligation on the majority to respect the religious differences of the minority or non-adherents. Van Schalkwyk[21] uses the example of a rugby match, where the majority of the players are Christian and one of the players is Muslim. It might be more appropriate to allow for a moment of silence where each player can observe in accordance with his own religion, rather than to have one of the Christian players pray. In such a way there is no coercive pressure to conform to a particular religion and the practice would not infringe religious freedom. Since learners cannot be completely free of indirect religious coercion, it is important how schools accommodate the diversity of learners' religious convictions in order to reduce the harmful effects of the coercion. Religious observances must be conducted in a way that ensures the equitable treatment of both majority and minority religions, and accommodating the beliefs of a religiously diverse pupil body.

In relation to the requirement of equitability, it does not necessarily require a school to have equal amounts of observances from all the different religions, but rather seeks to strike a balance between religious coercion on the one hand and the right to conduct religious observances in the public school setting on the other. As pointed out in a handbook on Basic Education Rights:

> It most probably also does not mean that each school must rotate between this wide set of possible religious observances in a manner that allows an equal number of observances per year or per term to each religion. This would be an extremely difficult standard for schools to meet.[22]

In the case of *Lawrence*, O'Regan J saw the equitable treatment of religions as a requirement distinct from voluntariness and emphasised the even-handed treatment of religions forms as the crucial element of the equity requirement. According to her:

> In determining what is meant by inequity in this context, it must be remembered that the question of voluntary participation is a consideration separately identified in section 14(2). The requirement of equity must therefore be something in addition to the requirement of voluntariness. It seems to me that, at the least, the requirement of equity demands the state to act even-handedly in relation to different religions.[23]

20 Van Schalkwyk *Religious Observances* 140.
21 Van Schalkwyk *Religious Observances* 141.
22 T Fish Hodgson 'Religion and Culture in Public Education in South Africa' in F Veriava (ed) *Basic Education Rights Handbook – Education Rights in South Africa* (2017) 194.
23 *S v Lawrence* para 122.

And further:

> Requiring that the government act even-handedly does not demand a commitment to a scrupulous secularism, or a commitment to complete neutrality. Indeed, at times giving full protection to freedom of religion will require specific provisions to protect the adherents of a particular religion as has been recognised in both Canada and the United States of America. For example, in the context of religious observances at local schools, the requirement of equity may dictate that the religious observances held should reflect, if possible, the religious beliefs of that particular community or group. But for religious observances at national level, however, the effect of the requirement is to demand that such observances should not favour one religion to the exclusion of others.[24]

Section 62 of the policy provides some examples of appropriate and equitable means of acknowledging the multi-religious nature of a school community, including the rotation of opportunities for observance, in proportion to the representation of different religions in the school; selected readings from various texts emanating from different religions; the use of a universal prayer; or a period of silence. Various forms of religious observance exist, some of which will be discussed in the next section.

Religious dress

The National Guidelines on School Uniforms[25] expressly provide for religious and cultural diversity, and freedom of expression:

> A school uniform or dress code should take into account religious and cultural diversity within the community served by the school. Measures should be included to accommodate learners whose religious beliefs are compromised by a uniform requirement.[26]

The guidelines further require school uniform policies to accommodate learners' free expression, provided that this does not contribute to disruption by substantially interfering with discipline or with the rights of others.[27] In *MEC for Education, KwaZulu-Natal and Others v Pillay*,[28] the Constitutional Court held that dress codes must be sufficiently flexible to accommodate religious and cultural

24 *S v Lawrence* para 122.

25 The *National Guidelines on School Uniforms GN 173, GG 28538* of 26 February 2006 adopted by the Minister under s8(3) of the South African Schools Act.

26 Section 29(1) of the *National Guidelines on School Uniforms.*

27 Section 29(3) of the *National Guidelines on School Uniforms.*

28 *MEC for Education, KwaZulu-Natal and Others v Pillay* 2008 (1) SA 474 (CC) para 114.

practices, unless there is real evidence that a departure will ‘threaten academic standards or discipline’.

Jewellery

Codes of Conduct at many schools contain strict rules about what jewellery and accessories may be worn at schools. At the same time, jewellery, including symbolic jewellery such as crosses, beads, studs or David stars, has an important place in cultural and religious practices. An important case dealing with freedom of religion in schools is the case of *MEC for Education: KwaZulu-Natal and Others v Pillay*. The case concerned the right of a learner to wear a nose stud to school. Sunali Pillay, a girl of South Indian descent and a learner at Durban Girls’ High School, returned after the holiday with a gold nose stud. It was against the school’s code of conduct and the school indicated that she should not be allowed to wear it. The school’s code of conduct provided that no jewellery may be worn at school other than a watch and one earring per ear. Ms Pillay took the school and the KwaZulu-Natal MEC for Education to the Equality Court alleging that they had unfairly discriminated against Sunali and had violated her religious and cultural rights. The Equality Court found that the school had not unfairly discriminated against Sunali, but on appeal to the High Court, the decision was overturned. The court held that the school had discriminated against Sunali and that the discrimination was unfair. The School and Department then appealed to the Constitutional Court. Langa CJ considered the first question and that was whether Sunali was part of an identifiable religion or culture and the religious and cultural significance of the nose stud. The evidence before the court showed that the wearing of a nose stud was a voluntary practice that formed part of Sunali’s South Indian Tamil Hindu culture, which itself was inseparably intertwined with Hindu religion and protected by the Equality Act. The court further held that the nose stud was an expression of both religion and culture.[29] The court noted that the school had taken meaningful steps to accommodate diversity in its community, and that uniforms and school rules served an important purpose in education. However, the court was of the view that this case was not about uniforms in general, but about a specific exemption to a uniform. According to the court:

> The discrimination has had a serious impact on Sunali and, although the evidence shows that uniforms serve an important purpose, it does not show that the purpose is significantly furthered by refusing Sunali her exemption. Allowing the stud would not have imposed an undue burden on the School. A reasonable accommodation would have been achieved by allowing Sunali to wear the nose stud. I would therefore confirm the High Court’s finding of unfair discrimination.[30]

29 See *Pillay* para 60.
30 *Pillay* para 112.

The court granted an order declaring that the refusal by the school to grant Sunali an exemption from the code unfairly discriminated against her and dismissed the appeal. In addition, the court ordered that the school, in consultation with learners, parents and staff, amend the code to provide for a procedure to reasonably accommodate religious and cultural practices.[31]

Hairstyles and headscarves

Through their codes of conduct and uniform policies, schools also regulate the hairstyles of learners. Problems tend to occur particularly in relation to Rastafarian learners, who are required to grow their hair and wear it in dreadlocks, in accordance with their religion. *In Antonie v Governing Body, Settlers High School*,[32] a grade 10 learner at Settler's High School in Bellville was suspended for wearing a cap and her hair in dreadlocks in conformity with her Rastafarian conviction. The school found this to be in defiance of the school rules. During a disciplinary hearing she was charged with serious misconduct. She was found guilty and suspended for 5 days. She then approached the court for the review and setting aside of the school's decision finding her guilty of serious misconduct. In relation to the code of conduct, no mention is made, under the heading of 'hair', to dreadlocks or anything similar. There is likewise no reference, in the discussion of clothing, to headgear. Therefore the court found that since the growing and wearing of dreadlocks was not prohibited by the school rules, the governing body failed to apply their minds to the provisions of the code.[33] The court was also of the view that the learner's behaviour was not 'something akin to immoral, promiscuous or shockingly inappropriate'.[34] The court found it a blatant absurdity to view dreadlocks and wearing of a cap as a serious misconduct and ordered the suspension to be set aside.[35]

In 2010, Lerato Motshabi, a learner at Navalsig High School in Bloemfontein, was ordered to cut her dreadlocks or to face expulsion from the school. The matter was reported to the South African Human Rights Commission (SAHRC).[36] In a similar case,[37] Odwa Sityata, a practising Rastafarian, who was a learner at Joe Slovo Engineering High School in Khayelitsha, was suspended from school after refusing to trim his dreadlocks. In 2013, another case involving a learner who was banished from her class room for wearing dreadlocks, ended up in

31 For some views on the *Pillay* case, see L du Plessis 'Religious Freedom and Equality as Celebration of Difference: A Significant Development in Recent South African Case-law' *Potchefstroom Electronic Law Journal* (2009) 12(4) 10–34; A Govindjee 'Of Nose Studs, Beards and Issues of Discrimination' *Obiter* (2007) 357–373.

32 *Antonie v Governing Body, Settlers High School* 2002 4 SA 738 (C).

33 *Antonie* 742 para12.

34 *Antonie* 743 para 19.

35 See further R Roos 'The Physical Appearance of Learners in Public Schools' *Journal of South African Law* (2003) 792.

36 V Vena 'Battle of the Dreads Rages on' *Mail & Guardian* (23 July 2010).

37 F Parker Pupil 'School Face Off Over Dreadlocks' *Mail & Guardian* (10 March 2011).

the Free State High Court.[38] Lerato, in conformity with her Rastafarian religion, wore dreadlocks. She was a learner at Leseding Technical School in Thabong, in Welkom in the Free State. She was not allowed to attend classes unless she cut in hair in line with the school's uniform code.[39] They approached the Equal Education Law Centre (EELC), a non-profit organisation working to protect learners' rights, who initiated urgent court proceedings in the Free State High Court. The Free State Department of Education was of the view that Lerato's Rastafarianism was not a seriously held belief. However, the court found in favour of Lerato and stressed the importance of religion.

> It cannot be overemphasised that religion is a very sensitive issue and that religious intolerance can ruin the whole country. One needs not look at the whole world, as good examples of what religious intolerance can do can be found in our own African continent, as in Northern Mali and Northern Nigeria. The courts of this country must be alert and proactive, and root out the evil of religious intolerance in any form. They should nip it in the bud wherever and whenever it raises its ugly head.[40]

The court found the school had discriminated against Lerato based on her religion, and violated her rights to freedom of religion, belief, expression and culture.

A similar problem arises in relation to religious and customary dress of Muslim women, particularly 'headscarves', including niqabs, hijabs and burkas. Wearing a headscarf is generally considered to be a manifestation of religion protected by the right to freedom of religion. Various cases have been reported in the news relating to religious dress and school uniforms. In 2013 and 2014, two schools[41] were forced to revise their uniform policy to accommodate learners wearing headscarves. In 2013, on the first day of the school year, a brother and sister at Eben Donges High School were asked by teachers to remove their headscarf and fez. According to the school, it was 'against the school's code of conduct for the children to wear the Islamic headgear'.[42] When they contacted the parents, they informed the school that it was part of their Islamic faith and that the children must wear the headgear. The Provincial Department of Education viewed the

38 *Radebe and Others v Principal of Leseding Technical School and Others* (1821/2013) [2013] ZAFSHC 111 (30 May 2013).

39 Paragraph 4.3.3 of the code of conduct reads as follows:

'Hairstyle must be neat and short. No elaborate style (such as parting, shaven paths, steps, dyes, fizzes, dreadlocks and hairpieces) are allowed. Girls may have long hair or simple braids, but long hair must be tied back out of the face'.

40 Para 21.

41 See Staff Writer 'W Cape School Denies Muslim Siblings Entry for Wearing Head Dress' *Mail & Guardian* (23 January 2013); See further A Tayob 'The National Policy on Religion and Education and Religious Dress Observances in South African Schools' in C Green *et al* (eds) *Religious Pluralism, Heritage and Social Development in Africa* (2017) 171–186.

42 M Jones 'School Under Fire over Fez Ban' *Cape Times* (24 January 2013). Online at: www.iol.co.za/capetimes/school-under-fire-over-fez-ban-1457846.

issue in a very serious light. They supported the parents and were of the view that 'schools should take religious and cultural diversity into account. We believe it is a simple matter to adjust dress codes to meet these requirements'.[43] Their parents complained to the SAHRC, who investigated the matter.

Religious symbols

Religious symbols in schools are often found in relation to school mottos and anthems. With reference to the case of *In re Certification of the Constitution of the Republic of South Africa 1996*,[44] Justice Ackerman[45] noted that when the Constitutional Court had to certify the 1996 Constitution, several objections were lodged against the reference to 'God' in the Preamble of the Constitution. The objections viewed the inclusion of '[m]ay God protect our people' as discriminatory against non-theists. However, the court was of the view that the invocation of the deity did not constitute any form of discrimination against non-theists. It also did not oblige non-theists to do anything in conflict with their beliefs or opinions, nor did it in any way limit them in the exercise of such beliefs or opinions. According to De Freitas, a 'God-free' preamble in a Constitution does not necessarily provide a more democratic or pluralistic situation when compared to a preamble that refers to 'God'.[46] Many international and European societies that stands for pluralism and tolerance do include reference to 'God' in their respective mottos, preambles or national anthems.[47]

There can be many interpretations of the term 'God', and for purposes of religious pluralism, it is important to note that it can also present a 'diverse and accommodative understanding regarding the word "God" that can and has been understood to embrace all of human beings and creation'.[48] Viewed in this manner, reference to 'God' is not only the expression of religious beliefs, but a much wider range of beliefs that may be expressed in the public sphere. According to De Freitas:

> By excluding 'God' from the picture, the idealistic aim of attaining absolute (and even substantial) accommodation is a misnomer. In the process one will be establishing some other underlying belief in a motto, a belief that is reflected in the motivations of those persons who feel that, in the name of pluralism, one has to move towards a supposedly more neutral or inclusivist direction. Excluding 'God' from the picture essentially excludes all of those

43 *Ibid.*
44 *In re Certification of the Constitution of the Republic of South Africa 1996*, 1996 (10) BCLR 1253 (CC) paras 203–204.
45 LWH Ackermann 'Some Reflections on the Constitutional Court's Freedom of Religion Jurisprudence' *NGTT* (2002) 43(1–2) 177; 180.
46 S de Freitas 'Mottos, Prayer and the Public University' *South African Journal on Human Rights* (2012) 28(2) 178.
47 See further De Freitas 2012 *NGTT* 180 and further.
48 De Freitas 2012 *NGTT* 182–183.

interest groups who find a reference to 'God' important and relevant for whatever reason (whether religious or non-religious).[49]

Numerous public schools in South Africa refer in their mottos to words such as 'God'; 'We Believe'; 'Faith'; 'In God is Truth' and many more. In the light of the argument above, public schools, as part of their religious observance and religious ethos, should not be prohibited from using these phrases. An approach prohibiting any reference to 'God' will in fact support an anti-theistic approach, as opposed to the cooperative model that the National Policy on Religion in Education in fact stands for.

Laerskool Randhart – judgment

The most recent case relating to religious observances in public schools is the case of *Organisasie vir Godsdienste-Onderrig en Demokrasie v Laerskool Randhart and Others.*[50] In 2017, the High Court ruled in favour of the Organisation for Religious Education and Democracy (*Organisasie vir Godsdienste-Onderrig en Demokrasie, OGOD*) in a matter concerning the promotion of religion in South African public schools. A voluntary organisation and pro-atheist group, OGOD, wanted to declare the religion policy of six schools unconstitutional. They approached the South Gauteng High Court, requesting it to rule against having one dominant religion observed at public schools. They claimed the Christian ethos of these schools (they were Randhart Primary School in Alberton, Baanbreker Primary School in Boksburg, Garsfontein Primary School in Pretoria, Linden High School in Johannesburg, Oudtshoorn High School and Langenhoven Gymnasium in Oudtshoorn) was unconstitutional. They further wanted the court to prohibit practices by a public school such as holding itself out as a Christian school; recording that its school badge represents the Holy Trinity; having religious instruction and singing; opening the school day with Scripture and explicit prayer dedicated to a particular God; referring to any deity in a school song; and having any value that includes learners to strive towards faith.[51] The primary issue in the *Randhart* case was whether a public school may hold out that it is exclusively a Jewish, or a Christian, or a Muslim, or a Buddhist, or an atheist school, and to what extent? The schools argued that they have a right of freedom of religion; and that they were entitled by law to have a religious ethos or character.[52] They further argued that their practices complied with the requirements of section 15(2) of the Constitution in that it was conducted under the required rules of the governing body and that it was on an equitable basis and attended by learners on a voluntary basis.

49 De Freitas 2012 *NGTT* 183.

50 *Organisasie vir Godsdienste-Onderrig en Demokrasie v Laerskool Randhart and Others* 2017 (6) SA 129 (GJ).

51 *Laerskool Randhart* para 6.

52 *Laerskool Randhart* para 12.

With reference to the legislative framework, and particularly the views of the Constitutional Court in the *Lawrence* judgment, the High Court found that public schools, as state institutions, cannot promote a single religion to the exclusion of others. According to the court, neither the Constitution nor the Schools Act confers on a public school or SGB the right to adopt the ethos of one single religion to the exclusion of others. Schools are required to adopt rules that provide for religious policies and for religious observances that are to be conducted on a 'free and voluntary' and on an 'equitable' basis.[53] The court declared it offends section 7 of the Schools Act for a public school:

> to promote or allow its staff to promote that it, as a public school, adheres to only one or predominantly only one religion to the exclusion of others; and to hold out that it promotes the interests of any one religion in favour of others.[54]

The judgment affirmed the principles of equality and religious diversity in public education in South Africa. The High Court recognised the important role that religion plays in the everyday life of all who live in South Africa. The court highlighted that there are ways to entrench unity in diversity, and that is to foster religious rights on an equitable basis. Important in this judgment is also that just because we require the government to act even-handedly does not necessitate secularism. The judgment made it clear that religious rights can still be observed in state institutions, subject to certain limitations. The judgment is therefore not a victory for secularism, as claimed by OGOD, but rather a recognition of South Africa's religious diversity. It creates the space for all religions to express their religious beliefs in the public sphere. The judgment does not compel public schools to stop all religious observances, but rather direct them to acknowledge religious diversity and that learners hold different beliefs. To that effect, schools must make sure that there is equal space and opportunity for learners of different faiths to express their religious beliefs. What about private education in South Africa and do the same principles apply to independent schools?

Independent schools

The Interim Constitution explicitly stated the right 'to establish, where practicable, educational institutions based on a common culture, language or religion'. Under the Interim Constitution, the Constitutional Court explained that this 'right' was one that entitled communities to establish their own religious schools, but did not require the state to do so. The final Constitution also provides for 'everyone' a 'right to establish and maintain, at their own expense, independent educational institutions'. It is important that, unlike the Interim Constitution, the final Constitution makes no mention of religion in this right. It simply requires

53 *Laerskool Randhart* para 91.
54 *Laerskool Randhart* para 102.

that independent schools do not discriminate based on race, are registered and 'maintain standards that are not inferior to standards at comparable public educational institutions'. Citizens do have the right, at their own expense, to establish independent schools, including religious schools, as long as they avoid racial discrimination, register with the state, and maintain standards that are not inferior to the standards of comparable public educational institutions.[55]

It is important to note that section 29(3) is qualified in that private schools may not discriminate on the basis of race and must be registered with the state. Currie and De Waal[56] have argued that private schools are not subject to section 15(2) of the Constitution, even where they receive the some form of subsidy from the state. Because of the horizontal application of the Bill of Rights, the right to freedom of religion also applies to private schools. However, section 29(3) read with section 31 of the Constitution allows private and religious schools to discriminate on the basis of gender, language, culture and religion in so far as it allows them to restrict admission to pupils from a particular religious group. This will apply to both religious education as well as religious observance, although they may not compel learners to attend.

Independent schools may deny admission to learners who refuse to subscribe to the school's mission statement and may advance particular religious and cultural beliefs and practices. However, they are still prohibited from unfairly discriminating against learners for reasons such as religion or culture. In relation to admissions, independent schools are subject to the Promotion of Equality and Prevention of Discrimination Act 4 of 2000 (PEPUDA) and may not discriminate against learners on the grounds set out in the Act. The Constitutional Court in *Gauteng Provincial Legislature In re: Gauteng School Education Bill*[57] emphasised that associations have the right to establish independent schools in order to preserve linguistic, cultural or religious beliefs and practices. The court interpreted section 32(c)[58] of the Interim Constitution to mean that 'constitutionally guaranteed space should be made available for private individuals to set up and maintain [establish] their own schools if they feel that their special cultural, language or religious needs are not being sufficiently catered for in the state system'.[59] According to Franklin,[60] this implies that independent schools:

> may be entitled to greater latitude than public schools when implementing a curriculum that demands that learners participate and adhere to certain

55 Section 29(3) of the Constitution of the Republic of South Africa.

56 Currie and De Waal *The Bill of Rights Handbook* 333.

57 *Gauteng Provincial Legislature In re: Gauteng School Education Bill of 1995* 1996 (3) SA 165.

58 Section 32(c) guaranteed everyone the right to establish, where practicable, educational institutions based on a common culture, language or religion, provided that there shall be no discrimination on the ground of race.

59 *Gauteng Provincial Legislature* para 78.

60 S Franklin 'Education Rights in Independent Schools' in F Veriava (ed) *Basic Education Rights Handbook – Education Rights in South Africa* (2017) 360.

> linguistic, religious and cultural practices. However, even in an independent school, certain practices may be limited in terms of the Constitution.

In *Christian Education SA v Minister of Education*,[61] an organisation of concerned Christian parents approached the High Court to challenge section 10 of the South African Schools Act, which prohibited corporal punishment in any school. They applied to the South-Eastern Cape Local Division of the High Court for an order declaring section 10 of the Schools Act unconstitutional and invalid in that it interferes with the right to freedom of religion and to cultural life to the extent that it prohibits corporal punishment in those independent schools. The High Court turned down the application and held that 'section 10 of the Schools Act did not constitute a substantial burden on religious freedom' and that 'corporal punishment in schools infringed the children's right to dignity and security of the person and was accordingly not protected by section 31 of the Constitution'. They were granted leave to appeal to the Constitutional Court. In the Constitutional Court, the Minister of Education argued that even at a private Christian school, allowing teachers to use corporal punishment to physically discipline children violated learners' right to dignity and their rights to freedom of security of the person. Sachs J highlighted the significance of religious and related rights and that for the appellants 'what is at stake is not merely a question of convenience or comfort, but an intensely held sense about what constitutes the good and proper life and their place in creation'.[62] After a careful analysis of the limitation clause, however, the court concluded that the prohibition on corporal punishment in the Schools Act, although limiting the right to freedom of religion of Christian parents, was reasonable and justifiable. The court dismissed the appeal.

A question that comes to mind is whether a school can expel learners who refuse to participate in school prayers or to comply with the dress code of the school? Judgments by our courts have indicated that religious institutions and religious schools have the right to suspend learners who have voluntarily subjected themselves to the rules and regulations of the school, set by the school governing body, and then refuse to abide by those rules.[63] In *Wittman v Deutscher Schülverein, Pretoria*,[64] the court confirmed the view that a school governing body of a Christian German independent school was entitled to expel a learner who was aware of the fact that she had to attend language and religious classes, but refused to attend the religious instruction classes and school prayers. According to the court:

> Does this mean that private parochial schools which do not receive State aid may not prescribe obligatory attendance at their morning prayers and confessional religious instruction classes? The answer is negative. Section 17 of the

61 *Christian Education South Africa v Minister of Education* 2000 (4) SA 757 (CC).
62 *Christian Education South Africa* para 37.
63 See further Malherbe (2002) *Tydskrif vir Suid-Afrikaanse Reg* 391 and further.
64 *Wittman v Deutscher Schülverein, Pretoria* 1998 (4) SA 423 (T).

> interim Constitution and s 18 of the Constitution recognise the freedom of association. Section 14(1) and s 15(1) respectively recognise the freedom of religion which includes the right to join others in worship, propagation of the faith, etc. Freedom of association entails the right with others to exclude non-conformists. It also includes the right to require those who join the association to conform with its principles and rules.[65]

The court justified the expulsion because the school's rules and regulations required the learner to attend religious classes; the learner had agreed to abide by the school's rules and regulations; and the learner was given the opportunity to 'opt out' by attending school elsewhere. According to the court:

> To deprive our society of that important unifying mechanism in order to spare the non- believer what seems to me the minimal inconvenience of standing, or even sitting in respectful non-participation, is as senseless in policy as it is unsupported in law.[66]

An important aspect to consider is always whether the impact of the discrimination is severe enough to justify intervention against a school's policy or practices. Often complex issues will have to be taken into account in order to decide whether there was in fact unfair discrimination. A court will assess the impact that the discrimination has on the learner, and the degree to which the affected learner is part of a group that suffers from patterns of discrimination. A court will also look at the degree of discrimination compared to the legitimate purposes it seeks to achieve and whether the school could have taken narrower means to achieve its purpose. It is important for the school to consider other means of accommodating the learner and a court will look at the extent to which the school has attempted to do that.[67]

An interesting case came before the Human Rights Commission in relation to the South African Board of Jewish Education (SABJE). Under the South African Schools Act, all schools controlled by SABJE are independent schools. Although SABJE-controlled schools did allow non-Jewish children to attend their schools and employ non-Jewish educators, they still insisted that all learners at the school should adhere to and abide by the requirements of a Jewish education. They must also undertake Hebrew language instructions, observe Jewish religious instructions and participate in all school-sponsored religious events. When learners apply to the school, the application forms make it clear that the goals of the schools 'are to inculcate respect for the Jewish religion, its traditions, customs and institutions and to further the Zionist aims of the Jewish people'.[68] Thus, parents and learners

65 *Wittman v Deutscher Schülverein*, 451 C-E.
66 para 66.
67 See further Franklin *Education Rights* 361 and further.
68 South African Human Rights Commission (SAHRC) Report *Public Inquiry Exclusionary Policies of Voluntary Associations: Constitutional Considerations* (2006) 7. Online at: www.sahrc.org.za.

admitted to the school are required to abide by the rules and policies and participate in all the activities of the school. When admitting learners to the school, they seek to maintain the Jewish identity of the school. The issue was whether the admission policies could be seen as discriminatory if an applicant who refuses to take Hebrew classes or Jewish religious instructions could be refused admission. It was argued on behalf of SABJE by Woolman that the school's admission policies do not amount to unfair discrimination. Even if the policy differentiates on a specified ground, the admission policy constitutes fair discrimination as it is grounded in the legitimate objectives of SABJE and its schools. The discriminatory admissions policy is necessary to achieve the legitimate object of SABJE of offering a Jewish education, including Hebrew language classes and Jewish religious instructions. With reference to the *Wittman* case discussed above, the conclusion was reached that:

> the constitutional right to set up and run an independent school grounded in culture, language or religion inevitably includes the right to exclude students who do not wish to adhere to school requirements that are grounded in language, culture or religion. Given the clear choice enjoyed by non-Jewish children to attend other private schools, the restrictive admission policies impact marginally on their dignity. The restrictive admission policies are however necessary in order to preserve the cultural and religious character of the schools.[69]

In a more recent example, a Muslim family have accused a Johannesburg school of acting in an unconstitutional and racist manner for not allowing their son to grow his beard as part of their Islamic practices. A legal opinion by the Department of Basic Education indicated that Ashton International College has acted unconstitutionally by refusing to allow the pupil to grow his beard. Ashton College, however, emphasised that it was an 'independent Christian school', where all prospective parents were informed of the institution's ethos. The school was thus Christian and private, where parents voluntarily accept, sign and agree to the particular school ethos and code of conduct before their child is registered. The school submitted 'while Christian, our school is multicultural in that students of all faiths are welcomed and all our students adhere to the same uniform and code of conduct requirements'.[70] In the light of the example above, it can be argued that the prohibition might be in line with the school's religious ethos and code of conduct, particularly because of the fact that it is an independent school. Although the specific code of conduct prohibits the growing of a beard, the prohibition does not amount to unfair discrimination, since it is in line with the legitimate objective of the school to adhere to its Christian ethos. In the light of the discussion above, independent schools should note that they are allowed to advance particular

69 Human Rights Commission 2006 *Exclusionary Policies* 8.

70 K Koko 'School in Hot Water over Refusal to Allow Muslim Boy to Grow Beard' *The Mercury* (23 October 2018).

linguistic, cultural or religious values, beliefs or practices, provided that they do not unfairly discriminate on any of the grounds, as set out in PEPUDA. Where independent schools receive a subsidy from the state, they may be more constrained in terms of what will constitute unfair discrimination in relation to religious education, practices and observances at their schools.

Conclusion

This chapter has clearly illustrated that the relationship between religion and education remains a contentious issue. Section 7 of the Schools Act, read with section 15(2) of the Constitution, establishes the framework for the drafting of rules on religious observances. As public schools constitute state-aided institutions, their governing bodies are subject to the requirements of section 15(2). The power of governing bodies to make rules on religious observances is not absolute. It is subject to the Constitution and legislation and, as is illustrated above, may be challenged in a court of law.

Religious expression in schools will always create tension because often it pits conflicting interests against one another. Learners have the right to express their religious and cultural views through their clothing and hairstyles, but schools also have a duty to maintain law and order and create safe learning environments for all learners in the school, by enforcing certain dress or disciplinary codes that may have the potential to limit the free expression of religious rights. It is not easy to strike a balance between creating a proper place for religious observances in schools and simultaneously maintaining an appropriately non-religious environment in public schools.

A measure of coercion will always be present in relation to religious observance. School governing bodies must make sure to structure religious observance at their respective schools in such a way as to ensure the least amount of coercive pressure on non-adhering learners or learners of minority religions, and in a manner that will allow for learners to refrain from participation without drawing attention. It is also important to note that religions do not always have to be treated in exactly the same way, but schools are prohibited from exclusively advancing the beliefs or teachings of a specific religion or religions to the exclusion of other religions. School governing bodies should engage relevant learners, parents and other stakeholders of the school when drafting the relevant school rules and policies. The relevant school rules on religious observance must avoid the potential of directly or indirectly coercing learners towards one religion at the expense of other religions. The rules must ensure the equitable and fair treatment of religions in order to promote the learners' constitutionally protected rights to dignity, equality and religious freedom.

Malherbe[71] reminds us of the fact that religious freedom does not mean freedom *from* religion, but rather freedom *for* religion. Society is therefore not protected from religion, but opportunity and space must be created for people to

71 Malherbe 2013 *NGTT* 6.

manifest their beliefs freely and in all spheres of life, even in schools. It is then also within this context that religious observance in the public sphere, including education institutions, must be interpreted in South Africa.

Bibliography

Ackermann LWH 'Some Reflections on the Constitutional Court's Freedom of Religion Jurisprudence' *NGTT* (2002) 43(1–2) 177–184.

Currie I and J de Waal *The Bill of Rights Handbook* 6 ed (2013) Cape Town: Juta.

De Freitas S 'Mottos, Prayer and the Public University' *South African Journal on Human Rights* (2012) 28(2) 176–195.

Du Plessis L 'Religious Freedom and Equality as Celebration of Difference: A Significant Development in Recent South African Case-law' *Potchefstroom Electronic Law Journal* (2009) 12(4) 10–34.

Fish Hodgson T 'Religion and Culture in Public Education in South Africa' in F Veriava (ed) *Basic Education Rights Handbook – Education Rights in South Africa* (2017) 185–204Johannesburg: Section27.

Franklin S 'Education Rights in Independent Schools' in F Veriava (ed) *Basic Education Rights Handbook – Education Rights in South Africa* (2017) 353–371, Johannesburg: Section27.

Govindjee A 'Of Nose Studs, Beards and Issues of Discrimination' *Obiter* (2007) 28(2) 357.

Jones M 'School Under Fire over Fez Ban' *Cape Times* (24 January 2013). Online at: www.iol.co.za/capetimes/school-under-fire-over-fez-ban-1457846.

Koko K 'School in Hot Water over Refusal to Allow Muslim Boy to Grow Beard' *The Mercury* (23 October 2018). Online at: www.iol.co.za/mercury/news/icymi-school-in-hot-water-over-refusal-to-allow-muslim-boy-to-grow-beard-17599872.

Mail & Guardian, staff writer 'W Cape School Denies Muslim Siblings Entry for Wearing Head Dress' *Mail & Guardian* (23 January 2013). Online at: https://mg.co.za/article/2013-01-23-high-school-denies-siblings-entry-for-wearing-head-dress.

Malherbe R 'Religion in School' *NGTT* (2013) 54(4) 1–10.

Malherbe R 'The Constitutionality of Government Policy Relating to the Conduct of Religious Observances in Public Schools' *Tydskrif vir Suid-Afrikaanse Reg (TSAR)* (2002) 391397.

Malherbe R 'The Right to Freedom of Religion in South African Schools: Recent Disturbing Developments' *International Journal for Education Law and Policy* (2004) 1(1–2) 248–257.

Parker F 'Pupil, School Face Off Over Dreadlocks' *Mail & Guardian* (10 March 2011). Online at: https://mg.co.za/article/2011-03-10-pupil-school-face-off-over-dreadlocks.

Robbers, G 2011. 'Religion in Public Education' Proceedings of the Conference Trier, 11–14 November 2010. (2011) Germany: European Consortium for Church & State Research.

Roos R 'The Physical Appearance of Learners in Public Schools' *Tydskrif vir Suid-Afrikaanse Reg (TSAR)* (2003) 4792–796.

Settler F 'Legal and Civic Contestations over Tolerance in South Africa's National Policy on Religion and Education' *Alternation* Special Edition 10 (2013).

South African Human Rights Commission (SAHRC) *Report Public Inquiry Exclusionary Policies of Voluntary Associations: Constitutional Considerations* (2006). Online at: www.sahrc.org.za.

Tayob A 'The National Policy on Religion and Education and Religious Dress Observances in South African Schools' in MC Green, Hackett RIJ, Hansen L and Venter F (eds) *Religious Pluralism, Heritage and Social Development in Africa* (2017) 171–186Stellenbosch: Conf-RAP.

The National Guidelines on School Uniforms GN 173, GG 28538 of 26 February 2006 adopted by the Minister under s8(3) of the South African Schools Act.

Van Schalkwyk C *The Constitutionality of Religious Observances in South African Public Schools* (LLM Thesis, University of Stellenbosch, 2016).

Vena V 'Battle of the Dreads Rages on' *Mail & Guardian* (23 July 2010). Online at: https://mg.co.za/article/2010-07-23-battle-of-the-dreads-rages-on.

7 Freedom of expression

Hate speech and blasphemy

Introduction

Section 16 of the Constitution guarantees the right to freedom of expression.[1] The importance of this right was emphasised by the Constitutional Court in *Islamic Unity Convention v Independent Broadcasting Authority*[2]

> South Africa is not alone in its recognition of the right to freedom of expression and its importance to a democratic society. The right has been described as 'one of the essential foundations of a democratic society; one of the basic conditions of its progress and for the development of every one of its members' … As such it is protected in almost every international human rights instrument. In *Handyside v The United Kingdom* the European Court of Human Rights pointed out that this approach to the right to freedom of expression is 'applicable not only to "information" or "ideas" that are favourably received or regarded as inoffensive or as a matter of indifference, but also to those that offend, shock or disturb … Such are the demands of that pluralism, tolerance and broadmindedness without which there is no "democracy society"'[3] (footnotes omitted).

1 16(1) of the Constitution of the Republic of South Africa. Section 16 reads as follows:
(1) Everyone has the right to freedom of expression, which includes
(a) freedom of the press and other media;
(b) freedom to receive or impart information or ideas;
(c) freedom of artistic creativity;
(d) academic freedom and freedom of scientific research.
(2) The right in subsection (1) does not extend to -
(a) propaganda for war;
(b)incitement of imminent violence; or
(c) advocacy of hatred that is based on race, ethnicity, gender or religion, and that constitutes incitement to cause harm.

2 *Islamic Unity Convention v Independent Broadcasting Authority and Others* (2002) (4) SA 294.

3 *Islamic Unity Convention* para 26.

The above approach and interpretation of the right to freedom of expression shows the importance of the right, but also emphasises the fact that it is not without any limitation. Section 16(2) therefore makes it clear that the right to freedom of expression does not extend to certain expressions. Section 16(2)(a) and (b) are respectively concerned with 'propaganda for war' and 'incitement of imminent violence'. Section 16(2)(c) is directed at what is commonly referred to as hate speech, namely expression or speech that amounts to 'advocacy of hatred' that is based on one or other of the listed grounds, namely race, ethnicity, gender or religion and that amounts to 'incitement to cause harm'. According to the Constitutional Court:

> There is no doubt that the State has a particular interest in regulating this type of expression because of the harm it may pose to the constitutionally mandated objective of building the non-racial and non-sexist society based on human dignity and the achievement of equality. There is accordingly no bar to the enactment of legislation that prohibits such expression. Any regulation of expression that falls within the categories enumerated in s 16(2) would not be a limitation of the right in s 16.[4]

The right to freedom of expression also goes hand in hand with the right to freedom of religion, which includes the right to be able to express one's beliefs and convictions. Therefore, every person and religious institution should have the right to freedom of expression in respect of religion.[5] For religious institutions, this right includes the right to make public statements and participate in public debate on religious grounds; to produce, publish and disseminate religious publications and other religious material; and to conduct scholarly research and related activities in accordance with their convictions.[6] The expression of religious beliefs and convictions should thus not be confined only to the private sphere, but the right must also extend to the public domain. The right to freedom of expression in relation to religious institutions can also include the right to share their convictions with other consenting persons and the right to have access to public media, access to which must be regulated fairly. Of particular importance in relation to freedom of expression and the prohibition on hate speech is the right to religious dignity, which includes not to be victimised, ridiculed or slandered on the ground of their faith, religion, convictions or religious activities. No person may advocate hatred that is based on religion, and that constitutes incitement to violence or to cause physical harm.[7] The dissemination of religion concerns itself with two aspects, the substance of the message as well as the method by which the message is spread. Where individuals or groups object to the message, or the manner in which it is disseminated or to both, it will inevitably lead to clashes. It is thus to

4 *Islamic Unity Convention* para 33.
5 Section 6 of the Religious Charter provides for this.
6 See section 6.1 of the Religious Charter.
7 See section 6.4 of the Religious Charter.

prevent the dissemination of religion in a manner that is offensive to others that certain laws and regulations, such as laws against blasphemy and hate speech have been enacted.[8] Within the context of the right to freedom of expression, this section will first discuss the offence of blasphemy in South Africa and then the prohibition against hate speech.

Blasphemy

The repealed censorship laws prohibited blasphemy in South Africa, although it remains a common law offence. Under the South African common law, blasphemy was a criminal offence and consisted of the 'unlawful and intentional publication of words or conduct whereby God is slandered'.[9] In *R v Webb*,[10] the court gave the following definition: 'Blasphemy … consists either in the denial of the existence of God or in slandering God'.[11] In *R v Webb*, X published a story in which a nun declared that she had an erotic ecstasy and imagined herself having carnal intercourse with Jesus. The court convicted him of blasphemy. Milton[12] described the essential elements of the crime of blasphemy as unlawfully, intentionally, publicly and acting contemptuously towards God. He argued that blasphemy cannot be committed by accident. Intention is an element of the crime and X must know or foresee the possibility that the conduct may be contemptuous of God and that at least one other person may become aware of it.[13] For the crime to constitute criminal defamation, there must be publication in that it outrages the feelings of a large section of the community. In relation to acting contemptuous towards God, Milton argued that it is the manner in which something is published that determines whether it is blasphemous. There must be an element of 'vilification, ridicule, or irreverence as would be likely to exasperate the feelings of others' and the action would be likely to shock an:

> ordinary member of the community: not just those of a person of strong religious feelings, but those of any one in sympathy with the Christian religion, whether he be a strong Christian or a lukewarm Christian, or merely a person sympathising with their ideals.[14]

It has been pointed out that the law of blasphemy is anomalous in that it only protects the religious feelings of Christians, and not those of members of other

8 A Krishnaswami *Study of Discrimination in the Matter of Religious Rights and Practices* (1960) 41.
9 SV Hoctor 'Criminal Law' in WA Joubert and M Kuhne (eds) *LAWSA* 3 ed (2017) 11 para 253.
10 *R v Webb* 1934 AD 493.
11 *R v Webb* 496.
12 JRL Milton *South African Criminal Law and Procedure* revised 2 ed (1990) 294.
13 Milton *Criminal Law* 294–295
14 Milton *Criminal Law* 296.

religions. Other religious groups may suffer similar feelings of outrage caused by an attack on the Supreme Being that they worship.[15]

In *Islamic Unity Convention v Independent Broadcasting Authority and Others*,[16] the South African Jewish Board of Deputies (the Board) complained to the Independent Broadcasting Authority (IBA) that an interview broadcast by radio 786, a community station owned by the Islamic Unity Convention (IUC), breached the relevant provision (clause 2[a]) in the Broadcasting Code that prohibits the broadcasting of material that is 'likely to prejudice relations between sections of the population'. The Jewish Board argued that the material that had been broadcast was likely to prejudice relations between Jews and other communities.[17] The IUC challenged the constitutionality of the relevant provision of the Code, claiming that it was a violation of the constitutional right to freedom of expression. Freedom of expression has been entrenched in section 16 of the Constitution and forms part of the Broadcasting Code. Section 16(2) sets out certain limitations to the right of freedom of expression, and particularly excludes the advocacy of hatred that is based on religion that constitutes incitement to cause harm.

The Constitutional Court held that this test in section 2(a) of the Broadcasting Code was in fact too wide and ruled that the test should be substituted with the limitation to freedom of expression as contained in section 16(2) of the Constitution of the Republic of South Africa. The court found that the prohibition was too intrusive and made serious inroads into the right to freedom of expression. The court upheld the appeal and declared the prohibition unconstitutional and invalid. The declaration of invalidity was however made subject to the proviso that no protection is given to the broadcasting of material that amounts to propaganda for war, the incitement of imminent violence or the advocacy of hatred that is based on race, ethnicity, gender or religion, and that constitutes incitement to cause harm.[18] As a result of this judgment, the Code of Conduct was amended and a new code came into operation on 7 March 2003. Therefore, the Broadcasting Complaints Tribunal must decide all complaints in the light of the limitations set out in section 16(2) of the Constitution, which is a strict test.

After the amended Code of Conduct came into operation, a case came before the Broadcasting Complaints Commission of South Africa in *Van Loggerenberg and another v 94.7 Highveld Stereo*.[19] In *Van Loggerenberg*, the Broadcasting Complaints Tribunal had to consider numerous complaints relating to a radio broadcast that had included a joke containing a sexual innuendo and which referred in a frivolous manner to a central event in the Christian faith. The court accepted the fact that in terms of the previous Code of Conduct, it was a contravention to broadcast material which was offensive to the religious convictions or

15 Hoctor 2017 *LAWSA* para 253.
16 *Islamic Unity Convention* 294.
17 *Islamic Unity Convention* para 2.
18 *Islamic Unity Convention* para 58.
19 *Van Loggerenberg and another v 94.7 Highveld Stereo* 2004 (5) BCLR 561 (BCT).

feelings of a section of the population. With reference to the *Islamic Unity Convention* case, the court had to apply the amended Code in terms of which the court should also consider the limitation to freedom of expression as contained in section 16(2) of the Constitution. Therefore, the joke complaint in *Van Loggerenberg* would only fail the test if it amounted to the advocacy of hatred based on religion and if the words constituted incitement to cause harm. In relation to blasphemy, the court had to answer the question as to whether the joke:

> cast contempt on God and are intended to hurt and ridicule the religious feelings of professing Christians or can be interpreted as a denial of the existence of God or the slandering of God. In the light of modern attitudes with regard to religion and to religious matters and beliefs, can the (joke) in question viewed in context be said to be so scurrilous or profane, or scoffingly irreverent, and contumelious that one may infer blasphemy.[20]

The majority was of the view that South Africa is not inhabited only by Christians, but by an amalgam of various cultures and religions that all enjoy equal protection under the Constitution. As such, in present-day modern South African society, the court held that although the words may be objectionable, offensive and ill-conceived, it is not so repugnant that one can infer that the words constitute blasphemy and further that the joke does not amount to the advocacy of hatred based on religion that constitutes incitement to cause harm.[21] According to the court:

> It is the majority's view that the impugned joke in present day South Africa cannot be said to be beyond the pale, to such extent that the joke would be regarded as blasphemous and constitute hate speech.[22]

The Tribunal dismissed the complaint and found that Section 16 of the Constitution and the Broadcasting Code have not been contravened. However, Professor Viljoen, in a minority judgment, found that the broadcast of the joke constituted advocacy of hatred based on religion and therefore contravened both the Code as well as section 16 of the Constitution. He based his view on the fact that the divine nature of Jesus is one of the main pillars on which the Christian religion is built and to subject this doctrine to 'ridicule and sexual innuendo will be considered by Christians, of which there are many in this country, to be blasphemy to such a degree that it is tantamount to the advocacy of hatred based on religion'.[23] He was further of the view that the Christian community would not tolerate the ridiculing of the doctrine of the divine nature of Christ. The requirement of section 16 of the Constitution that there must be incitement to cause harm, does, in his view, also not only refer to physical harm but can also include

20 *Van Loggerenberg* para 5.
21 *Van Loggerenberg* para 6.
22 *Ibid.*
23 *Van Loggerenberg* minority judgment para 1.

emotional or psychological harm. He found the incitement to cause in this case in the 'the frivolous manner in which this amazing and holy event in the Christian faith is ridiculed over the airwaves, thus constituting an assault on the religious convictions of adherents to the Christian faith'.[24]

Currently the common law crime of blasphemy still forms part of South African law and it has not formally been abolished by any legislation or declared to be unconstitutional.[25] Snyman[26] argues that the scope of the crime should be determined in the light of the role of religion in present-day society, because of the significant changes in the mores of society as well as their attitude towards religion. Thus, it must be interpreted restrictively. Hoctor[27] argues that it may very well be that the crime has been abrogated by disuse, and criminal law expert Burchell[28] advocates the abolition of the crime and that cases of blasphemy should be regarded as cases of incitement to religious hatred, which would apply to all religions equally.[29] Since the crime of blasphemy protects only the beliefs of Christians, it can be argued that it violates the right to equality. In the case of *Lawrence*, O'Regan J saw the even-handed treatment of religions as a crucial element of the requirement of treating religions equally. In light of the right to freedom of religion, an equitable solution might be to extend the definition of blasphemy to include protection for all religions, not just Christianity.[30]

Hate speech

Apart from section 16(2) of the Constitution that prohibits any expression that advocates hatred based on race, ethnicity, gender or religion, and that constitutes incitement to cause harm (the hate speech provision), section 10 of the Promotion of Equality and Prevention of Unfair Discrimination Act (PEPUDA) 4 of 2000 also prohibits hate speech. It specifically states that no person may publish, propagate, advocate or communicate words based on one or more of the prohibited grounds (including religion), with the intention to be hurtful; be harmful or to incite harm, or promote or propagate hatred. The Constitutional Court has repeatedly highlighted the interest of the state in regulating hate speech 'since it may cause harm to the constitutionally mandated objective of constructing a non-racial and non-sexist society which is based on common human dignity and attainment of equality'.[31]

24 *Van Loggerenberg* minority judgment para 2.
25 G Kemp et al (ed) *Criminal Law in South Africa* 3 ed (2018).
26 CR Snyman *Criminal Law* 2 ed (1989).
27 Hoctor 2017 *LAWSA* para 253.
28 J Burchell Principles of Criminal Law 5 ed (2016) 790–791.
29 See further MI Goolam 'The Cartoon Controversy: A Note on Freedom of Expression, Hate Speech and Blasphemy' *The Comparative and International Law Journal of Southern Africa* (2006) 39(2) 333–350.
30 This argument is also supported by G Van der Schyff 'The Right to Freedom of Religion in South Africa' (LLM dissertation, RAU, 2001) 112 and I Currie and J De Waal *The Bill of Rights Handbook* 6 ed (2013) 376.
31 *South African Human Rights Commission obo South African Jewish Board of Deputies v Masuku and Another* 2018 (3) SA 291 (GJ) para 35.

Where there is a clash between the right to freedom of expression and the right to freedom of religion, such a conflict must be resolved in terms of section 36 of the Constitution.

The hate speech provision of the Equality Act has been described as a provision that 'implements and clarifies the constitutional hate speech provision. While the Constitution puts these forms of expression outside constitutional protection, the Act clearly prohibits hate speech and creates rights. It provides remedies to counter the harmful effects of hate speech'.[32] Because of an increase in recent years of racist and various other incidents relating to racial hate and other forms of hate speech, the Department of Justice and Constitutional Development published the Prevention and Combating of Hate Crimes and Hate Speech Bill in 2016. This Bill adds to the existing measures such as the Promotion of Equality and Prevention of Unfair Discrimination Act in order to combat instances of racism, xenophobia and related intolerances. The Bill provides for the prevention of hate crimes and hate speech. It further aims to give effect to the Republic's obligations in terms of the Constitution and international human rights instruments concerning racism, racial discrimination, xenophobia and related intolerance, in accordance with international law obligations. It creates the offence of hate crime and the offence of hate speech and provides for the prosecution of persons who commit those offences and appropriate sentences.

Numerous complaints were lodged against the first draft of the Prevention and Combating of Hate Crimes and Hate Speech Bill, especially from religious organisations that were concerned that the Bill could be used to silence people of faith for saying things that could be regarded as offensive. The organisation FOR SA and other religious organisations advocated very hard for amendments to the original bill and for the inclusion of a 'religious exemption clause' that would exclude bona fide religious speech.[33]

The revised Prevention and Combating of Hate Crimes and Hate Speech Bill (the Bill) has recently been tabled before Parliament as an improved version of its 2016 predecessor. The Bill is better aligned to the Constitution in relation to its prohibition of certain forms of speech, namely speech that is harmful or incites harm, promotes or propagates hatred. It creates other protected categories beyond what is listed in the Constitution, such as HIV status, culture, sexual orientation and disability. The Bill criminalises hate speech but creates certain defences and includes a religious exemption clause. The new section 3(2)(d) states that the offence of hate speech does not apply in respect of anything done in good faith in the course of engagement in 'the bona fide interpretation and proselytising or espousing of any religious tenet, belief, teaching, doctrine or writings'. This is however subject to the requirement that such interpretation and proselytisation does not advocate hatred that constitutes incitement to cause harm. This exemption will also only apply to sermons and not to statements made by individuals.

32 As quoted by the court in *South African Jewish Board of Deputies* para 36.

33 N Badenhorst 'Revised "Hate Speech" Bill Expected to be Published for Comment Soon' *FOR SA* (19 September 2018).

This has been criticised by various religious organisations and challenges as a major concern, since it may preclude individual believers such as the Jehovah Witnesses, from sharing their faith with others. According to FOR SA:

> To limit the application of the religious exemption clause to sermons, implies that the conscience, convictions and beliefs of individual believers are somehow less sacred and worthy of protection than their pastors.[34]

With any fundamental right, there are boundaries to be drawn. A question that is often asked is what happens when the right to freedom of expression comes into conflict with the right to freedom of religion? With any clash between constitutional rights, they must be balanced against the limitation provisions of the Constitution, with reference to the particular circumstances of the case. The right to dignity, more specifically religious dignity, may also be important, as expressed in section 10 of the Constitution. When the state elevates one religion above others, it can be argued that the state infringes the religious dignity of the other religions. Malherbe[35] argues that the most blatant example of the violation of religious dignity would be where the beliefs, rituals or icons of a particular religion are ridiculed. What follows are a few examples of disputes that ended up in court.

In 2005, a series of cartoons, some depicting the Prophet Mohammed as a terrorist with a bomb, was published by a Danish newspaper, which elicited worldwide reaction in the Muslim community. The cartoons were also published in South Africa. The Jamiat-ul-Ulama of Transvaal, a voluntary religious association, approached the court to interdict Johncom Media Investments Ltd, a publisher of national newspapers, from publishing in any newspaper, magazine or other publication any, cartoons/caricatures/drawings of the Prophet Mohammed. In relation to the image of the Prophet Mohammed, the applicants was of the view that:

> Islam does not know a depiction of Prophet Mohammed (PBUH) and it is a principle of Islam that a production of the holy Prophet (PBUH) in drawings, paintings etc. are blasphemous. The drawings overstep even the bounds of a simple productive drawing but are characterised by insulting messages and innuendos that mock at and ridicule Islam and its founder. Prophet Mohammed (PBUH) is the cornerstone of every Muslim's existence.[36]

The court in *Jamiat Ul-Ulama of Transvaal v Johncom Media Investment Ltd* acknowledged the fact that the media plays a role of undeniable importance in a democratic society in order to provide citizens with information and serve as a

34 N Badenhorst 'Minister Says "Religious Exemption Clause" Will Only Protect Sermons' *FOR SA* (7 June 2018).

35 R Malherbe 'The Mohammed Cartoons, Freedom of Expression and the Infringement of the Right to Religious Dignity' *Tydskrif vir die Suid-Afrikaanse Reg* (2007) 2 333.

36 *Jamiat Ul-Ulama of Transvaal v Johncom Media Investment Ltd and Others* (1127/06) [2006] ZAGPHC 12 (3 February 2006) 4–5.

platform for the exchange of ideas. As powerful institutions tasked with the dissemination of information and ideas, they have a constitutional duty to act with vigour, courage, integrity and responsibility.[37] The court further highlighted the importance of the value of dignity in our constitutional framework and was of the view that a limitation on the freedom of the media may be justified in this case in the interest of human dignity. According to the court:

> These expressions advocate hatred and stereotyping of Muslims on the basis of immutable characteristics that is particularly harmful to the achievement of our core values as a nation, and reinforces and perpetuates patterns of discrimination and inequality.[38]

The court was of the view that if the pictures were to be published, it would 'demean the dignity of an individual whom the Muslim community hold in highest regard'.[39] The court granted the interdict and the respondents were restrained from publishing in any newspaper or publication any cartoons or drawings of the Prophet Mohammed. Malherbe[40] is of the view that the court in the *Jamiat Ul-Ulama* case could have argued that the cartoons amounted to 'incitement to cause harm', if 'harm' was defined to include more than mere physical harm. This argument could have been successful, based on the earlier case of *Van Loggerenberg* where it was argued that the reference to 'harm' in section 16 of the Constitution could also include emotional or psychological harm. If the cartoons did in fact violate the religious dignity of Muslims, Malherbe[41] argues that the court could then have regarded the cartoons to fall under the hate speech qualification, and they would not have been protected under the provision, because any expression that falls under the hate speech qualification would be excluded from the protection afforded by section 16(1) of the Constitution.

Another example relates to comments made against Jews during a lecture at the University of the Witwatersrand in 2009. Bongani Masuku, a member of the Congress of South African Trade Unions (Cosatu), made some threatening, inflammatory and derogatory comments about Jews who supported Israel. The South African Jewish Board of Deputies (SAJBD) accused Masuku of hate speech and lodged a complaint with the Human Rights Commission (SAHRC). The SAHRC found Masuku guilty of hate speech and he was ordered to apologise to the SAJBD, which he refused to do.[42] The case then went to the Equality Court and judgment was delivered in the case of *South African Human Rights Commission obo South African*

37 *Johncom Media Investment* 5.
38 *Johncom Media Investment* 8.
39 *Johncom Media Investment* 9.
40 Malherbe 2007 *Tydskrif vir die Suid-Afrikaanse Reg* 338.
41 *Ibid.*
42 See J Chabalala 'Bongani Masuku Guilty of Hate Speech, Must Apologise to SA Jewish Board of Deputies' *News24* (29 June 2017).
43 *South African Human Rights Commission obo South African Jewish Board of Deputies v Masuku and Another* 2018 (3) SA 291 (GJ) (29 June 2017).

Jewish Board of Deputies v Masuku and Another.[43] In Masuku's utterance, he said that 'the Zionists must be targeted, exposed, and that all must be achieved to subject Jews to perpetual suffering until they withdraw from the land of others'. He further calls for every Zionist to be made 'to drink the bitter medicine they are feeding our brothers and sisters in Palestine'.[44] Since it was confirmed that most Jewish people in South Africa, and indeed world over, regard themselves as Zionists, the court was of the view that these expressions by Masuku were held to be hurtful, harmful, incite harm and propagate hatred, and consequently amounted to hate speech. According to the court:

> not only does the utterance transgress the purview of s 10(1) of the Equality Act, but it clearly makes reference to the persecution and harm that allegedly happened to the Palestinians during the Gaza war. It can, with ease of construction amount to direct incitement to cause some harm to South African Jews.[45]

The court ordered Masuku to tender an unconditional apology to the Jewish community within 30 days of the order. Masuku and Cosatu was also ordered to pay the SAHRC's costs.

In another case, Oscar Bougaardt, a pastor in Mitchells Plain, was taken to court by the SAHRC following complaints about derogatory and offensive comments he had made against gay and lesbian people. In 2013, the SAHRC laid a complaint with the Equality Court against Bougaardt for alleged hate speech. They settled the case through mediation and he signed a statement that he will refrain from making similar comments again in future and the settlement was made an order of court, prohibiting Bougaardt from publishing hate speech on the grounds of sexual orientation. However, despite this court order, it was reported that Bougaardt continued to make hateful comments directed at gays and lesbians and the SAHRC approached the Equality Court for a contempt of court order against Bougaardt. The Western Cape Equality Court found that Bougaardt's comments were not protected by the right to freedom of religion, and found him to be in contempt of court for making hateful comments against gay men and lesbians. He was sentenced to imprisonment for a period of 30 days and the court suspended the sentence for a period of 5 years. Should Bougaardt not refrain from making any hateful comments, he will be imprisoned.[46] This judgment has highlighted the fact that although the draft Hate Crimes Bill provides for a religious exemption clause, religious beliefs and religious hatred cannot be a defence to liability for hate speech.

44 *South African Jewish Board of Deputies* para 49.
45 *Ibid.*
46 OY Ampofo-Anti 'Court Rules that Religion Cannot be Used as a Defence for Anti-gay Hate Speech' *Groundup* (15 June 2018).

Conclusion

It has been stated that 'it is a settled and trite approach in our law that, although the right to freedom of expression is inseparable from a normal democracy, it is however, neither an absolute nor limitless right nor is it a pre-eminent right'.[47] As pointed out by the court in *South African Jewish Board of Deputies v Masuku*:[48]

> The limitation of freedom of expression imposed by ss 10(1) and 11 and related provisions of the Equality Act under discussion, are not unreasonable and not unjustifiable in an open and democratic society based on human dignity, equality and freedom, when regard is had to all the relevant circumstances. The same should apply to s 12, which in its proviso essentially and potentially targets speakers who do not act *bona fide* and whose utterances have the damaging effects listed in s 10.

Blasphemy must also be interpreted within the limits of hate speech and where God is denigrated in such a manner as to constitute hate speech. This means that no one should be allowed to make any statements that advocate hatred or incite violence. It does not matter whether you are a pastor, priest, imam or individual believer, or whether the statements are made in public or from the pulpit. FOR SA, a Christian non-profit organisation, 'strongly condemn any such instances of "hate speech" – whether against another religion, members of the LGBT community or any other group of persons'.[49]

Bibliography

Ampofo-Anti OY Court Rules that Religion Cannot be Used as a Defence for Anti-gay Hate Speech *Groundup* (15 June 2018).

Badenhorst N Minister Says "Religious Exemption Clause" Will Only Protect Sermons *FOR SA* (7 June 2018).

Badenhorst NRevised "Hate Speech" Bill Expected to be Published for Comment Soon *FOR SA* (19 September 2018).

Burchell J *Principles of Criminal Law*5 ed (2016) Cape Town: Juta.

Chabalala JBongani Masuku Guilty of Hate Speech, Must Apologise to SA Jewish Board of Deputies *News24* (29 June 2017).

Currie I and J de Waal *The Bill of Rights Handbook* 6 ed (2013) Cape Town: Juta.

Goolam MI The Cartoon Controversy: A Note on Freedom of Expression, Hate Speech and Blasphemy *The Comparative and International Law Journal of Southern Africa* (2006) 39(2) 333.

Hoctor SV Criminal Law in WA Joubert and M Kuhne (eds) *LAWSA*3 ed (2017) para 11, South Africa: LexisNexis.

47 *South African Jewish Board of Deputies* para 26.
48 *South African Jewish Board of Deputies* para 29.
49 Badenhorst *Religious Exemption Clause* 2018.

Kemp G (ed) *Criminal Law in South Africa* 3 ed (2018) Cape Town: Oxford University Press.

Krishnaswami A *Study of Discrimination in the Matter of Religious Rights and Practices* (1960) New York: United Nations Publication.

Malherbe RThe Mohammed Cartoons, Freedom of Expression and the Infringement of the Right to Religious Dignity *Tydskrif vir die Suid-Afrikaanse Reg* (2007) 2332.

MiltonJRL *South African Criminal Law and Procedure* revised 2 ed (1990) Cape Town: Juta.

Snyman CR *Criminal Law* 2 ed (1989) Durban: Butterworths.

Van der Schyff G *The Right to Freedom of Religion in South Africa* (LLM dissertation, RAU, 2001).

8 Celebration of marriage

Introduction

Most countries recognise one or more forms of marriage. As pointed out by Krishnaswami:

> some recognize only marriage performed by the civil authorities, others give equal recognition to civil and to religious marriage and leave the parties free to make a choice between the two, while still others permit only a religious celebration of marriage either for all or for certain groups of the population.[1]

In South Africa, until almost the turn of the century, the legislature and courts refused to recognise polygamous marriages or unions, including African customary marriages or those concluded under Muslims and Hindu rites.[2] Marriage has been seen as not only a relationship of great significance to the parties concerned, but also as a relationship that has public significance.[3] It is not only valued by the parties themselves, but also by their families, society and the state. 'It has consequences both in the private and public sphere. Privately it offers reciprocal rights and duties of love and support between spouses; consequences and duties in relation to children and other important benefits'.[4]

1 A Krishnaswami *Study of Discrimination in the Matter of Religious Rights and Practices* 36–37.
2 J van der Vyver 'The Diversity of Religiously-based Marriages and Family Law within African Legal Systems' in P Coertzen et al (eds) *Law and Religion in Africa. The Quest for the Common Good in Pluralistic Societies* (2015) 230. In *Seedat's Executors v The Master (Natal)* 1917 AD 302, 309, Innes CJ held that 'Bearing in mind the essential characteristics of marriage, it is clear that the union in question was not a marriage as we understand. It was a relationship recognized no doubt by the legal system under which the parties contracted, but forbidden by our own and fundamentally opposed to our principles and institutions'.
3 See O Regan J in *Dawood and Another v Minister of Home Affairs and Others; Shalabi and Another v Minister of Home Affairs and Others; Thomas and Another v Minister of Home Affairs and Others* 2000 (3) SA 936.
4 *Women's Legal Centre Trust v President of the Republic of South Africa and Others, Faro v Bingham N.O. and Others, Esau v Esau and Others* 2018 (6) SA 598 (WCC) para 3.

Section 15 of the Constitution explicitly creates the possibility for the recognition of religious legal systems and marriages that are not inconsistent with the Constitution.[5] This is further entrenched in section 5 of the Religious Charter that gives every person the right to maintain traditions and systems of religious personal, matrimonial and family law that are consistent with the Constitution. It envisages that legislation that is consistent with the Constitution may be made to recognise marriages concluded under any tradition, or a system of religious, personal or family law, or to recognise systems of personal and family law under any tradition, or adhered to by persons professing a particular religion.

In 1998 Parliament enacted the Recognition of Customary Marriages Act 120 of 1998.[6] It came into force on 15 November 2000 and sought to correct the past discrimination against African women by officially recognising all African customary marriages in South Africa. Polygamy is also no longer an obstacle to the recognition of customary unions as valid marriages. The Act gives women in customary law marriages the same status and protection as women in civil law marriages. The Act also introduces equality between husband and wife into the marriage relationship. Section 6 provides that:

> A wife in a customary marriage has, on the basis of equality with her husband and subject to the matrimonial property system governing the marriage, full status and capacity, including the capacity to acquire assets and to dispose of them, to enter into contracts and to litigate, in addition to any rights and powers that she might have at customary law.

Both monogamous and polygynous customary marriages are now recognised as legal under the Act. Currently South African law recognises three forms of marriage, namely civil marriages, African Customary marriages and civil unions. Once Parliament has given effect to the judgment by the Western Cape High Court in *Women's Legal Centre Trust v President of the Republic of South Africa*,[7] Muslim

5 Section 15(3)(a) of the Constitution authorises legislation recognising marriages concluded under any tradition, or systems of religious personal or family law.

6 A complete analysis of this legislation falls outside the scope of this discussion. For further discussions see J Heaton 'Customary Marriages' in *South African Family Law* 3 ed (2010); C Himonga and A Pope '*Mayelane v Ngwenyama and Minister for Home Affairs*: A Reflection on Wider Implications' in A Claassens et al (eds) *Marriage, Land and Custom: Essays on Law and Social Change in South Africa* (2013); JG Horn and AM Janse van Rensburg 'Practical Implications of the Recognition of Customary Marriages' *Journal for Juridical Science* (2002) 27(1):54–69; RM Jansen 'The Recognition of Customary Marriages Act: Many Women Still Left out in the Cold' *Journal for Juridical Science* (2002) 27(2): 115–128; R Kovacs, S Ndashe, and J Williams 'Twelve Years Later: How the Recognition of Customary Marriages Act of 1998 is Failing Women in South Africa' in A Claassens et al (eds) *Marriage, Land and Custom: Essays on Law and Social Change in South Africa* (2013); JM Pienaar 'African Customary Wives in South Africa: Is there Spousal Equality after the Commencement of the Recognition of Customary Marriages Act?' *Stellenbosch Law Review* (2003) 2 256–272.

7 *Women's Legal Centre Trust v President of the Republic of South Africa.*

marriages will also be recognised as valid marriages under South African law. This section will briefly look at civil unions[8] and more particularly, religious marriages. In relation to the celebration and dissolution of marriage, conflict often arises between the prescriptions of religious law and those of secular law. As pointed out by Krisnaswami,[9] 'these conflicts occur because most religions or beliefs consider these questions to be within their competence, whereas the modern State assumes the right to regulate family relationships on the ground that the family is the basic unit of society'. Questions of marriage, law, religion and the Constitution have occupied the courts over a period of time. As pointed out by Sachs J in *Minister of Home Affairs v Fourie*, '"I do" bring the most intense private and voluntary commitment into the most public, law-governed and State regulated domain'.[10]

Civil unions

The Civil Union Act 17 of 2006 sets out the legal framework for same-sex couples to solemnise civil unions by way of either a marriage or civil partnership, and regulates the legal consequences of civil unions. Civil unions for same-sex spouses are thus regulated in the same way as civil marriages for opposite-sex spouses and bear the same consequences. However, according to section 8 of the Act, if a person chooses to register a civil union, that person may not conclude a marriage under the Marriage Act or the Customary Marriages Act as well. Similarly, a person who is married under the Marriage Act or the Customary Marriages Act may also not register a civil union. The legalising of same-sex marriages and subsequent enactment of the Civil Unions Act came as a result of the leading case of *Minister of Home Affairs v Fourie*,[11] when South Africa became the fifth country in the world and the first country on the African Continent to legalise same-sex marriages (civil unions). In *Fourie*, the court had to decide, first, whether the fact that no provision was made for same-sex marriages in any statute amounted to the denial of equal protection of the law and unfair discrimination by the state against homosexuals on the basis of their sexual orientation. Second, if such unfair discrimination were to be found, the court had to decide on an appropriate remedy.

In a unanimous decision, the Constitutional Court declared that the common law definition of marriage, and section 30(1) of the Marriage Act 25 of 1961, which excluded same-sex marriages, were inconsistent with sections 9(1) and 9(3) and section 10 of the Constitution that deal with the right to equality and the right to human dignity, respectively. In the words of Justice Albie Sachs, writing on behalf of the majority: 'To penalise people for being who and what they are is profoundly disrespectful of the human personality and violators of equality.

8 More on this type of marriage is discussed under the topic 'homosexuality' in relation to the appointment of religious leaders in Chapter 10.

9 Krishnaswami *Study of Discrimination* 36.

10 *Minister of Home Affairs v Fourie; Lesbian and Gay Equality Project v Minister of Home Affairs* 2006 (1) SA 524 (CC) para 63.

11 *Minister of Home Affairs v Fourie* 2006 (1) SA 524 (CC).

Equality means equal concern and respect across difference'.[12] One of the religious arguments put forward in the *Fourie* case was that marriage was by its very nature a religious institution and to change its definition would violate the freedom of groups whose religious identities are wrapped up in a heterosexual definition of marriage. This argument was in no uncertain terms rejected by the court. The court did however recognise that religious bodies play a large and important part in public life and that religion is not just a question of belief or doctrine, but that it is part of our temper and culture and for many believers a significant part of their life.[13]

The court went further to state that there is nothing in the matters before them that either directly or indirectly trenches in any way on the strong protection of the right of religious communities not to be obliged to celebrate marriages not conforming to their tenets.[14] Justice Sachs stated that 'judges would be placed in an intolerable situation if they were called upon to construe religious texts and take sides on issues which have caused deep schisms within religious bodies'.[15] He further emphasised that in an open and democratic society like South Africa, as contemplated by our Constitution, there must be mutually respectful coexistence between the secular and the sacred and that the function of the court is to recognise the sphere which each inhabits, not to force the one into the sphere of the other.[16] The court was clear that the acknowledgement by the state of the right of same-sex couples to enjoy the same status, entitlements and responsibilities as marriage law accords to heterosexual couples, is in no way inconsistent with the rights of religious organisations to continue to refuse to celebrate same-sex marriages. The two sets of interests involved do not collide; they coexist in a constitutional realm based on accommodation of diversity. Granting access to same-sex couples would in no way attenuate the capacity of heterosexual couples to marry in the form they wished and according to the tenets of their religion.[17] The outcome of the *Fourie* case was that the common law definition of marriage was found to be inconsistent with the South African Constitution and invalid because it did not permit same-sex couples to enjoy the status and the benefits coupled with responsibilities it accords to heterosexual couples. Furthermore, the court declared section 30(1) of the Marriage Act to be invalid to the extent that it gave effect to the exclusion of same-sex marriages. In order to remedy the situation Parliament was given 12 months to cure the defect through the implementation of legislation. As a result of this judgment, the South African Parliament reluctantly passed the Civil Union Act 17 of 2006 to extend marriage rights to same-sex couples. The Civil Union Act operates alongside the Marriage Act, with the effect that any individual in South Africa may conclude a marriage either in its

12 *Fourie* para 60.
13 *Fourie* para 90.
14 *Fourie* para 94.
15 *Fourie* para 92.
16 *Fourie* para 95.
17 *Fourie* para 98.

traditional form (under the Marriage Act) or in the form of a civil union (under the Civil Union Act).

An interesting development is a decision of the United States Supreme Court in *Obergefell v Hodges*,[18] a decision authored by Justice Anthony Kennedy, in which gay marriages were legalised nationwide in the United States on 26 June 2015. The brief facts of the case are that various petitioners, including James Obergefell, were same-sex couples who brought cases challenging either the denial of their right to marry or to have their marriage performed elsewhere recognised in their own state. Because only some states recognised same-sex marriages, many couples' legal status in relation to each other changed as they travelled between different states. The relevant section of the United States Constitution upon which they relied was section 1 of the Fourteenth Amendment, which forbids the state to 'deprive any person of life, liberty, or property, without due process of law; nor deny to any person within its jurisdiction the equal protection of the laws'. The petitioners argued that the actions by the various respondents violated the Fourteenth Amendment by either denying them their right to marry, or by denying the recognition of their marriage legally performed in another state. The view of the court was that the fundamental right to marry embraces all Americans – regardless of sexual orientation. The court was sharply divided and ruled by a majority of five to four in favour of the petitioners, stating that state bans on same-sex marriage violated due process and equal protection rights of the Fourteenth Amendment. According to the court:

> The Fourteenth Amendment requires States to recognize same-sex marriages validly performed out of State. Since same-sex couples may now exercise the fundamental right to marry in all States, there is no lawful basis for a State to refuse to recognize a lawful same-sex marriage performed in another State on the ground of its same-sex character.[19]

The case raised very important questions over how legalising gay marriages would affect religious institutions. The United States Supreme Court emphasised that 'the First Amendment ensures that religions, those who adhere to religious doctrines, and others have protection as they seek to teach the principles that are so fulfilling and so central to their lives and faiths'.[20] In responding to the concerns raised by many in relation to religious organisations, the majority of the court emphasised that religions and those who adhere to religious doctrines:

> may continue to advocate with utmost, sincere conviction that, by divine precepts, same-sex marriage should not be condoned. The First Amendment ensures that religious organizations and persons are given proper protection as they seek to teach the principles that are so fulfilling and so central to their

18 *Obergefell v Hodges*, 576 US (2015).
19 *Obergefell* 5.
20 *Obergefell* 5.

> lives and faiths, and to their own deep aspirations to continue the family structure they have long revered.[21]

The case has not only sharply divided the court itself but has also left the country sharply divided. Religious conservatives feel they are under siege and are looking for ways to fight back or protect themselves. It is interesting to note that the media mentioned that 'Kennedy's decision hints at matters beyond gay marriage and anticipates the next big high court showdown – a bitter national struggle pitting gay rights against religious liberty'.[22] It is exactly at this point where South Africa finds itself and in the *Fourie* case, the Constitutional Court was confronted with some of the same religious concerns and arguments as was raised in the case of *Obergefell v Hodges.* In drafting the Civil Unions Act in South Africa, religious communities and their views were accommodated. No minister of religion is forced to solemnise a civil union in accordance with the Civil Union Act and section 5 of the act provides that any religious denomination or organisation may apply in writing to the minister to be designated as a religious organisation that may solemnise marriages in terms of this Act. Once a denomination has been so designated, individual ministers from that denomination are then permitted to apply to be designated as a marriage officer in accordance with section 3 of the Civil Union Act.[23] It is important to note that a minister who is a marriage officer in terms of the Marriage Act does not automatically become a marriage officer in terms of the Civil Union Act. Like the Anglican Church of Southern Africa (ACSA) and the Methodist Church of Southern Africa (MCSA), the Dutch Reformed Church of South Africa (DRC) has not applied to be designated as a religious institution that may solemnise marriages in terms of the Civil Union Act and therefore DRC ministers are not eligible to apply to be designated as marriage officers in accordance with the Civil Union Act. In the light of the recent decision in *Gaum v Van Rensburg*, for the original 2015 decision of the General Synod to take effect, the DRC needs to apply in writing to the Minister for permission to solemnise same-sex unions, before individual ministers can legally solemnise these unions.[24] Reasonable accommodation for religious institutions in relation to the solemnisation of gay marriages has been described by Bonthuys[25] as follows:

21 *Obergefell* 27.

22 W Richey 'Gay Marriage Ruling Leaves Debate About Religious Liberty Wide Open' *Christian Science Monitor* (5 July 2015).

23 In accordance with section 3 of the Marriage Act 25 of 1961, the minister and any officer in the public service authorised thereto by him may designate any minister of religion of, or any person holding a responsible position in, any religious denomination or organisation to be, so long as he is such a minister or occupies such position, a marriage officer for the purpose of solemnising marriages according to Christian, Jewish or Muslim rites or the rites of any Indian religion.

24 *Gaum v Van Rensburg* (40819/17) [2019] ZAGPPHC 52 (8 March 2019), (see further discussion in Chapter 4 and Chapter 10).

25 E Bonthuys 'Reasonable Accommodation as a Mechanism to Balance Equality Rights and Rights to Religion in Family Law' *South African Public Law* (2010) 25 679.

> If the aim of reasonable accommodation is to serve as an exception to the application of formally equal rules which seeks to increase substantive social equality, then clearly it cannot apply in family law. The reason is that family law rules are not formally equal as between individuals and religious institutions. Religious institutions have the power to conclude marriages, to decide who to accept as members and to set the parameters of marriage and family life for their believers. Individual gay and lesbians do not have this ability. Using reasonable accommodation in this context reinforces the inequalities that the law itself has created.

This might hold true for public servants, but religious ministers should be given the choice or not to solemnise a civil union, as a manifestation of their right to freedom of religion. The legislation has thus accommodated religious views by creating an exemption for religious ministers. The question is what about public servants? Civil unions may be solemnised either by religious marriage officers, by *ex officio* marriage officers, or by designated marriage officers who are civil servants. In terms of section 2 of the Marriage Act 25 of 1961:

> (1) Every magistrate, every special justice of the peace and every Commissioner shall by virtue of his office and so long as he holds such office, be a marriage officer for the district or other area in respect of which he holds office.
>
> (2) The Minister and any officer in the public service authorised thereto by him may designate any officer or employee in the public service or the diplomatic or consular service of the Republic to be, by virtue of his office and so long as he holds such office, a marriage officer, either generally or for any specified class of persons or country or area.

In the case of civil marriages, the Marriage Act provides that a marriage officer *must* solemnise all marriages placed before him or her and is not allowed to refuse to solemnise a marriage on the grounds of conscience, religion or belief. However, the same marriage officer is permitted in terms of section 6 of the Civil Union Act to object on the grounds of conscience, religion and belief in respect of solemnising same-sex civil unions. By submitting this objection notice, the marriage officer is relieved of any obligation to solemnise such unions. Therefore, currently, other marriage officers (other than a religious marriage officer) may apply for exemption and in writing inform the Minister that he or she objects on the ground of conscience, religion and belief to solemnising a civil union between persons of the same sex. Such a marriage officer shall then not be compelled to solemnise such civil union.[26] A discrepancy arises, since the marriage officers envisaged in section 6 of the Civil Union Act are those who solemnise civil unions in their capacity as civil servants and are the same civil servants who as marriage officers have no legal rights to object to solemnising marriages under the Marriage

26 See section 6 of the Civil Union Act.

Act. Consequently, the Portfolio Committee on Home Affairs has adopted a draft Civil Union Amendment Bill in which they sought to repeal section 6 of the Act. The Bill was lodged by a Congress of the People (COPE) Member of Parliament (MP), Deidre Carter, after it came to her attention that some same-sex couples seeking the services of a marriage officer were being turned away from some Home Affairs offices. This happened particularly in rural areas, where marriage officers at those offices had been exempted in terms of section 6 of the Act from officiating over marriages between persons of the same-sex.[27] It has been argued that:

> On a symbolic level, by allowing civil marriage officers to turn same-sex couples away, the message is sent out that the state does not regard their relationship as equal to heterosexual relationships in status and worth.[28]

In the context of the public service, Kruuse[29] argues that a same-sex couple should be able to successfully challenge the constitutionality of the exemption provision in the Civil Union Act, should a civil marriage officer refuse to marry them. This might not be necessary, given the fact that the Portfolio Committee on Home Affairs in Parliament formally adopted the Civil Union Amendment Bill in November 2018.[30] The Bill was passed by the National Assembly in December 2018. The purpose of the Bill is to repeal section 6 of the Civil Union Act, which allows a marriage officer to inform the Minister that he or she objects on the ground of conscience, religion and belief to solemnising a civil union between persons of the same sex. The memorandum on the objects of the Civil Union Amendment Bill, 2018 concludes:

> In the context of South African same-sex partnerships, many same-sex couples may be obliged to have their marriages conducted by civil servants because the religious bodies they attend are unwilling to do so. The prevalence of homophobia in our society could mean that a large number of civil servants will avail themselves of the statutory right to lodge objections, resulting in same-sex marriage becoming available in theory only, especially in rural areas. This would clearly constitute undue hardship for same-sex couples. This therefore leads to a conclusion that section 6 of the Act limits the rights of same-sex partners to enter into a civil union, and this limitation cannot be justified in an open and democratic society. (footnotes omitted)

The Bill proposes a transitional period of 24 months for the Department of Home Affairs to enable officers an opportunity to be trained if it is passed, although some

27 D Spies 'SA's 'anti-gay' Marriage Officers: Fierce Debate Looms as MP Demands Change' *News24* (27 January 2018).

28 See H Kruuse 'Conscientious Objection to Performing Same-Sex Marriage in South Africa' *International Journal of Law, Policy and the Family* (2014) 28(2) 164.

29 Kruuse 2014 *International Journal of Law, Policy and the Family* 167.

30 Civil Union Amendment Bill [B 11–2018].

objections were raised against this transitional period. The amendment will also require the Minister of Home Affairs to ensure that there is a marriage officer, other than a marriage officer who had been granted exemption through the Civil Union Act, available to solemnise a civil union at every Department of Home Affairs office.[31] However, not everyone was in favour of this amendment. The African Christian Democratic Party (ACDP) opposed the Bill and claimed that the state was encroaching on churches. According to the ACDP leader:

> Our constitution protects freedom of conscience, religion and belief, and Parliament has a duty to see that people do not act against this conscience in places of work. No one should be forced to accept a moral wrong.[32]

Religious marriage officers are still exempted under the Civil Union Act, and the Repeal Act only applies to designated marriage officers who are civil servants.

Religious marriages

Religious believers all over the world, from Muslim, Jewish or Hindu traditions live according to their religious personal and family law. Apart from the Recognition of Customary Marriages Act, no other legislation has been enacted to legalise Muslim or Hindu marriages. Currently, parties to a religious marriage such as a Muslim, Hindu or Jewish marriage must also register their marriage either in terms of the Marriage Act or Civil Union Act, for it to be legally recognised. Under the Marriage Act, parties married by Muslim, Hindu and Jewish rites are able to access certain benefits of secular legislation if they enter into civil marriages. According to section 3 of the Marriage Act, the Minister may designate any minister of religion as a marriage officer for the purpose of solemnising marriages according to Christian, Jewish or Mohammedan rites or the rites of any Indian religion. Members of these religious groups have the choice of entering into a separate civil marriage before or after concluding their religious marriage, or to have their religious marriage solemnised by a person who is designated as a marriage officer under the Marriage Act. In 2014, the South African Government appointed 100 Imams as marriage officers under the 1961 Marriage Act.[33] As marriages officers, they can solemnise civil marriages of Muslim couples. However, they were still not empowered to conclude a marriage under the dictates of Islamic Law. In so far as section 3 excludes minority religions, members of other religious groups can possibly challenge this section as unconstitutional on the basis that it unfairly discriminates on the ground of religion.

31 C Maphanga 'Home Affairs Committee Adopts Civil Union Amendment Bill' *News24* (28 November 2018).

32 African News Agency (ANA) 'Refusing to Marry Gays May Become Illegal' *Cape Argus* (7 December 2018).

33 'Full Legal Status for Muslim Marriages in South Africa' *SAnews.gov* (2 May 2014).

Section 8 of the Promotion of Equality and Prevention of Unfair Discrimination Act 4 of 2000 prohibits unfair discrimination on the ground of gender. Section 8 (d) is of particular importance since it specifically states that no person may unfairly discriminate against any person on the ground of gender, including 'any practice, including traditional, customary or religious practice, which impairs the dignity of women and undermines equality between women and men, including the undermining of the dignity and well-being of the girl child'. In the light of this section, Van der Vyver[34] argues that due to the discriminatory practices inherent in Islamic and Hindu family law, 'it would be extremely difficult for Parliament to recognise marriages based on those religious systems while maintaining consistency with other provisions of the Constitution', in particular the right to freedom of religion, belief and opinion.

In relation to the recognition of Muslim marriages as valid under South African law, the South African Law Reform Commission issued a report in 2003 on Islamic Marriages and Related Matters[35] with a draft Bill on Islamic Marriages. The Bill emanated from an investigation by the South African Law Reform Commission (the SALRC) on Islamic Marriages and Related Matters. In its report, the SALRC made some legislative proposals in the form of a Muslim Marriages Bill. The aim of these legislative proposals was set out to provide statutory recognition of Muslim marriages in order to redress inequities and hardships arising from the non-recognition of these marriages. The Bill is applicable to persons who adhere to the Muslim faith and who elect to be bound by its provisions. It also contains an opting out provision for persons who do not wish to be bound by it. The Bill sets out a statutory framework for the legal recognition of Muslim marriages and their consequences. However, no further action was taken by government to pass this Bill into law and various court battles followed. The Women's Legal Centre Trust brought various applications in order to compel the legislature to enact the legislation.

In 2005, the South African Commission for Gender Equality in consultation with the Department of Justice and Constitutional Development drafted a Bill called the Recognition of Religious Marriages Bill (RRMB) in order to afford recognition to all religious marriages. The RRMB recommends that religious communities should regulate their own religious marriages but that the approach required under the Divorce Act should apply to the dissolution of religious marriages. However, there has been no public consultation with religious communities about the Bill and no progress has been made after that.

Before the most recent court application in the Western Cape High Court, courts dealt with various issues surrounding Muslim marriage, including issues relating to maintenance,[36] contractual obligations and actions for damages flowing

34 Van der Vyver *Religiously-based Marriages* 238.

35 South Africa Law Reform Commission 'Islamic Marriages and Related Matters' Project 59 (July 2003).

36 *Ryland v Edros* 1997 (2) SA 690 (C); *Khan v Khan* 2005 (2) SA 272 (T); *Volks NO v Robinson and Others* 2005 (5) BCLR 446 (CC).

from a Muslim marriage,[37] and succession.[38] In 2017, a case for the recognition of Muslim marriages and to have the Muslim Marriages Bill made law started in the Western Cape High Court in the case of *Women's Legal Centre Trust v President of the Republic of South Africa and Others.*[39] In the case, the Women's Legal Centre (WLC) approached the Western Cape High Court to compel the President, Parliament and the departments of Home Affairs and Justice and Correctional Services to have Muslim marriages recognised with the passing of the Bill. The WLC argued that by not recognising Muslim marriages under the common law, Muslim women are not afforded legal protection and do not have access to the courts to assert their rights. According to the Centre, the non-recognition of Muslim marriages has far-reaching implications and consequences for women in such marriages, as they do not have the protections offered to women in civil marriages. They argued that the state's failure to enact a legal framework to regulate Muslim marriages was in breach of a direct constitutional obligation to put reasonable measures in place to protect rights such as women's right to equality, dignity and access to courts.

In the course of its judgment, the court recognised the fact that the status of a spouse married in terms of religious tenets is not equal to that of a spouse married in terms of the Marriage Act, the Civil Union Act or the Customary Marriages Act. Therefore, according to Botha,[40] not only is there differentiation on the basis of religion, 'but also importantly, considering the historical vulnerability of women, on the basis of gender'. According to the court, the 'continued non-recognition of marriages solemnised according to Islamic tenets infringes on the rights to equality and dignity'.[41] In *Women's Legal Centre*, the court did not rule on the constitutionality of the existing Muslim Marriages Bill, although they acknowledged that legislation may be the most reasonable and effective way of protecting the rights implicated.[42] The court made it clear that it remains a choice for the executive and the legislature to decide what option to take, whether introducing a new Bill or vary current marriage legislation. Of importance is that the court reaffirmed the state's constitutional duty to take active measures to ensure that a legal framework is in place to provide the equal benefit and protection of the law to Muslim Religious marriages.

> As seen through the cases, the non-recognition of Muslim marriages is historic, persistent and unfulfilled since the beginning of democracy. This is not a single instance but rather a systemic failure by the state to provide recognition and regulation, potentially effecting millions of people around the country.

37 *Amod v Multilateral Motor Vehicle Accident Fund* 1999 (4) SA 1319 (SCA).

38 *Daniels v Campbell NO and Others* 2004 (5) SA 331 (CC).

39 *Women's Legal Centre Trust v President of the Republic of South Africa.*

40 C Botha 'On Legal Recognition for Religious Marriages' *Politicsweb* (20 September 2018).

41 *Women's Legal Centre Trust v President of the Republic of South Africa* para 179.

42 *Women's Legal Centre Trust v President of the Republic of South Africa* para 88.

> Marriage concerns a plethora of issues, from status to property, involving a wide range of laws, which are complex and fundamentally important.[43]

The court acknowledged the possibility of the legislation not being passed within the prescribed period and that it might be necessary for some judicial intervention by the court in the form of providing some default regime. This is particularly in relation to divorce issues that may leave women and children in Muslim marriages without protection and vulnerable.[44] In relation to these issues, the court allowed for various temporary provisions of the Divorce Act to be applicable. According to the court:

> The application of the Divorce Act would mean that from the religious point of view, whilst it may be that the Muslim marriage can be terminated by any method recognised under *Sharia* law; in its civil aspect, the union would be terminable under the Divorce Act.[45]

In exercising its jurisdiction, the divorce court should allow for some religious sensitivities and would need to be sensitive to the requirements of Islamic law. The court's temporary order would not prohibit spouses in Muslim marriages from conforming to *Sharia* prescripts if they so elect.[46] The Western Cape High Court ordered that the state be obliged to introduce legislation to recognise Muslim marriages as valid, and to regulate the consequences of these unions. The state was ordered to introduce and bring such legislation into operation within 24 months. The Muslim Judicial Council (MJC) has welcomed the decision by the Western Cape High Court and saw it as a milestone for Muslims as a minority group in South Africa. The significance of this judgment for them is the fact that the President has now been tasked to enforce the legislation. According to the deputy president of the MJC, they 'await the government to fulfil their constitutional obligation and facilitate the process to enact the legislation as soon as possible as per the court order'.[47] As highlighted by the court:

> It is hoped that the executive and the legislature would act without delay in bringing about legislation so as to eradicate the continuous hardships faced by women and children in Muslim marriages highlighted in this judgment.[48]

Waheeda Amien,[49] a Muslim scholar, is of the view that legislation such as the RRMB will not be able to provide sufficient protection for women in religious

43 *Women's Legal Centre Trust v President of the Republic of South Africa* para 180.
44 *Women's Legal Centre Trust v President of the Republic of South Africa* para 225.
45 *Women's Legal Centre Trust v President of the Republic of South Africa* para 227.
46 *Women's Legal Centre Trust v President of the Republic of South Africa* para 230.
47 African News Agency (ANA) 'MJC Welcomes Court Judgment on Muslim Marriages' *IOL News* (31 August 2018).
48 *Women's Legal Centre Trust v President of the Republic of South Africa* para 250.
49 W Amien 'Recognition of Religious Marriages in South Africa' *Opinions* (6 June 2018).

marriages, particularly Muslim marriages. She argues that government should rather enact the existing Muslim Marriages Bill as soon as possible and proceed to draft separate legislation for the recognition of the remaining minority religious marriages, provided that it needs to regulate the marriages and not only afford recognition. In an earlier contribution, she has argued that the Muslim Marriages Bill in its current form has the potential to result in a conflict between the right to freedom of religion and women's rights to equality. Nevertheless, she is of the view that the legislation can:

> ameliorate the position of Muslim parties by affording them the same legal status as their civil law counterparts. This will entitle them to enjoy similar civil benefits afforded to legal spouses. It will also allow women to enjoy the beneficial aspects of a Muslim marriage.[50]

Government will then need to embark on a proper consultation process with religious communities and civil society.[51] Since the Muslim Marriages Bill only applies to Muslim marriages, it may be argued that it is not fair to provide recognition of the tenets of one religious group and not to others. The RRMB applies to all religious marriages rather than to regulate specific elements of any particular religious law. Manjoo[52] argues that this approach makes it possible not only to address the problem of non-recognition of religious marriages, but at the same time treat all religions equally within the context of a single act.

In relation to Hindu marriages, South African law does not currently recognise marriages by Hindu rites and couples in a Hindu marriage who want to get divorced do not need to go to court, since all the legal consequences of a marriage do not apply to such marriages in South Africa. As a result, spouses can also not claim any of the legal consequence of divorce, such as maintenance, after the relationship has ended. In *Singh v Ramparsad*,[53] the court refused the application of Suchitra Singh to have her unregistered Hindu marriage recognised by the

50 W Amien 'Overcoming the Conflict between the Right to Freedom of Religion and Women's Rights to Equality: A South African Case Study of Muslim Marriages' *Human Rights Quarterly* (2006) 28 734; N Gabru 'Dilemma of Muslim Women Regarding Divorce in South Africa' *Potchefstroom Electronic Law Journal* 2004(2) 1–15; C Rautenbach 'Some Comments on the Current (and Future) Status of Muslim Personal Law in South Africa' *Potchefstroom Electronic Law Journal* 2004(2) 1–34; W Amien 'A South African Case study for the Recognition and Regulation of Muslim Family Law in a Minority Muslim Secular Context' *International Journal of Law, Policy and the Family* (2010) 24(3) 361–396.

51 For some other views on the recognition of Muslim marriages, see N Hoel 'Engaging Religious Leaders: South African Muslim Women's Experiences in Matters Pertaining to Divorce Initiatives' *Social Dynamics* (2012) 38(2) 184–200; JL Neels 'Constitutional aspects of the Muslim Marriages Bill' *TSAR* (2012) 3 486–506.

52 R Manjoo 'The Recognition of Muslim Personal Laws in South Africa: Implications for Women's Human Rights' Human Rights Program, Harvard Law School Working Paper Project Report (2007).

53 *Singh v Ramparsad* 2007 (3) SA 445 (DCLD).

court so that she could get a divorce. Hindu law does not permit divorce. Thus, she asked the court to find that a Hindu marriage falls within the ambit of the Marriage Act 25 of 1961 or, alternatively, within the ambit of the Divorce Act 70 of 1979. The court dismissed her action and held that the non-recognition of her marriage did not offend her dignity and that none of her constitutional rights have been compromised. The court was also of the view that neither the provisions of the Marriage Act or Divorce Act needs to be ruled unconstitutional.

In *Daniels v Campbell*,[54] the Constitutional Court extended the ambit of the Intestate Succession Act 81 of 1987 to the surviving partner to a monogamous Muslim marriage. However, since no challenge had been brought in respect of persons married under Hindu rites, this category of persons has been excluded from the provisions of the Intestate Succession Act. A few years later, in *Govender v Ragavayah NO and Others*,[55] the court ruled that the word 'spouse' as used in section 1 of the Intestate Succession Act includes the surviving partner to a monogamous Hindu marriage. The Govenders were married to each other according to the rites and customs of the Hindu religion. The marriage was monogamous in accordance with the rites, customs and traditions of the Hindu religion. However, they never registered the marriages in terms of the Marriage Act. Mr Govender then died without leaving a will and the executor in his estate prepared the estate accounts on the basis that his father and mother were the sole heirs. The applicant then approached the court to declare that the word spouse as used in the Intestate Succession Act should include a surviving partner to a monogamous Hindu marriage. With reference to various cases, to court stated was of the view that:

> In the light of what has been stated in all the cases, referred to above, I am of the view that there is judicial support for the proposition that a spouse of a 'marriage' by Hindu rites may well have the religious 'marriage contract' given some recognition by South African law for certain purposes.[56]

Although the court accepted that presently, in terms of our law, a Hindu marriage that has not been registered in terms of South African law is invalid, the court found that the validity of the marriage was not required for the relief that the applicant sought.[57] The court granted the order and declared the applicant to be a spouse for purposes of section 1 of the Intestate Succession Act. The Law Reform Commission started an investigation in the field of Family law and the law of persons (Project 100). One of these subprojects relates to 'Hindu marriages'. The aim of this investigation is to look into the recognition of Hindu marriages in order to afford these marriages full legal recognition and the same status as marriages concluded in accordance with civil rites. The Commission resolved at its

54 *Daniels v Campbell NO and Others* 2004 (5) SA 331 (CC).
55 *Govender v Ragavayah NO and Others* 2009 (3) SA 178 (D).
56 *Govender* para 41.
57 *Govender* para 42.

meeting of 5 December 2015 that the Hindu Marriages investigation should come back into the programme of the Commission. However, work on this investigation is on hold at the moment.[58]

Numerous pieces of legislation extended protection to spouses in religious marriages, such as the Domestic Violence Act 116 of 1998;[59] the Compensation for Occupational Injuries and Diseases Act 130 of 1993;[60] the Demobilisation Act 99 of 1996;[61] the Special Pensions Act 69 of 1996;[62] the Children's Act 38 of 2005;[63] and the Income Tax Act 58 of 1962.[64] The meaning of marriage has also been extended to religious marriages through various pieces of legislation, including the Civil Proceedings Evidence Act 25 of 1969;[65] the Criminal Procedure Act 51 of 1977;[66] the Taxation Laws Amendment Act 5 of 2001;[67] the Government Employees Pension Law 1996;[68] the Estate Duty Act 45 of 1955;[69] the Child Care Act 74 of 1983, as amended by the Child Care Amendment Act 96 of 1996.[70] In the Constitutional Court case of *Moosa N.O. and Others v Minister of Justice and Correctional Services*,[71] the court held that section 2C(1) of the Wills Act 7 of 1953 is to be read as including the following words 'for the purposes of this sub-section, a "surviving spouse" includes every husband and wife of a monogamous and polygamous Muslim marriage solemnised under the religion of Islam'.[72]

Conclusion

One of the problems that have been identified is that of non-recognition of religious marriages. If religious marriage ceremonies were to be prohibited, this

58 South Africa Law Reform Commission Report *Family Law and the Law of Persons* Project 100 (2016/ 2017) 37.
59 Section 1(vii)(a)–(b) extends the protection to spouses in religious marriages and/or unmarried cohabitants.
60 Section 1(xv)(c).
61 Sections 1(c) and 7.
62 Sections 2 and 31(2)(a)(ii).
63 Sections 1, 20, 231(1)(a)(ii), (c).
64 See the definition of 'spouse' in section 1.
65 Section 10A recognises religious marriages for the purposes of the compellability of spouses as witnesses in civil proceedings.
66 Section 195(2) recognises religious marriages for the purposes of the compellability of spouses as witnesses in criminal proceedings.
67 It inserts a wider definition of 'spouse' into the Transfer Duty Act 40 of 1949, which exempts from transfer duty property inherited by the surviving spouse in a religious marriage.
68 See the definition of 'spouse'
69 Section 4(q) read with the definition of 'spouse' in section 1 exempts from estate duty property accruing to the surviving spouse in a religious marriage.
70 Section 1(d) widens the definition of 'marriage' to include any marriages concluded in accordance with a system of religious law.
71 *Moosa N.O. and Others v Minister of Justice and Correctional Services and Others* 2018 (5) SA 13 (CC).
72 *Moosa* para 210.

would undoubtedly be considered an infringement of the right to freedom of religion and discriminatory against persons belonging to religious groups. In South Africa this is a problem faced in particular by the Muslim community, but also other religious communities. The Muslim community is also still deeply divided internally regarding the exact scope and application of the recognition of Muslim marriages and whether it is desirable to bring all aspects within the confines of the Constitution. Particularly Muslim women are in favour of protecting all aspects of Muslim personal law under the Constitution, as observed by Moosa:[73]

> Even though the final Constitution promotes and protects the human rights of women through national machinery, their powers do not extend beyond the Constitution. Gradual social reform within the Muslim community, along with active participation by Muslim women, appears to be more realistic safeguards and long-term solutions for effective improvement to the status of Muslim women.

It has been argued that we need a legislative solution that provides for the recognition of all religious marriages, while avoiding codifying any particular religion.[74] As a general rule, no member of a religious community 'should be prevented from having marriage rites performed in accordance with the prescriptions of his religion or belief, nor be compelled to undergo a religious marriage ceremony not in conformity with his convictions'.[75]

Bibliography

African News Agency (ANA) "MJC Welcomes Court Judgment on Muslim Marriages" *IOL News* (31 August 2018). Online at: www.iol.co.za/news/south-africa/western-cape/mjc-welcomes-court-judgment-on-muslim-marriages-16828177.

African News Agency (ANA) "Refusing to Marry Gays May Become Illegal" *Cape Argus* (7 December 2018).

Amien W 'A South African Case study for the Recognition and Regulation of Muslim Family Law in a Minority Muslim Secular Context' *International Journal of Law, Policy and the Family* (2010) 24(3) 361–396.

Amien W 'Overcoming the Conflict between the Right to Freedom of Religion and, Women's Rights to Equality: A South African Case Study of Muslim Marriages' *Human Rights Quarterly* (2006) 28729–754.

Amien W 'Recognition of Religious Marriages in South Africa' *Opinions* (6 June 2018).

Bonthuys E 'Reasonable Accommodation as a Mechanism to Balance Equality Rights and Rights to Religion in Family Law' *South African Public Law* (2010) 25666–681.

Botha C 'On Legal Recognition for Religious Marriages' *Politicsweb* (20 September 2018). Online at: www.politicsweb.co.za/opinion/legal-recognition-for-religious-marriages.

73 N Moosa 'The Interim and Final Constitutions and Muslim Personal Law: Implications for South Africa Muslim Women' Stellenbosch Law Review (1998) 9(2) 205.
74 Manjoo 2007 *Human Rights Program* 28.
75 Krishnaswami *Study of Discrimination* 38.

'Full Legal Status for Muslim Marriages in South Africa' *SAnews* (2 May 2014).

Gabru N 'Dilemma of Muslim Women Regarding Divorce in South Africa' *Potchefstroom Electronic Law Journal* (2004) 7(2) 1–15.

Heaton J 'Customary Marriages' in *South African Family Law*3 ed (2010) South Africa: LexisNexis.

Himonga C and A Pope 'Mayelane v Ngwenyama and Minister for Home Affairs: A Reflection on Wider Implications' in A Claassens, D Smythe and G Bradfield (eds) *Marriage, Land and Custom: Essays on Law and Social Change in South Africa* (2013) South Africa: Juta.

Hoel N 'Engaging Religious Leaders: South African Muslim Women's Experiences in Matters Pertaining to Divorce Initiatives' *Social Dynamics* (2012) 38(2) 184–200.

Horn JG and AM Janse van Rensburg 'Practical Implications of the Recognition of Customary Marriages' *Journal for Juridical Science* (2002) 27(1) 54–69.

Kruuse H 'Conscientious Objection to Performing Same-Sex Marriage in South Africa' *International Journal of Law, Policy and the Family* (2014) 28(2) 150–176.

Jansen RM 'The Recognition of Customary Marriages Act: Many Women Still Left out in the Cold' *Journal for Juridical Science* (2002) 27(2) 115–128.

Kovacs R, S Ndashe and J Williams 'Twelve Years Later: How the Recognition of Customary Marriages Act of 1998 is Failing Women in South Africa' in A Claassens, D Smythe and G Bradfield (eds) *Marriage, Land and Custom: Essays on Law and Social Change in South Africa* (2013) South Africa: Juta.

Krishnaswami A *Study of Discrimination in the Matter of Religious Rights and Practices* (1960) New York: United Nations Publication.

Manjoo R *The Recognition of Muslim Personal Laws in South Africa: Implications for Women's Human Rights* Working Paper Project Report, Human Rights Program, Harvard Law School (2007).

Maphanga C 'Home Affairs Committee Adopts Civil Union Amendment Bill' *News24* (28 Nov 2018). Online at: www.news24.com/SouthAfrica/News/home-affairs-committee-adopts-civil-union-amendment-bill-20181128.

Moosa N 'The Interim and Final Constitutions and Muslim Personal Law: Implications for South Africa Muslim Women' *Stellenbosch Law Review* (1998) 9(2) 196–206.

Neels JL 'Constitutional Aspects of the Muslim Marriages Bill' *TSAR* (2012) 3486–506.

Pienaar JM 'African Customary Wives in South Africa: Is there Spousal Equality after the Commencement of the Recognition of Customary Marriages Act?' *Stellenbosch Law Review* (2003) 2256–272.

Rautenbach C 'Some Comments on the Current (and Future) Status of Muslim Personal Law in South Africa' *Potchefstroom Electronic Law Journal* (2004) 7(2) 1.

Richey W 'Gay Marriage Ruling Leaves Debate About Religious Liberty Wide Open' *Christian Science Monitor* (5 July 2015). Online at: www.csmonitor.com/USA/Justice/2015/0705/Gay-marriage-ruling-leaves-debate-about-religious-liberty-wide-open.

South Africa Law Reform Commission *Islamic Marriages and Related Matters* Project 59 (July 2003).

South Africa Law Reform Commission *Report 'Family Law and the Law of Persons'* Project 100 (2016/2017).

Spies D 'SA's "anti-gay" Marriage Officers: Fierce Debate Looms as MP Demands Change' *News24* (27 January 2018).

Van der Vyver J 'The Diversity of Religiously-based Marriages and Family Law within African Legal Systems' in P Coertzenet al (ed) *Law and Religion in Africa. The Quest for the Common Good in Pluralistic Societies* (2015) 225Stellenbosch: SUN Media.

9 Financial regulation

Introduction

Many of the complaints outlined in the CRL Rights Commission's Report on the commercialisation of religion related to financial abuses, misappropriation of funds and non-compliance with legislation, particularly of a financial and governance-related nature. Further to this report, in January 2018, the Commission recommended that religious organisations should pay income tax. The South African Revenue Service (SARS) indicated that they will engage with religious institutions about paying tax. The decision follows preliminary investigations conducted by SARS and the engagement with the recommendations made by the CRL Rights Commission. Reports were also filed that suggested that certain religious organisations and practitioners are not in compliance with tax laws, although SARS acknowledged the fact that a number of religious organisations were indeed complying with their tax obligations.[1] Although religious institutions are exempted from various tax and other financial duties, they should still abide by tax laws. The organisation Freedom of Religion South Africa (FOR SA) holds the position that 'freedom of religion cannot be used as an excuse or reason to disobey or evade the law of the land, including the tax laws'.[2] They are of the view that a change in the law could highlight financial abuses that occur in the religious sector. This chapter will explain the current legislative framework relevant to religious institutions, with a particular emphasis on financial requirements. Since many religious organisations operate as non-governmental organisations NGOs (and often non-profit organisations (NPOs)), the chapter will also briefly outline some aspects of financial regulation in the non-profit context. The chapter will conclude with some discussion and examples relating to financial abuses and non-compliance with the relevant laws, and proposals for the financial regulation of the religious sector.

1 SARS Legal Counsel 'SARS' Compliance intervention in Religious Sector' SARS media release (26 January 2018). Online at: www.sars.gov.za.
2 K Pillay 'Religious Bodies May Have to Pay Tax' *The Witness* (2 February 2018).

Legislative framework

Religious institutions, like many NPOs, play a significant role in society by sharing some of the responsibility for social and development needs of society, and in that manner relieving the financial burden that would otherwise fall on the state. According to a tax exemption guide for public benefit organisations in South Africa, 'tax benefits are designed to assist NPOs by augmenting their financial resources and providing them with an enabling environment in which to achieve their objectives'.[3]

In South Africa, religious, charitable and educational institutions of a public character used to be fully exempt from income tax[4] and other taxes. Religious institutions may apply to SARS to be exempted from the payment of Income Tax and certain other taxes in terms of section 10(1) (cN) of the Income Tax Act 58 of 1962,[5] read together with the provisions of section 30. These sections introduced the concept of a public benefit organisation (PBO)[6] carrying on a public benefit activity (PBA).[7] The Commissioner will approve an organisation as a PBO only if its sole or principal object is to carry on one or more PBAs and it complies with all the conditions and requirements of section 30. In terms of the definition of a PBO in section 30(1), a PBO must be constituted as a Non-Profit Company (NPC) incorporated in South Africa, a trust established in South Africa, an association of persons formed or established in South Africa, or a branch of a foreign tax-exempt organisation. The sole or principal object of a PBO must be the carrying on of one or more PBAs and not for the purpose of conducting commercial business activity in order to use the profits derived from the business undertaking or trading activity to fund the PBA. Part I of the Ninth Schedule sets out the various PBAs. Part 5 deals with Religion, Belief or Philosophy, and it includes activities such as the promotion or practice of religion which encompasses acts of worship, witness, teaching and community service based on a belief in a deity; the promotion and/or practice of a belief; and, the promotion of, or engaging in, philosophical activities. Once tax exemption status has been granted to a religious institution, certain requirements need to be complied with. The organisation as a PBO must conduct all activities in a non-profit manner with a philanthropic or altruistic intent. The activities should not be intended to directly or indirectly promote economic self-interest of any person, including a religious leader or practitioner, other than by way of the normal and reasonable remuneration paid

3 SARS Legal Counsel 'Tax Exemption Guide for Public Benefit Organisations in South Africa' *Issue 5* (26 January 2018) 3.

4 Section 10(1)(f) was repealed by section 21(1)(a) of the Taxation Laws Amendment Act 30 of 2000, with effect from 15 July 2001, subject to certain provisos regarding extended exemption.

5 Section 21(1)(c) and section 35(1) of the Taxation Laws Amendment Act 30 of 2000 introduced section 10(1)(cN) and section 30, respectively. These amendments came into operation on 15 July 2001.

6 'PBO' means a 'public benefit organisation' as defined in section 30(1) approved by the Commissioner under section 30(3).

7 'PBA' means a public benefit activity listed in Part I of the Ninth Schedule.

for services rendered. Religious institutions may not distribute any funds, directly or indirectly, to any person if it is not in the course of performing their religious activity.[8] The activity must further be carried on by the organisation for the benefit of, or be widely accessible to, the general public at large, including any sector thereof. However, it may not exclusively be for the benefit of a small and exclusive group.[9] A religious organisation engaging in a PBA for the benefit of a certain sector of the general public, such as a school established for persons of the Hindu, Muslim or Christian faith, will qualify.[10]

In addition to being exempt from the payment of income tax on certain receipts and accruals, PBOs will also enjoy the benefit of being exempt from other taxes and duties. PBOs will be exempt from Donations Tax. Any donation made by or to a PBO are exempt from the payment of donations tax.[11] They will also be exempt from estate duty. Any property bequeathed to a PBO is excluded from the value of the estate and not subject to estate duty.[12] In terms of transfer duty, the Transfer Duty Act 40 of 1949 levies transfer duty on a sliding scale on the value of any property acquired by any person.[13] A PBO is exempt from the payment of transfer duty on any property acquired provided that the whole or substantially the whole of the property is used for the purpose of carrying on one or more PBAs.[14] The transfer of property by a PBO to a separate entity controlled by that PBO may also qualify for an exemption from transfer duty.[15] The Income Tax Act also contains provisions relating to dividends tax.[16] Dividends tax applies to any dividend paid by a company on or after 1 April 2012 and it is treated as a separate tax from income tax. A PBO that is the beneficial owner of a dividend is exempt from dividends tax, provided that they submit a declaration to the company that declared and paid the dividend, to the effect that it is exempt from dividends tax.[17] Under the Securities Transfer Tax Act 25 of 2007, securities transfer tax is levied, but is not payable if a security is transferred to a PBO.[18] Skills development levy is a compulsory levy to fund education and training under the Skills Development Levies Act 9 of 1999. According to the SARS Tax exemption guide,[19] a PBO is exempt from the payment of this levy if it:

- is registered as an employer and its annual payroll will not exceed R500 000 in the following 12 months;[20]

8 See SARS Legal Counsel, *SARS media release.*
9 Paragraph (*c*)(i) of the definition of 'public benefit organisation' in section 30(1).
10 *Tax Exemption Guide for Public Benefit Organisations in South Africa* 7.
11 Income Tax Act – section 56(1)(h).
12 Section 4(h) of the Estate Duty Act.
13 See further *Tax Exemption Guide for Public Benefit Organisations in South Africa* 38.
14 Section 9(1)(c) of the Transfer Duty Act.
15 Section 9(1A) of the Transfer Duty Act.
16 See sections 64D–64N.
17 Section 64F(1)(c) and section 64FA(1)(a).
18 Section 8(1)(d) of the Securities Transfer Tax Act.
19 *Tax Exemption Guide for Public Benefit Organisations in South Africa* 41.
20 Section 4(b) of the Skills Development Levies Act.

- solely carries on PBAs 1, 2(a), 2(b), 2(c), 2(d) and 5;[21] or
- solely provides funds to a PBO that solely carries on the above PBAs.[22]

In relation to capital gains tax, a capital gain or loss applies when a person or organisation disposes of an asset. Up until years of assessment commencing on or after 1 April 2006, PBOs enjoyed complete exemption from income tax and capital gains tax. However, following the introduction of partial taxation, PBOs no longer qualify for full exemption from capital gains tax. According to the exemption guide:

> as from the first day of their first year of assessment commencing on or after 1 April 2006 any capital gain or capital loss made by a PBO on the disposal of an asset which has been used for a business undertaking or trading activity or substantially the whole of which has been used in such an undertaking will not be disregarded.[23]

In relation to municipal property rates, religious organisations such as places of public worship and the official residence are excluded from payment of rates in terms of the Municipal Property Rates Act 6 of 2004, as amended. In terms of section 17(1)(i) of the Act, a municipality may not levy a rate on properties registered in the name of and used primarily as a place of public worship[24] by a religious community, including an official residence[25] registered in the name of that community which is occupied by an office-bearer[26] of that community who officiates at services at that place of worship. The exclusion from rates lapses if the property is disposed of by the religious community owning it. If they no longer use the property as a place of worship or as an official residence, the exclusion from rates will also lapse.[27]

21 Section 4(c)(i) of the Skills Development Levies Act.
22 Section 4(c)(ii) of the Skills Development Levies Act.
23 *Tax Exemption Guide for Public Benefit Organisations in South Africa* 41.
24 'Place of public worship' means property used primarily for the purposes of congregation, excluding a structure that is primarily used for educational instruction in which secular or religious education is the primary instructive medium: Provided that the property is
(a) registered in the name of a religious community;
(b) registered in the name of a trust established for the sole benefit of a religious community; or
(c) subject to a land tenure
25 'official residence', in relation to places of public worship, means.
(a) a portion of the property used for residential purposes: or
(b) one residential property, if the residential property is not located on the same property as the place of public worship, registered in the name of a religious community or registered in the name of a trust established for the sole benefit of a religious community and used as a place of residence for an office bearer.
26 'office bearer', in relation to places of public worship, means the primary person who officiates at services at that place of worship.
27 Municipal Property Rates Act section 17(5)(a).

As outlined above, PBOs are thus entitled to numerous tax and other rates benefits. PBOs are further entitled to receive tax-deductible donations and to have donor deductible status. Any donation made to these organisations can be deducted from individuals' taxable income. However, according to section 18A of the Income Tax Act, the PBO should be involved in the activities specified by SARS in this section, which focuses on health, education and welfare. Section 18A of the Act excludes certain payments or transfers, such as 'tithes and offerings' to churches or other faith-based organisations, if it is in support of their religious activities.

Since the practice of religion is excluded, contributions and donations to religious organisations and churches are not tax deductible from the donor or contributor's taxable income. A PBO would also not be exempted from the obligation to deduct or withhold employees' tax and must register like any other employer for employees' tax purposes. In addition, a PBO will also be liable for Unemployment Insurance Fund (UIF) contributions unless it qualifies for other exemptions. According to a recent tax statement, SARS raised concerns in relation to violations of tax laws by religious institutions. They expressed concerns that proper taxes on trading activities that are unrelated to religious activities are not being paid as required by legislation. A number of religious institutions have also issued tax-deductible receipts in terms of section 18A of the Income Tax Act, for donations towards religious activities, which is not permitted in terms of the Income Tax Act.[28]

It is important to note that registration as an NPO is not a condition for approval as a PBO, since the registration as an NPO under the NPO Act is a voluntary registration lodged with the Directorate of NPOs. However, all registered NPOs must keep accounting records in line with the standards of the generally accepted accounting practice of its income, expenditure, assets and liabilities. They are also required to draw up financial statements within six months of its financial year-end. These statements must include an income and expenditure statement, and a balance sheet reflecting its assets and liabilities. In terms of sections 18 and 19, it is obligated to submit annual reports within nine months of the end of its financial year. The next section will briefly focus on religious institutions in the non-profit context.

NGOs and financial regulation

Religious organisations are among the most important of non-profit, public benefit organisations and their activities have expanded from traditional roles into much wider areas of public welfare. As charitable organisations, however, the danger is that the more they operate in the public sphere and are dependent on public funds, the greater the need for accountability and the potential for a loss of independence and vitality. Because they are relying to a large extent on state funding, does it mean that the state can interfere in the affairs of the organisation and violate the autonomy of these organisations?

28 *SARS media release.*

One of the roles of religious organisations is the provision of services, as these are predominantly service-driven organisations. Faith-based organisations (FBOs) are often NPOs that are involved in some or other form of service delivery, including religious education, charity, elderly care, health services and missionary work. Many of these organisations have religious objectives, either to provide religious education, or to be involved in missionary work. Some of them are funded by churches or congregations to run religious schools or old-age homes, and some have no religious objectives at all, but are inspired by religious values. Most of these organisations, especially in the field of social services, are fully dependent on the state for funding.

It is widely held that a stable and active civil society aids in poverty alleviation and civil society capacity building, enhancing public debate and participation and the promotion of democracy. In South Africa, 'many Community Service Organisations (CSOs) are filling the gaps by providing socio-economic and basic services that the state is unable to provide and in some cases have taken over the functions of the state'.[29] Many of these organisations are well embedded in local communities, flexible and more able to meet the needs of poor communities, since they are often in a better position to identify innovative development alternatives within their own community. Through their role in service delivery, these organisations provide both qualitative and financial benefits for the state. Despite these benefits, it seems that there is still the perception within government that these organisations 'are only an irritant' and treated by government as '*spaarwiele*' (spare wheels).[30] However, the Non-prof Organisations Act 71 of 1997 explicitly states: 'Within the limits prescribed by law, every organ of state must determine and coordinate the implementation of its policies and measures in a manner designed to promote, support and enhance the capacity of non-profit organisations to perform their functions'.[31]

The more religious or faith-based organisations are dependent on outside funding, especially government funding, the greater the pressure on the organisation to sacrifice religious beliefs, practices and independence. The paradox lies in the fact that while government is eagerly seeking out private religious alternatives for service delivery, private religious organisations increasingly turn to government for funds, but they are unwilling to sacrifice their unique position and autonomy as religious organisations in the community.

One of the biggest challenges that community organisations face is a lack of funding. As the Coalition on Civil Society Resource Mobilisation of the Charities Aid Foundation Southern Africa has observed:

> South African civil society is currently facing a funding crisis. This has resulted in a multiplicity of sustainability and institutional development challenges.

29 Coalition on Civil Society Resource Mobilisation 'Critical Perspectives on Sustainability of the South African Civil Society Sector' (2012) 44.

30 *Critical Perspectives* 45.

31 Non-prof Organisations Act section 3.

> Reasons for these circumstances include declining international funding, leadership and identity changes and the apparent unwillingness of government to meet its responsibilities to the sector. Government has been particularly remiss about its obligations regarding legislated and budgeted resource flows to CSOs. As a result of the above, the sustainability of many important CSOs is seriously compromised, a situation that has been exacerbated by the prevailing economic recession.[32]

During the apartheid era in South Africa, civil society organisations played an important role not only in trying to mitigate the effects of apartheid, but also as opposition to the government of the time. International donors often channelled their funds through credible South African agencies, of which some of the largest agencies happened to be religious organisations, such as the South African Council of Churches and the South African Catholics Bishops Conference.[33] Due to a decline in funding through ineffective government structures, most organisations now have to rely on other forms of funding and donations. According to Archbishop Emeritus Desmond Tutu:

> Charity organisations, which represent 30 per cent of the social services in the country, had R3 billion less to spend on the crucial causes because of the recession! Five hundred Thousand needy South Africans, many of them women and children, have been plunged into despair as the country's charities battle a funding crisis.[34]

Public funding often requires religious organisations to conform to reporting and other requirements that can contribute to FBOs becoming more secularised when they become dependent on public funds.

The South African Council of Churches (SACC) is of the view that any voluntary association (including religious organisations) should qualify for public funds if they provide a service to the public or at least a section of the public. In their view, 'an association that admits any person who subscribes to and supports its aims and objectives can be classified as an open association and should [...] be entitled to public funding'.[35] If an organisation's objectives are constitutionally permissible goals, they should be eligible to apply for state funding and 'then the state is precluded from denying funding to that body solely because it disapproves of its policies, practices, or activities'.[36]

32 *Critical Perspectives* 5.
33 *Critical Perspectives* 9.
34 According to Archbishop Emeritus Desmond Tutu in a letter to the South African Media Industry, available on the home page of The Giving Organisation. Online at: http://thegivingorganisation.org/.
35 South African Human Rights Commission (SAHRC) Report *Public Inquiry Exclusionary Policies of Voluntary Associations: Constitutional Considerations* (2006) Online at: www.sahrc.org.za.
36 Human Rights Commission 2006 *Exclusionary Policies.*

The issue of funding and welfare organisations came before the Free State High Court in the case of *Association of Welfare Organisations and Non-Governmental Organisations v MEC for Social Development Free State*.[37] The judgment affirmed the responsibility of government to offer financial support to organisations that render statutory services, and provided guidelines on how the responsibility between the state and NPOs should be shared in order to prevent the state from abdicating its constitutional and statutory duties. The judgment recognised the major contribution of NPOs in the provision of welfare services in South Africa and endorsed the fact that government must accept and take responsibility for providing these services and fulfilling their constitutional obligations.

In its report, the CRL Rights Commission highlighted the non-compliance with legislation, specifically relating to religious institutions status as NPOs in terms of the NPO Act and PBOs in terms of the Income Tax Act, as some of the main issues contributing to financial abuses. One of the proposals made by the Commission in its report was the amendment of existing legislation in order to compel religious institutions to register as a NPO, a NPC or a PBO. In relation to the non-compliance with existing laws, the Commission found that 'some churches are not registered either with the Department of Social Development as either NonProfit Organizations or with SARS as Public Benefits Organizations'. And further that some religious organisations 'operate freely without registration' and 'some that are registered with Department of Social Development do not even report yearly to the Department as required by law'.[38] They recommended the better enforcement of legislation, in particular the NPO Act and the Income Tax Act. It is important to note that registration as a NPO under the NPO Act is voluntary. Only churches and religious institutions that have opted for registration under the Act will need to comply with its requirements. The Act provides for the necessary legal mechanisms and penalties in the event of non-compliance. The Department of Social Development should therefore cancel a religious institution's registration as a NPO if there is non-compliance with the provision of the Act, however, this is not happening. The problem again seems to be both the con-compliance as well as the non-enforcement of the existing laws.

Financial abuses and proposed financial regulation

The CRL Rights Commission identified numerous problems associated with the commercialisation of religion and financial abuses in their report. The various problems were categorised under various headings. In relation to financial abuses, the problems under three of those categories were particularly relevant for the

37 *Association of Welfare Organisations and Non-Governmental Organisations v MEC for Social Development Free State and Others* (1719/2010) [2010] ZAFSHC 73 (5 August 2010).

38 Final Report on 'The Commercialisation of Religion and Abuse of People's Belief Systems' by the Commission for the Promotion and Protections of the Rights of Cultural Religious and Linguistic Communities (CRL Rights Commission) April 2017: 25.

purpose of financial regulation, namely the commercialisation of religion, non-compliance with the law and the non-enforcement of the law. In its report, the Commission proposed the broad-scale regulation of religion in South Africa. In order to achieve that, they proposed that existing legislation should be amended to compel all religious institutions to register, or by creating new legislation that would establish statutory regulatory bodies responsible for regulating religious institutions and practitioners through registering and licencing. The report explained the rationale for the study as gaining a deeper understanding of the funding and financial accounting practices of religious communities, such as: sources of income, budgeting and expenditure allocations, assets and liabilities, tax and other statutory deductions, compliance with the legislative systems, processes and procedures for financial accounting.[39] The report identified various issues pertaining to religious leaders and organisations and specifically in relation to financial regulation, the following issues were raised:

- the failure of religious institutions to register as NPOs and to maintain financial records;
- the 'deliberate exploitation of poor and vulnerable people because of the commercialisation of religious practices, through assumption of divine/missionary right to directly or indirectly solicit and receive gifts/offerings/tithes in cash or in kind from their members (e.g. earnings, pension pay-outs, movable property, immovable property, etc.) without commitment to responsible financial management and accounting';
- loopholes in legislation and a lack of enforcement, including financial regulations and legislation;
- the 'refusal to use banking facilities and keeping money collected in safes in the institutions';
- 'the use of personal bank accounts as the institutions' account';
- 'earning funds as entertainers and not as religious practitioners'.[40]

In the summary findings of the report,[41] the Commission highlighted numerous financial abuses. The report argued that examples, ranging from bank speed points where people can swipe bank cards during ceremonies to charging exorbitant fees for blessings and prayers, was *prima facie* evidence of the commercialisation of religion. Institutions were also not complying with existing financial laws, such as not registering with SARS as PBOs, ignoring financial reporting requirements as required by law or not declaring or avoiding tax.[42] Various governance structures within the various religious institutions also lacked proper governance

39 *Commercialisation Report* 10.

40 See *Commercialisation Report* 19.

41 See *Commercialisation Report* 25–27.

42 For some interesting insights into financial accountability practices in churches, see E Goodchild *Best corporate Governance Practices: Financial Accountability of Selected Churches in the Free State Province* (M dissertation, University of the free State, January 2016).

structures that can deal with financial issues, and in some cases, the finance committee was made up of the spiritual leader, his wife and some of his friends. Various issues were also raised in relation to the flouting of banking rules, such as not banking the collections received, banking collections into personal accounts of the religious leaders, and the lack of fiduciary committees such as finance, internal audit and financial management. Some religious institutions violated the Reserve Bank Rules by taking money out of the country without the necessary permissions and often there is no clear separation between the religious activity and business activity of the institution. In relation to financial abuses by religious leaders, and activities that constitute the commercialisation of religion, it must be noted that financial or other donations are often given voluntarily by members to religious institutions. As pointed out by some commentators in relation to the report, 'there has always been an economic dimension to religious belief and practice',[43] In fact, section 11 of the Religious Charter states that 'every person has the right, for religious purposes and in furthering their objectives, to solicit, receive, manage, allocate and spend voluntary financial and other forms of support and contributions. The confidentiality of such support and contributions must be respected'. Unless members are coerced into doing so, it is a legitimate exercise of their constitutionally protected right to freedom religion. As pointed out by FOR SA and the South African Council for the Protection and Promotion of Religious Rights and Freedoms:

> Again, while we understand the CRL's need to want to do something about the 'commercialisation' of religion and abuse of people's belief systems, which unfortunately is a reality, the reality also is that the vast majority of religious institutions and practitioners in South Africa do not perpetrate such abuses and are compliant with the law. It does not make sense, and there is no rational justification for, the far-reaching regulation of all religious institutions in South Africa represented by the CRL's recommendations, because of the few who are abusing their freedom.[44]

In relation to financial abuses, the CRL Rights Commission can assist religious communities by educating and informing them of their legal and constitutional rights and creating awareness of existing laws and regulations that apply in the case of financial reporting and tax compliance. The educational and informative role of the CRL Commission can particularly assist the poorer religious communities in the remote and rural areas of South Africa, where people are potentially more vulnerable to exploitation and abuse by religious leaders.[45]

43 Comments on the CRL Rights Commission's Report on the 'Commercialisation' of Religion, submitted by Freedom of Religion South Africa (FOR SA) and the South African Council for the Protection and Promotion of Religious Rights and Freedoms (28 February 2017) 27.

44 *Comments Commercialisation of Religion* 40.

45 See also *Comments Commercialisation of Religion* 62.

In relation to issues of a lack of fiduciary committees such as finance, internal audit and financial management, religious institutions should be educated and equipped to deal with financial governance matters, such as the keeping of financial records; splitting personal and business activities; running of bank accounts and other financial-related matters. An interesting example of how the church has dealt with issues of financial misuse in the church, can be found in the case of Bishop Ngewu and the Anglican Church of Southern Africa, which came before the courts in various judgments. In *Bishop Mlibo Ngewu v The Anglican Church of Southern Africa*,[46] the court mainly focused on the issue of financial mismanagement within the Anglican Church of Southern Africa and the procedures and processes employed by the church to deal with it. The applicant was a Bishop for the Diocese of Umzimvubu of the Anglican Church of Southern Africa. In December 2010, the Metropolitan of the Church ('the Metropolitan') received complaints about the applicant's leadership of the Diocese relating to alleged financial mismanagement. The concerns were expressed as follows:

> The situation in the Diocese of Umzimvubu is extremely tense and there is a very real sense of fear of the Bishop … Governance and transparency are sadly missing from the Diocese and there is a very real sense of autocracy about how things are done. The Diocese has been run into the ground financially.[47]

After unsuccessful attempts to resolve the issues through pastoral means, the Synod of Bishops appointed a task team in accordance with Canon 21(3)[48] tasked with a forensic audit. In consultation with the applicant, they also decided to place the Diocese under administration.[49] The applicant agreed in a letter to the Metropolitan 'to temporarily relinquish his episcopal responsibility with a view to a Provincial Task Team appointed by the Synod of the Church investigating and mediating the conflict within the Diocese'.[50] The church subsequently appointed a fraud investigation team who recommended that the Bishops of the Church

46 *Bishop Mlibo Ngewu v The Anglican Church of Southern Africa and Ten Others* [2016] ZAKZPHC 88. For a comprehensive discussion of this case, see EH van Coller 'The Church, the Bishop and the Missing Money. A Reflection on the Case of Bishop Ngewu and the Anglican Church of Southern Africa' *Oxford Journal of Law and Religion* (2017) 6(3) 610–618.

47 *Bishop Mlibo Ngewu* para 6.

48 Canon 21(3) reads as follows:
When the Synod of Bishops becomes aware of events, developments or reasons which indicate to it that in its opinion the affairs of a Diocese merit an inquiry or investigation in relation to possible support, or other action that might need to be taken by the Diocese or the Province or both, it shall have the power to appoint a task team to inquire into or investigate these matters at the cost of the Common Provincial Fund. The task team shall report its findings and recommendations directly to the Synod of Bishops. The Synod of Bishops shall make whatever decision it feels appropriate in the circumstances in consultation with the Diocese concerned.

49 *Bishop Mlibo Ngewu* para 8.

50 *Bishop Mlibo Ngewu* para 9.

should charge the applicant 'for reckless conduct, misappropriation, breach of trust and failure to fulfil canonical duties'.[51] The Provincial Task Team appointed by the Bishops made a final report. The Synod meeting on 30 September 2013 did however not support their proposals and resolved that the applicant should stand trial under Canon 38.[52] In accordance with Canon 38(3)(a) the Metropolitan proceeded to appoint a Board of Preliminary Inquiry, who concluded:

> there was sufficient evidence to support a *prima facie* finding that the applicant had mismanaged funds, been negligent in relation to the Church's funds and property, misappropriated or misused Church funds, managed Church finances inappropriately and provoked dissension in the congregation, committed a breach of trust and promoted dissension.[53]

The Metropolitan then informed the applicant that they had decided to proceed with a trial against him in terms of Canon 38. The applicant was served with Articles of Presentment or disciplinary charges and a Court for the Trial of a Bishop ('the Tribunal') was duly appointed in terms of Article XIII of the Constitution and Canon 36(1) and (3). Having dismissed various points raised *in limine* by the applicant, the Tribunal held that the trials should proceed to consider the merits of the disciplinary charges. It is accordingly this decision to proceed with the trial that was before the court on review in *Bishop Mlibo Ngewu v The Anglican Church of Southern Africa*. The applicant also sought to review and set aside the decision of the Archbishop of Cape Town and Metropolitan to institute disciplinary proceedings against him. Since the Tribunal had not considered the merits of the charges against the applicant, the main issue before the court was 'whether this court can interfere in the Tribunal's unconcluded proceedings'.[54]

With reference to various cases, the court confirmed the view that 'a Court will only interfere in unconcluded proceedings if a *grave injustice* will occur and it is necessary to intervene to attain justice' (emphasis added).[55] The applicant raised issues in relation to high costs, flawed process, that the decision was unlawful and that the appointment of the panel was not in accordance with the principles of natural justice.[56] In order to determine whether there was any indication of a 'grave injustice' to merit an intervention, the court considered all these issues and was of the view that 'the applicant has failed to satisfy this Court that it should intervene in reviewing the proceedings of the Tribunal'.[57] The court found no reason to determine whether proper procedures were in fact followed, since it found that there was a *prima facie* case pending before the Tribunal and that the

51 *Bishop Mlibo Ngewu* para 13.
52 *Bishop Mlibo Ngewu* para 16.
53 *Bishop Mlibo Ngewu* para 22.4.
54 *Bishop Mlibo Ngewu* para 35.
55 *Bishop Mlibo Ngewu* para 39.
56 See *Bishop Mlibo Ngewu* para 40.
57 *Bishop Mlibo Ngewu* para 43.

Tribunal should proceed to determine the merits of this case against the applicant. For the court to intervene at this stage would be 'premature and unjustified'.[58] The court dismissed the application with costs.

The case was however significant in respect of dealing with issues of financial mismanagement in the church. The process in the Diocese of Umzimvubu, which began in 2010, involved at least 13 Bishops, the Provincial Treasurer, the Provincial Executive Officer, Synod of Bishops and Metropolitan of the Church and the Archbishop of Cape Town. The case of Bishop Ngewu is riddled with references to financial mismanagement and the misappropriation of funds. A substantial lack of accounting records and internal accounting controls were reported. *Prima facie* evidence was found against Bishop Ngewu, ranging from negligence in relation to the church's funds and property, misappropriated or misused church funds to committing a breach of trust and promoted dissension. Many of these issues related to the aspects of financial abuse, highlighted by the CRL Rights Commission in its report.

As pointed out earlier, article 11 of the Religious Charter relates to the religious rights of persons and religious institutions to raise and manage funds and contributions. Like all voluntary associations, a religious institution has the right to perform different actions to further its objectives, and to receive, manage and spend money for that purpose. It is however expected of religious institutions to govern themselves in financially sound, responsible and transparent ways and to act in the best interest of their members. They are also required to abide by existing financial laws and regulations. The Anglican Church, particularly in the case of Bishop Ngewu, took various steps to try and resolve the issues. They requested the Provincial Treasurer to investigate and report on the various concerns. Subsequently the Metropolitan took pastoral steps and appointed a pastoral team to meet with the Bishop. They proceeded to appoint a task team to investigate and address the various issues in the Diocese, including the commencement of a forensic audit. The Diocese was placed under administration pending the investigation. The Archbishop also appointed a Vicar General and forensic auditors. The Synod of Bishops then appointed another Provincial Task Team and resolved that the Applicant should stand trial under Canon 38. The Metropolitan appointed a Board of Preliminary Inquiry and informed the applicant that they had decided to proceed with a trial in terms of Canon 38. It is clear that the church did everything possible to address the issues in relation to financial mismanagement within the church.

The Commission highlighted in their report the need for the religious sector to be regulated, particularly in relation to financial management. Some views that were expressed in the report was that 'government should insist that all churches are first registered as NPOs before they operate to prevent profiteering given that there is no shareholding involved'.[59] In order to achieve this, it was suggested that

58 *Bishop Mlibo Ngewu* para 44.

59 Draft Report 'An investigative Study of the Commercialisation of Religion in the Republic of South Africa' *Study commissioned by the Commission for the Promotion and*

the government needs to 'pass high level legislation stipulating that for a religious institution to operate, it needs to be registered as an NPO and by registering, it becomes compliant. Thereafter how the institutions operate should be left to individual religions'.[60] Concerns have been raised by various churches in relation to the proposed regulation in that religious communities and leaders argue that churches are already 'over-regulated' and that this can create the danger of violating communities' right to freedom of religion. Religious institutions are already subject to various administrative and financial laws they have to comply with. It has been argued that there is no need for further financial and administrative regulation by the state.

> Instead of creating more regulatory laws churches have to comply with, pastors who swindle money or place people's health or lives in danger under the guise of 'religion' should be caught using the existing tax, immigration, criminal and other laws.[61]

The Anglican Church of Southern Africa has illustrated with this judgment that it is possible for churches to have proper procedures in place to deal with issues of financial impropriety within the church in a proper and transparent manner. In this way, they can still further their religious objectives without the fear of state interference or extra financial regulation, by making sure that they govern themselves in an accountable and transparent manner. A religious association must therefore also exercise its disciplinary authority in accordance with the requirements as laid down in the constitution, but also in accordance with the rules of natural justice. A court shall not interfere where an association has acted in accordance with its own rules. Churches who thus do not act in a financially sound manner, do not have procedures in place to act against financial abuse or neglect to act against a corrupt pastor, will be subject to scrutiny by the courts.

In relation to financial impropriety, Scrooby[62] noted that the judgment in *Ngewu* highlighted 'the importance of the Synod of Bishops (SoB) in the investigation of impropriety in the Dioceses of the Anglican Church Southern Africa'. Through the judgment, the leadership of the Archbishop of Cape Town and the Metropolitan of the Anglican Church of Southern Africa was put in the spotlight in their campaign against corruption and financial impropriety that has unfortunately also found its way into the church. Through various processes within the church, they sought to deal with it in a proper, procedurally fair and transparent way in accordance with the internal canons and constitutional provisions. This approach highlights the fact that although the right to freedom of religion allows

Protection of the Rights of Cultural, Religious and Linguistic Communities (August 2016) 124.

60 *Draft Commercialisation Report* 124.

61 N Badenhorst 'CRL Rights Commission Says it is "willing to talk, but not willing to stop"' *FOR SA* (20 Nov 2015).

62 D Scrooby 'The Bishop of the River of Hippopotamuses and the Archbishop of Cape Town' *Law & Religion UK* (20 March 2017).

churches to manage and spend money to further their objectives in a manner that they see fit, it still needs to be done in a responsible, financially sound and transparent manner. However, it is important to note that issues of church doctrine and governance should be left to the church to determine domestically, as far as is possible, without interference from the court. The court should only become involved in a dispute where it is strictly necessary to do so and it should refrain from determining doctrinal issues, in order to avoid religious entanglement. This was clearly the approach taken by the courts in the case of *Ngewu*.

This example also ties in with some of the problems highlighted in the CRL Rights Commission report, in particular the fact that numerous churches and religious institutions had no proper disciplinary codes or codes of conduct. The report highlighted a general lack of good governance, such as the commitment to responsible financial management and accounting and a lack of good governance structures within churches and religious institutions.

Despite the numerous problems with the CRL Rights Commission's recommendation for the establishment of peer review committees,[63] they did recommend the establishment of a 'code of good conduct'. According to their proposal, this code should not impede doctrinal differences, but 'ensures that the religion complies with section 15, 18, 31 and 33 of the Constitution that ensures sound financial governance that is accountable to the followers of the religion and that ensures that abuses do not occur within the religion'.[64] In its comments, FOR SA and the South African Council for the Protection and Promotion of Religious Rights and Freedoms endorsed the CRL Rights Commission's recommendation of adopting a 'Code of Ethics', which religious institutions and practitioners are encouraged (but not legally compelled) to voluntarily subscribe to. They further recommend that the code should be developed by the religious sector itself.[65] Towards the middle of 2018, the South African Council for Religious Rights and Freedoms proposed a draft Code of Conduct for Religions in South Africa, which is currently being circulated for comments. In relation to financial regulation, the draft code proposes that religious institutions and practitioners subscribe to the following:

> 17 We shall act with honesty, integrity, due diligence and transparency in respect of our finances and financial management.
>
> 17.1 We shall refrain from unlawful, corrupt, manipulative or misleading conduct when soliciting contributions or securing funds from members, external donors or other sources.
>
> 17.2 We shall respect the interests and well-being of givers and not pressurise them in any way into giving beyond their means. We shall not minister to anyone in a financially manipulative or exploitative manner.

63 See for more details the *Comments Commercialisation of Religion* and G Du Plessis 'The Constitutionality of the Regulation of Religion in South Africa – Untoward Restrictions of the Right to Religious Freedom?' *South African Law Journal* forthcoming.

64 *Commercialisation Report* 35.

65 *Comments Commercialisation of Religion* 64.

> 17.3 We shall not misappropriate funds, and shall honour and use gifts and contributions only for the purpose for which they were received, and shall communicate regularly with givers to acknowledge and confirm such contributions and expenditures
>
> 17.4 We shall avoid conflicts of interest and shall declare personal interests where appropriate.
>
> 17.5 We shall keep accurate financial statements in accordance with accepted financial practices. We shall subject our financial statements to independent audit at least annually.
>
> 17.6 We shall act transparently and, while maintaining confidentiality in respect of support and contributions, shall make our financial affairs openly available to our members or supporters in whatever way appropriate.
>
> 17.7 We shall make ourselves accountable to our members or supporters in respect of management and finances in whatever way appropriate.
>
> 17.8 Except insofar as we are entitled to reasonable remuneration, compensation or other income, we shall refrain from enriching ourselves in any way out of the funds of our institution, and from acting corruptly and fraudulently.
>
> 17.9 Where applicable, we shall make full disclosure of taxable income, and make diligent payment of taxes due.

Creating new legislation will not necessarily solve the problem. The Commission has in fact acknowledged the fact that existing legislation should be better enforced.[66] Particularly in relation to financial abuses, legislation to deal with most of the highlighted issues does in fact exist. Where a religious institution conducts purely business activities, the existing company legislation[67] (particularly where such institutions are registered as private or non-profit companies) can be used, or the existing tax legislation[68] for instances of tax avoidance by not registering for tax or not declaring the specific business activities. By refusing to use bank facilities, paying money into personal accounts or violating Reserve Bank Rules, various existing laws are available, ranging from banking laws[69] to applying existing criminal laws relation to fraud, theft or corruption.[70]

The *Ngewu* case has thus illustrated that by having proper procedures in place, a religious institution can effectively deal with financial abuses through their own proper channels. A code of conduct, as outlined above, may also assist institutions in creating a culture of good governance and proper financial practices within their institution. In the absence of proper processes or procedures, the Commission can play an important role. In its report, the Commission makes the following valid recommendation, by stating:

66 *Draft Commercialisation Report* 28.
67 The Companies Act, 2008.
68 The Income Tax Act 58 of 1962.
69 For example, the Banks Act 94 of 1990 and the applicable banking regulations; The Reserve Bank Act 90 of 1989.
70 See also the Prevention and Combating of Corrupt Activities Act 12 of 2004.

> Although religious organizations exist as voluntary organizations; the CRL Rights Commission should provide essential assistance in helping organizations to get their house in order and to ensure compliance with existing legislation and propose new legislation. The current disregard of fiduciary responsibilities is a serious concern.[71]

Conclusion

Instances of financial abuse and financial misconduct threaten the financial sustainability of churches and religious institutions, as well as their ability to assist in the provision of social services. It must also be noted that the state has a responsibility in carrying out its financial duties, ranging from collecting taxes and revenues, to administering and enforcing good corporate governance practices across all institutions in South Africa, through applicable statutes and regulations. As pointed out:

> a State cannot be precluded from carrying out obligations which it has assumed as a result of taking over property belonging to a religion or belief, nor from contributing funds towards the preservation of religious structures of historic or artistic value, and from using revenue derived from general taxes for these purposes.[72]

When it comes to financial regulation and good financial practices within churches and religious institutions, let us be reminded that 'no organisation should be exempt from accountability standards in the name of a higher calling'.[73]

Bibliography

Badenhorst N 'CRL Rights Commission Says it is "willing to talk, but not willing to stop"' *FOR SA* (20 November 2015).

Coalition on Civil Society Resource Mobilisation, 'Critical Perspectives on Sustainability of the South African Civil Society Sector' (2012). South Africa: Jacana Media.

Draft Report 'An Investigative Study of the Commercialisation of Religion in the Republic of South Africa' Study commissioned by the Commission for the Promotion and Protection of the Rights of Cultural, Religious and Linguistic Communities (August 2016).

Du Plessis G 'The Constitutionality of the Regulation of Religion in South Africa – Untoward Restrictions of the Right to Religious Freedom?' *South African Law Journal* forthcoming.

71 *Draft Commercialisation Report* 29 para 15.4

72 Krishnaswami A *Study of Discrimination in the Matter of Religious Rights and Practices* (1960) 30.

73 Statement made by Marian Walsh (State Senator of Massachusetts and voted one of Boston's 100 most powerful women) (John F Kennedy Presidential Library, 2008)) regarding the corporate governance of churches, as quoted by Goodchild *Financial Accountability* 116.

Final Report on 'The Commercialisation of Religion and Abuse of People's Belief Systems' Study commissioned by the Commission for the Promotion and Protections of the Rights of Cultural Religious and Linguistic Communities (April 2017).

Freedom of Religion South Africa (FOR SA) and South African Council for the Protection and Promotion of Religious Rights and Freedoms *Comments on the CRL Rights Commission's Report on the 'Commercialisation' of Religion* (28 February 2017).

Goodchild E *Best corporate Governance Practices: Financial Accountability of Selected Churches in the Free State Province* (Master's dissertation, University of the Free State, January 2016).

Krishnaswami A *Study of Discrimination in the Matter of Religious Rights and Practices* (1960) New York: United Nations Publication.

Pillay K 'Religious Bodies May Have to Pay Tax' *The Witness* (2 February 2018).

SARS Legal Counsel 'Tax Exemption Guide for Public Benefit Organisations in South Africa' *Issue 5* (26 January 2018)

SARS Legal Counsel 'SARS' Compliance intervention in Religious Sector' SARS media release' (26 January 2018). Online at: http://www.sars.gov.za.

Scrooby D 'The Bishop of the River of Hippopotamuses and the Archbishop of Cape Town' *Law & Religion UK* (20 March 2017).

South African Human Rights Commission (SAHRC) Report *Public Inquiry Exclusionary Policies of Voluntary Associations Constitutional Considerations* (2006). Online at: www.sahrc.org.za.

Van Coller EH 'The Church, the Bishop and the Missing Money. A Reflection on the Case of Bishop Ngewu and the Anglican Church of Southern Africa' *Oxford Journal of Law and Religion* (2017) 6(3) 610–618.

10 Religious leaders

Introduction

When it comes to religious institutions and their respective leaders, section 9.1 (c) of the Religious Charter provides for the right of every religious institution to:

> in accordance with the principles of tolerance, fairness, openness and accountability to regulate its own internal affairs, including organisational structures and procedures, the ordination, conditions of service, discipline and dismissal of office-bearers and members, the appointment, conditions of employment towards and members, the appointment, conditions of employment and dismissal of employees and volunteers, and membership requirements.

Article 6 of the UN Declaration on the Elimination of All Forms of Intolerance and of Discrimination Based on Religion or Belief[1] echoes these sentiments, affirming that the right to freedom of religion includes the right to 'train, appoint, elect or designate by succession appropriate leaders called for by the requirements and standards of any religion or belief'.[2] This chapter will first attempt to answer the question as to whether a religious minister can be regarded as an employee of the church or not. Then, the discussion will focus on religious ministers and discrimination and the right of religious organisations to appoint or not to appoint office holders, with specific reference to the example of homosexuality. The chapter will conclude with a brief example of access to public institutions by religious ministers in the form of chaplaincies.

Employment status

Different denominations such as the Dutch Reformed Church, Reformed Church and Anglican Church, all have different positions in relation to the question of whether a minister of religion is an employee of the church or not.[3] As early as

1 A/RES/36/55 (25 November 1981).

2 Para g.

3 For some further views on the employment position of religious ministers, see EH Van Coller ''n Regsvergelykende Blik op die Diensverhouding van 'n Predikant' *Dutch*

1976 in the important case of *Theron v Ring van Wellington van die NG Sendingkerk in Suid-Afrika*[4] the court took the view that the relationship between the minister and the church council was labour related because it was clear that the minister entered into an employment contract. This contract had to be read subject to the relevant provisions of the Church Order and it was clear the claim was based on the fact that the relevant contractual provisions had to be interpreted and enforced.[5] Jansen JA made it clear that the contract of employment must still be read in accordance with the Church Order. The case of *Schreuder v Nederduitse Gereformeerde Kerk Wilgespruit & others*[6] is of great importance for the Dutch Reformed Church. Rev. Schreuder was unfairly dismissed by the church in 1996 in terms of section 12 of the Church Order.[7] He was of the view that he was unfairly dismissed in terms of the Labour Relations Act.[8] The court had no problem in defining the relationship between the minister and the church as a contractual employment relationship.[9] The court was of the view that the intention of the contract of employment (beroepsbrief) was to create contractual duties in the form of an employment contract between the minister and his congregation.[10] The implication of the decision in *Schreuder* for the Dutch Reformed Church is that all employment relations (including the contract of employment of a minister) will be subject to the current labour law and read and interpreted in terms of current Labour legislation. Within the Dutch Reformed Church, the contract of employment (beroepsbrief) in section 7b.1 of the Church Order constitutes the offer of employment and it is seen as a normal contract of employment similar to that of a gardener, secretary or cleaner. The court in *Wagenaar v United Reformed Church*[11] is of the view that a *beroepsbrief* complies with all the requirements in order to be classified as a contract of employment.

Reformed Theological Journal/Nederduits Gereformeerde Teologiese Tydskrif (NGTT) (2013) 54(3&4) 1–14; Van Coller EH 'Religious Ministers – Working for God or Working for the Church? A Reflection on Universal Church of the Kingdom of God v Myeni and Others' *Oxford Journal of Law and Religion* (2017) 6(1) 187–193.

4 *Theron v Ring van Wellington van die NG Sendingkerk in Suid-Afrika* 1976 (2) SA 1 (A).

5 *Theron v Ring van Wellington* para 26D.

6 *Schreuder v Nederduitse Gereformeerde Kerk Wilgespruit & andere* 1999 BLLR 713 (LC).

7 '12.1 Indien ′n leraar nie sy gemeente verder tot stigting kan dien nie, mag die ring na ondersoek, waarin beide die kerkraad en die betrokke leraar aangehoor word, die band tussen leraar en gemeente losmaak indien daar, volgens die oordeel van die ring, billike voorsiening vir die leraar gemaak is.

12.2 Billike voorsiening word deur die ring in oorleg met die betrokke kerkraad of instansie en die betrokke leraar bepaal. ′n Uitbetaling van ses maande se lewensonderhoud en toelaes asook reëlings in verband met pensioendekking vir hierdie periode word as voldoende beskou'.

8 Labour Relations Act 66 of 1995.

9 *Schreuder* para 25.

10 *Schreuder* para 20.

11 *Wagenaar v United Reformed Church* SA [2005] 1 BALR 127 (CCMA) para 7.

Within the Reformed Church of South Africa the *beroepsbrief* is not seen as a contract of employment but merely as the expression of various sections (4, 5 and 11 in particular) of the Church Order applicable to the calling and care of its ministers.[12] In *Church of the Province of Southern Africa (Diocese of Cape Town v CCMA)*[13] the court was of the view that:

> The crucial question is whether, at the time the parties concluded the offer and acceptance, they *intended* to create a legally binding contractual relationship i.e. the mere fact of an offer and acceptance did not equate to a binding contractual relationship; the offer and acceptance had to be accompanied by the *intention* to create the contract.

Based on an interpretation of the *Nederlandse Geloofsbelydenis* [Belgic Confession] the Reformed Church is of the view that ministers should *not* be regarded as employees of the church.[14] According to them the arrangement with ministers is, in accordance with the self-definition of the church, is an internal ecclesiastical matter, based on religious convictions and therefore not subject to the national labour legislation.[15] The employment relationship in the Reformed Church of South Africa is therefore not regulated by a contract but in terms of the internal law of the church.[16] According to section 1 of the Church Order of the Reformed Churches in South Africa, in order

> to maintain good order in the Church of Christ, it is necessary that there should be: offices; assemblies; supervision over doctrine, sacraments and ceremonies; and church discipline. Ministers of the Word are called to do so, before they are permitted to proclaim the Word and administer the sacraments.[17]

The view of the Anglican Church in South Africa is very similar to that of the Reformed Church and therefore the case of *Church of the Province*[18] is of great importance. An Anglican priest was suspended on a ground of misconduct after a disciplinary hearing. He retained his status as priest but would receive no salary. He was of the view that in effect his suspension was in fact an unfair dismissal. He

12 According to article 11 of the Church Order: 'Die kerkraad wat die kerk verteenwoordig, is verplig om sy bedienaars van die Woord met behoorlike onderhoud te versorg en mag hulle nie die onderhoud weerhou of hulle uit hulle diens ontslaan sonder kennis en goedkeuring van die klassis met advies van die deputate van die partikuliere sinode nie'.

13 *Church of the Province of Southern Africa (Diocese of Cape Town) v CCMA & others* [2001] 11 BLLR 1213 (LC) 1223 para 24.

14 J Smit and D Du Plooy 'Reëling van die Gereformeerde Predikant se Diens – ′n Arbeidsregtelike of ′n Interne Kerklike Aangeleentheid? *In die Skriflig* (2008) 61. See further Church Order sections 4 and 5.

15 Smit & Du Plooy 2008 *In die Skriflig* 61.

16 See further J Smit 'Die Beroepsbrief in die Gereformeerde Kerke in Suid-Afrika – ′n Kontraktuele Werksaanbod?' *In die Skriflig* (2007) 586 and further.

17 See article 2 and 3.

18 *Church of the Province* 1227.

took his case to the Commission for Conciliation, Arbitration and Mediation (CCMA) who made an order declaring the dismissal as unfair. The Anglican Church took the case to the High Court claiming that the CCMA made a mistake since the relationship between the church and the priest in not an employment relationship and that the CCMA therefore did not have the jurisdiction to decide the case. According to the Anglican Church:

> a priest is not regarded as the servant of the Church: while the Church provides the framework for the priest's work (through the constitution and canons), the priest is regarded as working for God, and i.e. the relationship between the priest and the Church cannot be regarded as one of employment. The applicant simply, according to it, provided the sphere within which priests serve God arising out of their calling. It is for that reason, so applicant argued, that priests are said to be called of God and serving God and offering their lives to God – this precludes the Anglican Church generally, and the applicant in particular, from speaking of employing priests.[19]

The court came to the conclusion that:

> a contract of employment is necessary for purposes of establishing an employment relationship and that there was no legally enforceable contract of employment between the applicant and the third respondent, the parties are not an employer and employee as defined by the LRA and consequently the first respondent has no jurisdiction to entertain the alleged dispute referred to it by the third respondent.[20]

In the 2005 case of *Wagenaar v United Reformed Church*[21] a minister of the United Reformed Church was dismissed by his congregation. After considering both the *Screuder* case as well as the *Church of the Province* case the court came to the conclusion that the minister did have a contractual relationship with the church and that he was an employer in terms of the Labour Relations Act. The decision highlighted the conflicting views of the court and the fact that there is *no* general rule in South Africa regulating the employment relationships of ministers of religion. According to the court:

> It seems that there is no general rule in South Africa as to whether a Minister of Religion is an employee or not. Nor is there likely to be. Different denominations have different teachings and ideologies. In my view each case depends upon the facts.[22]

19 *Church of the Province* 1217 para xiii.
20 *Church of the Province* 1217 para 40.
21 *Wagenaar v United Reformed Church*.
22 *Wagenaar* 139F.

The court took the same view in a Scottish case of *Macdonald v Free Presbyterian Church of Scotland*.[23] According to the court:

> Deacons, Elders and Ministers are ordained to their respective offices within the Free Presbyterian Church and each is an office-holder and that therefore the claimant is an office-holder by virtue of his ordination. His rights and duties are defined by the office he holds and not by any contract. He is not an employee of the respondent.[24]

And further:

> [Judge MacKenzie's] conclusion is consistent with recognition of the principle that, in the case of a church whose foundation and structure shows a belief that it is not appropriate, in the case of important offices including that of Minister, to set up a legal relationship that is subject to control by the Civil Magistrate.[25]

The Labour Relations Act 66 of 1995 (LRA) and the Basic Conditions of Employment Act 75 of 1997 (BCEA) were amended in 2002. Section 200A of the LRA and section 83A of the BCEA introduced a rebuttable presumption as to whether a person is an employee and therefore covered by the Act. A person is presumed to be an employee if any one of the seven factors listed in section 200A[26] of the LRA is present in the relationship between that person and the person for whom they work or to whom they render services. It is not a requirement that all of these factors must be present; one is sufficient to create such a relationship. An interesting case, with reference to this section, came before the courts in the case of *Universal Church of the Kingdom of God*,[27] where the Labour Court (court *a quo*) and the Labour Appeal Court had to deal with

23 *Macdonald v Free Presbyterian Church of Scotland* 2009 ET S/11071 (28 May 2009).
24 *Macdonald* para 81.
25 *Macdonald v Free Presbyterian Church of Scotland* [2010] UKEAT S/0034/09/BI (10 February 2010) 42.
26 A person who works for, or renders services to, any other person is presumed, until the contrary is proved, to be an employee, **regardless of the form of contract**, if any ***one*** or more of the following factors is present:
i.the manner in which the person works is subject to the control or direction of another person
ii.the person's hours of work are subject to the control or direction of another person
iii.in the case of a person who works for an organization, the person is a part of that organization
iv.the person has worked for that other person for an average of at least 40 hours per month over the last 3 months
v.the person is economically dependent on the other person for whom that person works or renders services
vi.the person is provided with tools of trade or work equipment by the other person; or
vii.the person only works for or renders services to one person (emphasis added).
27 *Universal Church of the Kingdom of God v Myeni and Others* (DA 3/14) [2015] ZALAC 31 (28 July 2015).

the matter of whether a pastor who is in the voluntary service of the church is an employee of the church or not. A pastor of The Universal Church of the Kingdom of God referred an unfair dismissal dispute to the CCMA after his service was terminated on the ground of alleged misconduct. The church argued that the pastor was not an employee of the church and that the CCMA had no jurisdiction to hear the matter. The arbitrator disagreed and found the dismissal to be unfair. The church was not happy with the outcome of the arbitration process and approached the Labour Court to review and set aside the arbitration award. In the Labour Court Steenkamp J held that the arbitrator was correct in his finding that the pastor was an employee of the church. The church was granted leave to appeal to the Labour Appeal Court.

The court *a quo* based most of its decision on section 200A of the Labour Relations Act (LRA), which creates a rebuttable presumption as to who is an employee for the purposes of the LRA. The court assessed the relationship between the church and the pastor against the factors listed in section 200A and found that the church failed to rebut the presumption in section 200A of the LRA. The court referred extensively to developments in English law. Steenkamp J clearly interpreted the decisions by the United Kingdom Supreme Court to mean that the *manner* in which the minister is engaged and the rules governing the service as well as the *intention* of the parties must be taken account against the specific factual background. However, he still proceeded to consider the relationship between the pastor and the church, mainly with reference to the presumptions outlined in section 200A, despite his reference to numerous cases highlighting the importance of considering the specific merits and facts of each case to establish whether the parties did intend an employment relationship. In the specific circumstances it was clear from the facts that neither the pastor nor the church had the necessary and deliberate intention to enter into any legally binding contract, but these facts were ignored by the court *a quo*. The church relied heavily on the 2001 case of *Church of the Province* (discussed above). The court distinguished the earlier judgment in the *Church of the Province* case and noted that the case was decided before the introduction of section 200A of the LRA in 2002. In the *Church of the Province* case, an Anglican priest was suspended on grounds of misconduct after a disciplinary hearing. The CCMA declared the dismissal as unfair and the church took the case to the High Court, claiming that the CCMA made a mistake because the relationship between the church and the priest was not an employment relationship and that the CCMA therefore did not have the jurisdiction to decide the case. The court came to the conclusion that in order to establish an employment relationship there must be a contract of employment and as there was no legally enforceable contract between the parties, there was no employer and employee relationship between them. What was important in this case was that the arbitrator determined the issue on the assumption that there was a contract between the parties without determining whether that was the case and the court thus found that there was no *intention* to create an employment contract. The court *a quo* chose rather to rely on the *Schreuder* case (discussed above), where the court was of the view that the *intention* of the contract of employment was to create contractual duties in the form of an employment contract between the minister and his congregation. In the latter case, however, there was a clear *intention* to create a contract of employment, which was neither the case in *Church of the Province* nor in *Universal Church of the Kingdom of God*. The approach taken in *Church of the Province* is important for purposes of the argument in the Labour Appeal Court, where the church submitted that the only question relevant was whether the parties had the necessary *intention* to conclude any contract or to be bound by it and, if there was no such intention, that section 200A of the LRA did not apply. On appeal, Ndlovu JA took the view that, on a proper interpretation of section 200A as well as the code of good practice that came into force in 2006, both required the existence of an employment contract or some form of contractual arrangement, whether in writing or not and regardless of the form thereof. The Labour Appeal Court therefore proceeded to ask whether there was any legally enforceable agreement in place between the pastor and the church. From their conduct and the language used in the agreement, it was clear that the necessary intention (*animus contrahendi*) did not exist and the court correctly held that no contractual obligations existed between the pastor and the church. The appeal was upheld and the decision of the court *a quo* set aside. This case supports the view of the earlier decision in *Wagenaar* (discussed above), highlighting the conflicting views in both the *Schreuder* and *Church of the Province* cases and the fact that there seems to be no general rule in South Africa as to whether a Minister of Religion is an employee or not. The constitutional right to freedom of religion allows religious organisations and churches to give meaning to and to define the various positions in the church, including the position of minister according to their own religious views. Each case should therefore be judged on its own merits and facts. This view seems to be supported by the Labour Appeal Court in the case of *Universal Church of the Kingdom of God*.

Discrimination and the right of religious institutions to appoint office holders

Introduction

As outlined earlier, the right to freedom of religion includes the right of religious organisations to appoint their religious leaders in accordance with their own religious convictions. But what about the right to equality and non-discrimination and where a church refuses to appoint or ordain homosexual office holders based on their religious views. Are they allowed to discriminate? The issue of equality and non-discrimination in general, with reference to the case of Johan Strydom was discussed in Chapter 4. This section will briefly outline some of the difficult issues in relation to religious ministers in particular, when it comes to the right of religious organisations to appoint or not to appoint office holders. The issue of homosexuality will be used as an example, with reference to some of the mainline churches in South Africa.[28]

Religious beliefs vary widely around the question of the Bible and same-sex relationships and issues of homosexuality, gay priests and gay marriages. Although it has been stated that South Africa holds the most liberal attitude towards homosexuality on the continent, most churches in South Africa do not recognise same-sex marriages. Almost all the mainline Christian churches in South Africa recognise a marriage as only between a man and a woman and that marriage as an institution is reserved for heterosexual people only. These churches include: the Anglican Church of Southern Africa (ACSA), the Methodist Church of Southern Africa (MCSA) and the Dutch Reformed Church of South Africa (DRC). The KwaZulu-Natal Christian Council published a research document in 2015 on the topic of homosexuality in the main line churches in South Africa.[29] The research was based on the position within various main line churches in South Africa, including MCSA, the Evangelical Lutheran Church of Southern Africa (ELCSA), the Moravian Church of South Africa, the United Evangelical Lutheran Church of Southern Africa (UELCSA), DRC, ACSA, The Church of Jesus Christ of Latter-day Saints, the Baptist Union of Southern Africa (Baptist Church), the Roman Catholic Church, the Seventh-day Adventist (SDA) and the United Congregational Church of Southern Africa (UCCSA). From the responses received from the churches it was evident that almost all the denominations agree that it is sinful to discriminate against and persecute homosexual people, although they still take the view that marriage officers should not be compelled to act against their consciences or the principles of their religious bodies.

Denominations such as the Baptist Church, the Roman Catholic Church, The Church of Jesus Christ of Latter-day Saints, the Uniting Presbyterian Church and many others that are against homosexuality base their views on scripture and the definition of 'marriage' to mean a relationship or lifelong union between one man and one woman and ordained of God. Many of the denominations have indicated that they will not bless same-sex unions, although some churches, such as the Methodist and Anglican churches will provide loving support and care for same-sex couples. They also view homosexuality as incompatible with biblical teaching. Other denominations, such as the DRC and the UCCSA, are still debating and investigating the issue of homosexuality. The fact that homosexuality is open to debate is highly contested, and it is clear that in denominations such as the Catholics, Lutherans, SDA, Baptist Church and Moravians the issue of same-sex

28 This section is based on two earlier publications, and expanded on, in EH van Coller 'Homosexuality and the Churches: Controversies and Challenges' in P Coertzen (eds) *Religious Freedom and Religious Pluralism in Africa: Prospects and Limitations* (2016) 307–324; EH van Coller 'Homoseksuele Predikante: ´n Regs- en Morele Dilemma' *LitNet Akademies* (2013) 10(3) 678–706.

29 'Homosexuality in South Africa. Research on the Response of the Main Line Churches to Homosexuality in South Africa' *KwaZulu-Natal Christian Council* (7 August 2015).

marriages is not acceptable and that it is a closed debate. On the other hand, the Methodists, UCCSA and the DRC are open to debate, and they encourage spiritual leaders to engage in ongoing biblical and theological reflection and to assist religious leaders and members 'to cultivate attitudes and acquire skills that enable them to minister the grace of God to openly to homosexual persons'.[30]

In October 2018, the Southern Synod (church council) of the Uniting Reformed Church in Southern Africa (URCSA) took a decision that will permit gay marriage. After years of deliberation, they took the decision to ordain homosexual members and to marry them.[31] This decision came a mere month after the Anglican Diocese of Saldanha Bay became the first Diocese in Southern Africa to vote in favour of blessing same-sex couples in civil unions.[32] Important discussions have taken place around homosexuality in some South African churches that have dominated the news and media lately due to their views and decisions within the Church. They are the ACSA, but more particularly the DRC and the MCSA. The next section will outline some of discussions that have taken place.

Anglican Church

The ACSA continues to struggle with the issue of marriage equality. The official stance of the Anglican Church is that the church neither marries same-sex couples, nor ordains or licenses priests or deacons who live in same-sex unions. This view is in line with the practice of the worldwide Anglican Communion, and the General Synod of the church has adopted a resolution in which they state that they have accepted Resolution 1.10 of the Lambeth Conference 1998 as the basis for their engagement with the issues of human sexuality. According to this resolution, the church, in view of the teaching of scripture, upholds faithfulness in marriage between a man and a woman in lifelong union, and believes that abstinence is right for those who are not called to marriage. The church rejects homosexual practice as incompatible with scripture and cannot advise the legitimising or blessing of same -sex unions nor ordaining those involved in same-gender unions, but calls on all their people to minister pastorally and sensitively to all irrespective of sexual orientation. In the light of this resolution, the ASCA affirms the view that God calls them to love and minister to all people, regardless of their sexual orientation, while at the same time upholding God's standards of holiness.

The church indicated that they are committed to engaging in a process of listening to the whole variety of experiences and viewpoints so as to increase their understanding of these issues and to work towards finalising the Guidelines for pastoral ministry in response to civil unions as soon as possible. During the synod of the Diocese of Cape Town in July 2009, the bishops were requested to provide guidelines for the pastoral care of those in committed same-sex relationships. The Synod of Bishops of the ACSA confirmed in a statement of 9 September 2009 that 'Christian marriage is a lifelong union between one man and one woman … clergy unable to commit to another in a

30 *Ibid.*
31 N Daniels 'Church Backs Same-sex Couples' *Cape Times* (30 October 2018).
32 See further under the discussion relating to the Anglican Church.

Christian marriage partnership are called to a life of celibacy'.[33] Two years later, the Synod of Bishops of the ACSA drafted proposed pastoral guidelines for civil unions.[34] In the proposed pastoral guidelines, the ACSA aims to reflect upon the factors that they see as particularly shaping and guiding their pastoral response to issues relating to civil unions.

The ACSA, like many other denominations, are guided by scripture and their relevant church documents such as their Canons, the Book of Common Prayer and Anglican Prayer Book 1989, the Resolutions of Provincial Synod and Provincial Standing Committee, The Anglican Covenant and Statements of the Synod of Bishops. In relation to marriage and the church, the ACSA is guided by their church's teaching on the marriage of Christians, which is made clear in the Marriage Service in the Book of Common Prayer, the Anglican Prayer Book 1989 and in the Canons. Canon 34, 'Of Holy Matrimony', begins with this affirmation: 'The Church of the Province of Southern Africa affirms that marriage by divine institution is a lifelong and exclusive union partnership between one man and one woman'.[35]

The ACSA therefore affirms that the partnership between two persons of the same sex cannot be regarded as a marriage in the eyes of God, and that consequently they have not recognised such unions. According to their Canons, a licensed single or divorced cleric who wants to enter a civil union will not be permitted to retain their licence if they entered this union. The Canons further require such a person to remain celibate outside marriage. This also applies to an unlicensed cleric whose ordination is recognised as valid and who seeks a licence, but whom is already in a civil union. The Canons prescribe that such a person should not be licensed. Clergy are further not permitted to bless such unions, or, where they are state marriage officers, to conduct such unions.

Although a civil marriage between same sexes is not legal in any of the countries in the southern part of Africa, other than South Africa, the Anglican Church in the southern part of Africa has taken a small step towards accepting gay people in 'faithful, committed relationships'. The Anglican Diocese of Cape Town, which includes Anglican bishops from South Africa, Lesotho, Swaziland, Mozambique, Namibia, St Helena, Tristan da Cunha and Angola, passed a resolution in 2009, asking the church's bishops to provide pastoral guidelines for gay parishioners living in 'covenanted partnerships'.[36] However, the House of Bishops of the ACSA has still been unable to come to a common mind on the issue of gay blessings. According to an official statement by the Anglican Church of Southern Africa,[37] they accept the fact that they are not of one mind on the matters of

33 A Hunter 'Marriage, Proposed Pastoral Guidelines' *Discussion Document* (2 October 2015).

34 Synod of Bishops of the Anglican Church of Southern Africa 'Pastoral Guidelines in Response to Civil Unions within the Wider Contexts of Marriage and Human Sexuality' (2012).

35 *Pastoral Guidelines* 3.

36 'Church Makes Key Decision on Gay Couples' *IOL news* (23 August 2009).

37 'Anglican Church of Southern Africa considers Pastoral Response to Civil Unions' (Statement issued by the Office of the Anglican Archbishop of Cape Town) *Anglican News* (4 October 2013).

homosexuality, but the church has urged its bishops to provide guidelines for giving pastoral care to same-sex couples who have entered civil unions under South African law.

Early in 2016, Archbishop Thabo Makgoba stated that the Anglican bishops from across Southern Africa have resolved, through the adoption of guidelines, that gay and lesbian partners who enter same-sex civil unions under South African law should be welcomed into congregations as full members of the church.[38] However, these guidelines still do not provide for the baptism of children of same-sex couples and do not extend to that of marrying same-sex couples or allowing its clergy to enter them. In September 2016, the provincial synod of the ACSA, which is the church's top legislative body, voted against the introduction of blessing services for same-sex marriages. The church indicated that the matter could be taken up again at the next provincial synod in 2019 and at the next worldwide meeting of Anglican bishops in 2020.[39] As a result of this decision in 2016, Archbishop Thabo Makgoba began establishing a commission on human sexuality and the Synod bishops were asked to prepare a report on the issue. The mandate of the Commission is to present to Provincial Synod 2019 a proposal enabling the church 'to minister to those in same-sex unions and the LGBTI Community in the context in which ACSA operates in Southern Africa'.[40]

In October 2018, the Anglican Diocese of Saldanha Bay, who represents Anglicans in a large region ranging from the northern suburbs of Cape Town to the Namibian border, has taken the historic step of agreeing to bless same-sex couples. Members of the Diocese's synod overwhelmingly voted 104 to 4 in favour of praying and blessing same-sex couples in civil unions. This decision by the Saldanha Bay Diocese made it the first Diocese in the ACSA to take this step. However, their decision is still subject to approval by the Provincial Synod and the Diocese will only be able to officially start blessing same-sex couples until (and if) this is approved by the Anglican Church of Southern Africa. The ACSA will hold its next Provincial Synod in September 2019.[41]

Methodist Church of Southern Africa (MCSA)

The Methodist Church also does not recognise same-sex marriages and the discussion and engagement on issues of homosexuality within the Methodist Church has been going on for some time now. According to the church, it is incorrectly assumed that the church has no formal statement on homosexuality. In fact, the

38 'Anglican Church Says Yes to Homosexuals' *eNCA* (22 February 2016).

39 M Raborife 'Anglican Church Votes Against Blessings for Same-sex Couples' *News24* (30 September 2016).

40 See Pastoral Letter from the Synod of Bishops *Bishopscourt Media* (28 September 2017).

41 L DeBarros 'What Does the Saldanha Bay Diocese's Same-sex Union Decision Mean?' *Mambagirl News* (17 October 2018).

position on homosexuality within the MCSA has evolved over a number of years and various conference resolutions have been adopted on the issue. Already at the conference of 2001, the MCSA adopted a foundational principle in the same-sex debate, stating that they seek to be a community of love rather than rejection. At the conference of 2003, a discussion guide on Christians and same-sex relationships was adopted as a tool for the church's engagement on this issue, and was referred to the Methodist people for their study, comment and response. This discussion generated a robust debate and it became clear that there are widely divergent convictions on this issue within the MCSA, on the side of both clergy and laity. Following these different views and with a view of recognising the different convictions within the church, the MCSA committed itself at the Conference of 2005 'to an ongoing journey of discovering what it means to be part of a church which embraces many different and even opposing views on this issue'.[42] They also affirmed the view that the one body of the church is 'enriched and strengthened by the differing views and perspectives of its members'.[43] The Connexional Executive of 2006 reaffirmed the 2005 conference resolutions on the same-sex debate, and directed that 'until conference has pronounced on the matter, the MCSA continues to recognise marriage as only between a man and a woman, and urged ministers to refrain from officiating at same-sex unions'.[44] The conference of 2007 declared its determination not to permit different viewpoints around the same-sex debate to further divide the church, and sought 'a way forward that both respects and holds in tension differing views among our ministers and people'.[45] The conference further resolved that:

> any decision and subsequent action on the issue of civil unions between same-sex partners must await the outcome of the ongoing process of engagement as specified by Conference 2005 ... and, in the interim, expects Methodist ministers to continue to offer pastoral care to homosexual individuals.[46]

In accordance with the conference resolutions of 2011, the MCSA, in fact, has adopted a very clear position on this issue, which affirms the view of the 2001 conference in that the MCSA is seeking to be a community of love rather than rejection. The MCSA recognises the diversity of conviction within the church when it comes to same-sex relationships, and celebrates this diversity as a challenging but potentially life-giving gift. The church is also calling for an ongoing process of respectful dialogue and truthful engagement between those holding differing views – not with the intention of ultimately having one mind

42 Methodist Church of Southern Africa *Yearbook* (2006) para.8.3.
43 *Yearbook* (2006) para 8.5.5 (as per para 2.27, *yearbook* 2011).
44 *Yearbook* (2007) para 4 (as per para 2.27, *yearbook* 2011).
45 *Yearbook* (2008) para 2.5.1 (as per para 2.27, *yearbook* 2011).
46 *Yearbook* (2008) para 2.5.1.(vi) (as per para 2.27, *yearbook* 2011).

on this issue, which is unlikely, but rather to come to a deepened understanding of what it means to be the one body of Christ. The church also recognises its ongoing pastoral responsibility to homosexual people. What is clear from the views above is that the MCSA is a church with divergent convictions on this issue and that there is a current theological inconsistency within the MCSA, such that it allows this divergence of conviction to be held without the freedom for such divergence of conviction to be exercised. Discussions within the church on these issues are ongoing.[47]

However, these views and procedures adopted by the MCSA in relation to homosexuality ended up in a court battle with one of their own ministers. The MCSA suspended Ecclesia de Lange in January 2010 from her post at a Cape Town congregation after she entered into a same-sex marriage with her partner. She was accused of not adhering to 'the policy and practice of the church', in that she had breached Clause 4.82 of the Laws and Discipline (L&D) of the church by announcing her intention to enter into a same-sex civil union. The L&D is binding on the church, its ministers and its members. Clause 4.82 says that, 'Ministers shall observe and implement the provisions of the Laws and Discipline and all other policies, decisions, practices and usages of the Church'. She was further accused of violating certain sections of the 2008 year book, in particular Paragraph 2.5.1(vi):

> Any decision and subsequent action on the issue of civil unions between same-sex partners must await the outcome of the ongoing process of engagement as specified by Conference 2005 [...] and, in the interim, expects Methodist ministers to continue to offer pastoral care to homosexual individuals.[48]

The substance of the disciplinary charge was that the De Lange had defied the policies, decisions, practices and usages of the church that only recognise marriage between one man and one woman. She was found guilty by a District Disciplinary Committee. She appealed to the Connexional Disciplinary Committee who upheld the verdict and resolved that she be discontinued from the ministry of the church. She then instituted legal proceedings in the Western Cape High Court. The Western Cape High Court dismissed her case against the Methodist Church and ordered her to submit her case for arbitration. She was, however, granted leave to appeal to the Supreme Court of Appeal (SCA). The SCA dismissed her appeal in a unanimous judgment in *De Lange v Presiding Bishop, Methodist Church of Southern Africa*.[49] In so far as De Lange asked the SCA to declare that she had

47 'Any decision and subsequent action on the issue of civil unions between same-sex partners must await the outcome of the ongoing process of engagement as specified by Conference 2005 [...] and, in the interim, expects Methodist ministers to continue to offer pastoral care to homosexual individuals'. *Yearbook* (2011) chapter 2 para 2.27.

48 *Yearbook* (2008) para 2.5.1 (vi).

49 *De Lange v Presiding Bishop, Methodist Church of Southern Africa* 2015 (1) SA 106 (SCA).

been unfairly discriminated against, the SCA held that De Lange had failed to lay a factual basis in support of this claim in her papers before the Court and, in fact, had expressly abandoned this claim. The court thus did not have to decide this issue and, as a result, it was not necessary for the court to 'engage with the collision between the rights to freedom of association and religious freedom on the one hand, and the right to equality on the other'.[50] The SCA dismissed De Lange's appeal and she was granted leave to appeal to the Constitutional Court (CC).

In the Constitutional Court, De Lange argued that the church's reliance on the rule proscribing ministers from entering into same-sex marriages contravened her right to equality under the Constitution, which prohibits unfair discrimination based on marital status or sexual orientation. She further argued that arbitration was an inappropriate forum for the dispute, in light of her constitutional claims and because the arbitration process was biased and lacked practical effect. In a unanimous judgment written by Moseneke DCJ, the court found that since De Lange had unequivocally disavowed her unfair discrimination claim before the High Court, she could not now raise the claim for the first time on appeal. The court further concluded that the doctrine of constitutional subsidiarity requires that an unfair discrimination claim must be heard by the Equality Court first.[51] The court dismissed the appeal.

Dutch Reformed Church of South Africa (DRC)

The issue of allowing same-sex unions had been discussed in the DRC since the 1980s. In 2007, the church took significant steps when it changed its policy to include gay pastors. The 2007 decision reaffirmed the view that all people, irrespective of sexual orientation, are included in the love of God and are accepted as members of the church on the basis of their baptism and faith. The General Synod reaffirmed the decision that, based on scripture, a marriage is understood only as the union between one man and one woman and that homosexual unions are not accepted as an alternative to marriage. Paragraph 39.7 of the 2007 decision marked a significant departure from previous decisions in that, although it still recognised a marriage as only between a man and a woman, it allowed for gay theology students to be licensed and ordained, as long as they commit to a life of celibacy.[52] Section 39.8 went further to state that the General Synod recognises the discretion of individual congregations to deal with the different views on homosexuality '*in die gees van Christelike liefde*' (in the spirit

50 *De Lange* para 29.

51 *De Lange v Presiding Bishop of the Methodist Church of Southern Africa for the time being and Another* 2016 (2) SA 1 (CC) para 30.

52 According to Section 39.7 'Die verlening van predikantsbevoegdheid is ʹn funksie van die Algemene Sinode. Die Sinode besluit dat homoseksuele gelegitimeerdes wat ʹn selibate lewenstyl beoefen tot die predikantsamp toegelaat word'. [It is a function of the General Synod to license and ordain a Minister. The Synod decides that it will allow for gay theology students to be licensed and ordained, as long as they commit to a life of celibacy.]

of Christian love).[53] The General Synod affirmed the Bible as point of departure within this debate on homosexuality. In the beginning of October 2015, the debate took a surprising turn when a 64 per cent majority of the church's General Synod voted in favour of acknowledging same-sex marriages and having openly gay church members serve in the church, which had previously been forbidden. The DRC, as one of the mainstream churches in South Africa, became one of the first denominations to make this difficult decision.

The resolution[54] reconfirmed, as point of departure, the equality of all people irrespective of their sexual orientation and committed itself to maintaining the human dignity of all people. It declared that hetero- and homosexual persons who live in a personal, faith-obedient relationship with the Lord, could fully participate in all the privileges of the church as a covenant community. What is important to note is that the decisions of 2004, 2007 and 2013 concerning 'marriage' were reconfirmed in the 2015 synod – namely that only the union of one man and one woman is considered as a marriage. This view is in line with the church's previous views and that of the main denominations in South Africa. The important part of the resolution was the decision to give recognition to the status of civil unions between persons of the same sex that were characterised by love and fidelity and the provision for pastors who see their way open to solemnise such unions. The same Christian ethical standards would have applied to all persons with regard to licencing and ordination and gay pastors would no longer have been required to proof celibacy.

The same as in many other denominations, the General Synod acknowledged the diversity of opinions within the DRC concerning same-sex unions and therefore confirmed the right of church councils to formulate and exercise their own viewpoints and practices. In terms of this decision, local churches would have had the discretion not to allow same-sex unions and individual churches would not have been forced to follow the ruling. Church councils would have had the discretion to deal with different opinions concerning same-sex relationships in a congregation in a spirit of Christian love. It has been stated that: 'Church councils and congregations are like families. They will eventually decide how they will go about it. They know the context, they know the situation, they know about the faith of these people, so they can decide on that'.[55]

Unfortunately, at an extraordinary meeting of the General Synod in November 2016, the DRC reversed its 2015 decision to allow the recognition of same-sex unions. The church reaffirmed its view that marriage was instituted by God as a

53 Dutch Reformed Church of South Africa 'Agenda, Part III of the 13th meeting of the General Synod of the DRC' (June 2007) 204–205 paras 12.2 & 12.3. The 2007 decision was taken on the basis of recommendations by the task team on homosexuality and referred to a commission consisting of ten moderators of the different synods.

54 Dutch Reformed Church of South Africa 'Resolution of the General Synod' (9 October 2015).

55 'Dutch Reformed Church to Recognise Gay Marriage, South Africa' *eNCA* (20 October 2015).

sacred and lifelong union between one man and one woman and that any sexual intercourse outside such a solid formal marital relationship does not meet Christian guidelines. The effect of the 2016 decision is that a gay or lesbian person can only be a minister in the DRC if he or she is celibate, and ministers are not permitted to solemnise same-sex civil unions.

DRC Minister and gay activist Laurie Gaum, together with other concerned LGBT members of the church, brought a legal challenge against this decision in the Pretoria High Court, wanting the 2016 decision set aside and declared unconstitutional, from both a procedural and a substantive point of view. The applicants argued that the church did not follow the correct procedures when they made the decision and the decision should thus not stand due to procedural misconduct. From a substantive point, they argued that the decision violated their right to equality and that the decision constituted discrimination on the basis of sexual orientation. On this point, although the church accepted the discrimination, they argued that it constitute fair discrimination in the light of the right to freedom of religion. A full bench (Judges Raulinga, Potterill and Molefe) of the Pretoria High Court heard the case on 21 August 2018 in the case of *Gaum vs Dutch Reformed Church of South Africa*.[56] In *Gaum*, the court was confronted with two main arguments, one procedural and one substantive in nature. In relation to the procedural aspect, the applicants argued that the 2016 decision was procedurally flawed and that the church did not follow its own rules, set out in the Church Order. They therefore argued that the decision was invalid. On the basis that the church did not explicitly set aside the 2015 decision, when they adopted the 2016 decision, the court found that the church acted contrary to church practice. The decision was accordingly set aside.

Interestingly, the court proceeded to deal with the substantive issues, although strictly speaking, the 2016 decision, which the applicants argued to be discriminatory, has already been set aside by the court. The court was of the view that 'although the matter should end herewith, the parties requested the court to decide the substantive issue'.[57] This might also be a reason why the judgment on the substantive issues were flawed in numerous respects (all of which will not be argued here). It was almost as if the court decided that any further comments or arguments by the court in relation to the substantive issues would be made *obiter dictum*, and would not have any further effect in relation to the decision that has already been set aside. This approach was very unfortunate.

On the substantive issues, the applicants argued that the 2016 decision unfairly discriminated against gays and lesbians on the basis of sexual orientation and that it therefore violated section 9(3) of the Constitution (the right to equality). The court found that it was unfair to exclude members of the church from the full and equal enjoyment of all rights and freedoms that the church offers. Although the church accepted that the 2016 decision constituted discrimination on the basis of

56 *Gaum and Others v Van Rensburg NO and Others* (40819/17) [2019] ZAGPPHC 52 (8 March 2019).

57 *Gaum* para 61.

sexual orientation, they did not discharge the onus of proving that the discrimination was in fact fair, neither did they put up any argument suggesting that their conduct can be justified under the limitation clause. Similar to the approach taken in the *Strydom* case, discussed in Chapter 4, where the DRC did not discharge the onus that rested on them to prove to the court that a particular function of the church was a religious function, this is again an example where the church did not prepare a proper argument to justify their decision and did not learn from their mistakes. According to the court:

> Gaum is correct that in the opposition to the application the Church has set out no facts as to why the discrimination is fair. … Parties must not have a *laisse fair* attitude to opposition in these matters, trusting argument will save them.[58]

In possible future cases dealing with similar issues, a court could find in favour of the church, provided that they engage in a proper balancing of rights exercise, and the church presents a well-structured argument, supported by its followers, which was clearly not the case in *Gaum*. According to De Vos:[59]

> Although the court did not clearly make this argument, I suspect the reason why it was easy for the court in the *Gaum* case to rule that the Dutch Reformed Church had unfairly discriminated against gays and lesbians is because the actions of the church itself made it clear that the church was conflicted about the issue and that it did not hold a particularly strong *religiously-inspired* view that its religious doctrine required it to discriminate against gays and lesbians.

Although the DRC has indicated that they have decided not to the appeal the court's ruling, the judgment, particularly on the substantive issues, may pose a severe threat to the autonomy of churches and religious institutions in South Africa. Although it does not compel all churches in South Africa to marry gay couples, it creates a dangerous precedent and the approach taken by the court departed quite substantially from established case law on this point. One can just hope that any future dispute of a similar nature will be better argued by a court of higher standing, such as the Supreme Court of Appeal, or ideally the Constitutional Court.

58 *Gaum* para 69.

59 P de Vos 'Why Court ruled against Dutch Reformed Church in Same-sex Marriage case and what it may mean for other Churches who Discriminate Against Gays and Lesbians' Constitutionally Speaking Blog (12 March 2019). Online at: https://constitutionallyspeaking.co.za/why-court-ruled-against-dutch-reformed-church-in-same-sex-marriage-case-and-what-it-may-mean-for-other-churches-who-discriminate-against-gays-and-lesbians/.

Chaplaincies

Access to institutions such as schools, universities, hospitals, prisons and the armed forces are often provided for in the form of chaplaincies and is an important task performed by various church and religious leaders. Rivers[60] describes a chaplaincy as 'a position held by a minister of religion within an organization or institution in order to provide spiritual services to its members or inmates'. In relation to educational institutions, ministers of religion are allowed access to schools to take part in religious activities, such as religious instruction or religious observances in public schools,[61] provided that it is done in accordance with legislative requirements and in consultation with the particular institution. Religious communities often use school facilities for religious observances or religious instruction classes. Legislation allows public schools to make their facilities available to religious communities for such purposes. Where schools do make their facilities available to religious communities, this must be done in a way that is fair and equitable to all communities that apply. The policy on religion and education also allows for religious observances to be held during school times at events officially organised by the school, such as visits by different religious miniseries during school assembly or special prayer gatherings. This is a form of chaplain services provided to educational institutions by religious ministers. Chaplain services are further often associated with institutions where religious leaders offer spiritual guidance to a restricted community, whose members might find it difficult to access the service normally provided, particularly prisons, military facilities or hospitals.

International Law contains detailed regulations for the provision of chaplaincies under the Geneva Convention and the various protocols. South Africa enacted the Implementation of the Geneva Conventions Act 8 of 2012 in order to enact the Conventions into law as is required by section 231(4) of the Constitution. An example of chaplain services is found in the Geneva Convention for the amelioration of the condition of the wounded and sick in armed forces in the field of 12 August 1949. Numerous references are made to chaplains. Article 24 states for instance that chaplains attached to the armed forces shall be respected and protected in all circumstances and shall not be deemed prisoners of war (sec 28). The Geneva Convention Relative to the Treatment of Prisoners of War of 12 August 1949 (Third Convention) states that chaplains must be granted all facilities necessary to provide for the religious ministration to prisoners of war.[62] Prisoners of war are also entitled to be granted complete latitude in the exercise of their religious duties, including attendance at the service of their faith.[63] Article 35 allows for chaplains who fall into the hands of the enemy power and who remain or are retained with a view to assisting prisoners of war, to minister to them and to exercise freely their ministry among prisoners of war of the same religion. Prisoners of war who are ministers of religion shall be at liberty to minister freely

60 J Rivers *The Law of Organized Religions* (2010) 207.
61 See Chapter 6.
62 Article 33.
63 Article 34.

to the members of their community.[64] The Additional Protocols also contains provisions aimed at enhancing the protection of chaplains and other religious personnel.

On a domestic level, the Defence Act 42 of 2002 provides for religious observance in the Defence Force. The Minister may, subject to section 31 of the Constitution, determine the rules and related policies for religious observance in the Defence Force in consultation with the Chief of the Defence Force. In South Africa, the first national military force was established in 1912. No provisions were made for chaplains in the Union Defence Forces (UDF) and chaplain services were provided by civilian clergy.[65] With the outbreak of the First World War, South Africa joined the Allied forces. Chaplains were appointed in Simon's Town on 16 August 1916, which were recorded as the official founding of the military chaplaincy in South Africa, although no formal structure was created. Formal recognition for the chaplaincies was given when the South African Corps of Chaplains was established in 1946, though the South African Government Proclamation 204 of 18 October 1946.[66] With the start of the new constitutional dispensation, two policy documents were implemented: the Defence White Paper of 1996 and the Defence Review of 1997. When the then Minister of Defence, Joe Modise, presented the White Paper on Defence to Parliament on 8 May 1996, he envisaged that:

> In accordance with the Constitution, the SANDF shall promote freedom of religion and shall cater for the different religious views of its members on an inter-denominational basis. Religious observances shall be conducted on an equitable basis, and attendance at such observances shall be free and voluntary. The Chaplains Service shall regulate religious policy and practice in accordance with departmental policy and in consultation with the Religious Advisory Boards which represent different faiths.[67]

In terms of these policies, chaplains were assigned to different units and religious observances were conducted on an equitable and interdenominational basis, similar to the approach advocated for religious observances in public schools. Observances were thus also voluntary, although attendance of

64 Article 36.

65 I Bredenkamp and A Wessels 'A Historical Perspective on Military Chaplaincy Services in the South African National Defence Force (SANDF), 1998–2012' *Journal on Contemporary History* (2012) 37(2) 244.

66 Bredenkamp & Wessels 2012 *Journal on Contemporary History* 245.

67 According to the drafting memorandum, online at: www.gov.za/documents/nationa l- defence-white-paper. For some views on the Defence White Paper and the Defence Review, see further J Winkates 'The Transformation of the South African National Defence Force: A Good Beginning' *Armed Forces & Society* (2000) 26(3) 455–469; L Nathan 'The 1996 Defence White Paper: An Agenda for State Demilitarisation?' in J Cock and P Mckenzie (eds) *From Defence to Development* (1989) 41–57; G Shelton and C Alden 'Brave New World: The Transformation of the South African Military' Comparative Strategy (1998) 17: 346 and further.

chaplains' hours remained compulsory.[68] Different faith groups were represented, including different Christian denominations, and chaplains from the Muslim, Hindu and Jewish faith. With the establishment of the South African National Defence Force (SANDF), chaplain services were expanded to include other religious denominations, such as the African churches, which resulted in a much broader and inclusive religious diversity. Maj Gen (Rev) FFS Gqiba of the Anglican Church took office as the first black Chaplain General in South Africa on 1 October 1998.[69] Currently, the Chaplain Service renders a ministry to soldiers and their families and chaplains provide spiritual leadership, ethical guidance and social support to members of the SANDF. According to its mission statement:

> The Chaplains Service representing a cross-section of the religious communities in SA, provides spiritual leadership to DOD members at home and on deployment in order to build human capacity that enhances spiritual, ethical and human wholeness. It does so within the context of religious diversity, taking cognisance of the transformation imperatives of the DOD and in support of democratic peace-building in Africa.[70]

A similar position exists currently in relation to chaplaincies in the Department of Correctional Services, where there was a shift from a mainly Christian-dominated approach to a more multi-religious approach to spiritual services. The Correctional Services Act 111 of 1998 provides for the establishment, functions and control of the Department of Correctional Services. The Act contains several provisions relating to religion and belief. A prisoner must be allowed freedom of conscience, religion, thought, belief and opinion.[71] The Act also states that a prisoner may attend religious services and meetings held in the prison, provided that it is free and voluntary and no prisoner may thus be compelled to attend religious services or meetings or to take part in religious practices. Prisoners are also allowed to have religious literature in their possession.[72] Where practicable, places of worship must also be provided at every prison for prisoners of all religious denominations.[73] Section 13(2) of the Act requires that the Department must give prisoners the opportunity of communicating with and being visited by their chosen religious counsellor. In 2012, the Correctional Services Regulations with amendments incorporated[74] was promulgated, that also provide that subject to prescriptions, an inmate may be allowed to wear certain attire or dress for religious or cultural

68 Bredenkamp & Wessels 2012 *Journal on Contemporary History* 246.
69 Bredenkamp & Wessels 2012 *Journal on Contemporary History* 244.
70 See www.chaplain.mil.za/about.html.
71 Section 14(1).
72 Section 14(2).
73 Section 14(3).
74 GNR.323 of 25 April 2012: Promulgation of Correctional Services Regulations with amendments incorporated (Government Gazette No. 35277).

purposes.[75] Certain accommodations for work on Sundays or other religious days of rest may also be granted, as prescribed.[76]

One of the directorates in the Department of Corrections is the spiritual care directorate. Chaplaincies falls under this directorate and are also referred to as spiritual care managers. The chaplaincy component of the spiritual care services is responsible for providing spiritual care to offenders under the supervision of the Department of Corrections, in partnership with churches, religious institutions and other faith-based and community organisations. The Department also drafted a spiritual care policy to assist the Department in rendering effective spiritual care services to offenders. The policy outlines 15 principles that are important in relation to the religious rights of inmates.[77] These principles emphasis the rights of offenders to freedom of conscience, religion, belief and opinion. Religious tolerance should be respected and no offender shall be discriminated against on the basis of his religion. This also means that the spiritual practices of offenders, as a manifestation of religious beliefs, should be respected. Every church/faith shall be granted the opportunity to minister/care to the spiritual care of its members or adherents in correctional facilities, provided that participation in these spiritual care programmes should be voluntary.

Conclusion

This chapter has outlined some important but also difficult issues associated with the position of a religious leader, whether it is related to their appointment or the tasks they performed. For any party, including a religious minster, a contract of employment is necessary for purposes of establishing an employment relationship in order to be subject to the relevant labour laws. If no such employment relationship exists, the court will have no jurisdiction to entertain a dispute in terms of labour law. The right to freedom of religion, as contained in the Constitution, further allows religious organisations and churches to give meaning to and to define the various positions in the church, including the position of ministers according to their own religious views. With reference to the different views within various denominations and some case examples, it is clear that there is no general rule as to whether a Minister of Religion is an employee or not. Different denominations have different teachings and ideologies and each individual case should therefore be judged on its own merits and facts. The courts must be sensitive to the *sui generis* nature of churches and should not impose specific legal or labour relationship onto churches if it is in conflict with their own religious views.

75 Regulation section 5(2).

76 Regulation section 23(6)(a).

77 Spiritual Care Policy (Spiritual Care Directorate, Department of Correctional services: Pretoria), as quoted from M Mkhathini 'A Critical Analysis of the Chaplaincy in the South African Department of Correctional Services after 1994' (PHD, Faculty of Theology, University of Pretoria, 2016). See a discussion of the various principles on 74–81.

This section has further outlined the complexity of the issue of homosexuality, particularly in relation to the appointment of religious leaders. These are difficult issues, not only in the DRC, the ACSA and the MCSA, but within faith communities throughout the world and in almost every denomination. The majority of organised religions in South Africa differentiate between people in some way or another on many different grounds, including gender, sex, conscience, belief and sexual orientation. There is a need for religious organisations and religious leaders to be involved in an ongoing processes of engagement and to reflect on issues of homosexuality, in the light of religious, moral and constitutional values. Religious leaders must be empowered to engage with issues of diversity and religious pluralism, through their ministry and chaplaincy.

Bibliography

'Anglican Church of Southern Africa Considers Pastoral Response to Civil Unions' (Statement issued by the Office of the Anglican Archbishop of Cape Town) *Anglican News* (4 October 2013). Online at: www.anglicannews.org/news/2013/10/anglican-church-of-southern-africa-considers-pastoral-response-to-civil-unions.aspx.

'Anglican Church Says Yes to Homosexuals' *eNCA* (22 February 2016). Online at: www.enca.com/south-africa/anglican-church-says-yes-homosexuals.

Bredenkamp I and A Wessels 'A Historical Perspective on Military Chaplaincy Services in the South African National Defence Force (SANDF), 1998–2012' *Journal on Contemporary History* (2012) 37(2) 242–267.

'Church Makes Key Decision on Gay Couples' *IOL news* (23 August 2009). Online at: www.iol.co.za/news/south-africa/church-makes-key-decision-on-gay-couples-456065.

Daniels N 'Church Backs Same-sex Couples' *Cape Times* (30 October 2018).

DeBarros L 'What Does the Saldanha Bay Diocese's Same-sex Union Decision Mean?' *Mambagirl News* (17 October 2018). Online at: www.mambaonline.com/2018/10/17/what-does-the-saldanha-bay-dioceses-same-sex-union-vote-mean/.

De Vos P 'Why Court ruled against Dutch Reformed Church in Same-sex Marriage case and what it may mean for other Churches who Discriminate Against Gays and Lesbians' *Constitutionally Speaking Blog* (12 March 2019). Online at: https://constitutionallyspeaking.co.za/why-court-ruled-against-dutch-reformed-church-in-same-sex-marriage-case-and-what-it-may-mean-for-other-churches-who-discriminate-against-gays-and-lesbians.

Dutch Reformed Church of South Africa *Resolution of the General Synod* (9 October 2015). Online at: www.kaapkerk.ac.za.

'Dutch Reformed Church to Recognise Gay Marriage, South Africa' *eNCA* (20 October 2015). Online at: www.enca.com/south-africa/dutch-reformed-church-recognise-gay-marriage.

Dutch Reformed Church of South Africa *Agenda, Part III of the 13th meeting of the General Synod of the DRC* (June 2007) 204–205 paras 12.2 & 12.3.

GNR 323 of 25 April 2012: Promulgation of Correctional Services Regulations with amendments incorporated (*Government Gazette* No. 35277).

KwaZulu-Natal Christian Council 'Homosexuality in South Africa. Research on the Response of the Main Line Churches to Homosexuality in South Africa' (7 August 2015). Online at: http://kzncc.org.za/homosexuality-in-south-africa.

Hunter A *Marriage, Proposed Pastoral Guidelines* (Discussion Document) (2 October 2015).

Methodist Church of Southern Africa *Yearbook* (2006); (2011).

Mkhathini M *A Critical Analysis of the Chaplaincy in the South African Department of Correctional Services after 1994* (PHD, Faculty of Theology, University of Pretoria, 2016).

Nathan L 'The 1996 Defence White Paper: An Agenda for State Demilitarisation?' in J Cock and P Mckenzie (eds) *From Defence to Development* (1989) 41–57South Africa: David Philip Publishers.

*Pastoral Letter from the Synod of Bishops*Bishopscourt Media (28 September 2017). Online at: https://anglicanchurchsa.org/pastoral-letter-from-the-synod-of-bishops-september-2017/.

Raborife M 'Anglican Church Votes Against Blessings for Same-sex Couples' *News24* (30 September 2016). Online at: www.news24.com/SouthAfrica/News/anglican-church-votes-against-blessings-for-same-sex-couples-20160930.

Rivers J *The Law of Organized Religions* (2010) London: Oxford University Press.

Shelton G and C Alden 'Brave New World: The Transformation of the South African Military' *Comparative Strategy* (1998) 17346.

Smit J 'Die Beroepsbrief in die Gereformeerde Kerke in Suid-Afrika – ´n Kontraktuele Werksaanbod?' *In die Skriflig* (2007) 586.

Smit J and D Du Plooy 'Reëling van die Gereformeerde Predikant se Diens – ´n Arbeidsregtelike of ´n Interne Kerklike Aangeleentheid?' *In die Skriflig* (2008) 61.

Synod of Bishops of the Anglican Church of Southern Africa *Pastoral Guidelines in Response to Civil Unions within the Wider Contexts of Marriage and Human Sexuality* (2012). Online at: http://anglicanchurchsa.org.

Van Coller EH 'Homosexuality and the Churches: Controversies and Challenges' in P Coertzen (eds) *Religious Freedom and Religious Pluralism in Africa: Prospects and Limitations* (2016) 307–324. Stellenbosch: SUN media.

Van Coller EH ''n Regsvergelykende Blik op die Diensverhouding van 'n Predikant' *Dutch Reformed Theological Journal/Nederduits Gereformeerde Teologiese Tydskrif (NGTT)* (2013) 54(3,4) 1–14.

Van Coller EH 'Homoseksuele Predikante: 'n Regs- en Morele Dilemma' *LitNet Akademies* (2013) 10(3) 678.

Van Coller EH 'Religious Ministers – Working for God or Working for the Church? A Reflection on Universal Church of the Kingdom of God v Myeni and Others' *Oxford Journal of Law and Religion* (2017) 6(1) 187–193.

Winkates J 'The Transformation of the South African National Defence Force: A Good Beginning' *Armed Forces & Society* (2000) 26(3) 455–469.

11 Other religious exemptions and reasonable accommodation for religious practices

Introduction

Section 2.2 of the Religious Charter states that every person has the right to have their convictions reasonably accommodated. A broad and inclusive approach to religious freedom acknowledges the plural and multi-religious nature of the South African society, and promotes not the mere tolerance, but a reasonable accommodation of all views and convictions in society. In certain circumstances, laws should allow for religious exemptions, in cases where something is contrary to a person or institutions' religious beliefs. According to Lenta,[1] religious exemptions refer to:

> exemptions from facially neutral laws of general application (that is to say, laws that do not intentionally target religious believers for adverse treatment) granted on the grounds that such laws impose a burden on certain religious believers that is not brought to bear on other citizens. This burden arises because the laws in question require (sometimes as a condition of their receiving a benefit or availing themselves of some opportunity) that religious believers act in a way that is inconsistent with their religious beliefs or refrain from engaging in practices motivated by such beliefs.

Religious exemptions in various contexts have been discussed throughout various chapters in this book, in for instance the context of education, marriage laws, religious dress and other religious manifestations. The Constitutional Court has also extensively dealt with religious exemptions in cases such as *Pillay, Christian Education* and *Prince*. In relation to the right to manifest a religion as part of the right to freedom of religion, South African courts[2] have adopted a subjective test for determining whether conduct constitutes a manifestation of religion that needs to be protected. This test protects any conduct based on sincerely held religious beliefs and does not necessarily require those relying on the right to freedom of religion to prove that the conduct is an objective requirement of their religion.

1 P Lenta 'Is there a Right to Religious Exemptions?' *South African Law Journal* (2012) 129 304.
2 See for instance *MEC for Education, KwaZulu-Natal v Pillay* 2008 1 SA 474 (CC).

However, it must be a sincere belief and not just a personal preference. In *Christian Education South Africa v Minister of Education*, the Constitutional Court held that individuals have no automatic right to be exempt from generally applicable laws on the basis of religious beliefs.[3] A court can refuse a claim for an exemption where the legislation serves an important interest. In *Christian Education*, an association of private schools claimed an exemption from legislation prohibiting corporal punishment from being administered in schools on the basis that it infringed their right to freedom of religion. They refused the claim for exemption because the legislation was found to serve an important interest, namely the protection of children from abuse.[4] Similarly, in the *Prince* case, the Constitutional Court refused to grant an exemption when a Rastafarian requested an exemption from drug legislation to allow him to use dagga as part of his religious observance.

Where members of religious groups claim religious exemptions from general laws or regulations, it is often very difficult for decision-makers to know how to deal with such claims. In order to ascertain whether there is room for an exemption, Lenta[5] proposes that it is necessary to interrogate the reasons for having the rule or provision in the first place and then to determine whether the objectives which the rule or provision is intended to achieve will be frustrated by allowing for an accommodation. If a female Muslim employee wishes to wear a headscarf in the workplace, which goes against the employer's dress code, it only seems fair that there should be an accommodation to permit Muslim women to wear headscarves in the workplace, unless the law or regulation is so compelling as to rule out an accommodation. This may be in the case of safety or where it violates other's rights or places an undue hardship on an employee or for severe practical difficulties.

This chapter will briefly discuss some other examples of reasonable accommodation that has not been discussed under any of the other sections. Although some of the examples may relate to individual claims of religious accommodation, it may also be of importance to religious communities and their members. On a more private level, the chapter will look at reasonable accommodation in relation to abortion and the compulsory prevention or treatment of disease. One a more public level, the last section will look at reasonable accommodation in relation to the taking of an oath and military service.

Abortion

In the context of abortion, religious objections to performing abortions has been described as a legal right:

3 *Christian Education South Africa v Minister of Education* 2000 (4) SA 757 (CC) 779 para 35.

4 *Christian Education South Africa* 785–786 para 50.

5 Lenta 2012 *South African Law Journal* 299.

> where an individual otherwise has a duty to comply with a legally sanctioned obligation, such as being conscripted into active military service, taking a religious oath before legal proceedings or performing a certain healthcare procedure such as an abortion, but feels the duty is unethical. If performing the duty affronts the individual's genuinely held beliefs in a critical way, whether the beliefs are moral, religious or nonreligious, political or non-political, refusing to comply with the duty can be legally justified. Recognition of the right to conscientious objection serves to absolve the conscientious objector from performing the legal duty.[6]

Objections can thus be on religious or conscientious belief grounds. This is in line with section 15 of the Constitution that guarantees the right to freedom of conscience, religion, thought, belief and opinion. Reasonable accommodation in relation to the solemnisation of same-sex marriages have been discussed under the section dealing with Marriage, where it was shown that specific legislation, in the form of the Civil Unions Act (although not without criticism), exempt civil marriage officials from refusing to solemnising same-sex marriages on the grounds of conscience, religion and belief. However, this exemption has now been repealed by the Civil Union Amendment Bill, 2018 and only religious marriage officers are now exempt from solemnising same-sex marriages. There is no express exemption available in terms of the Choice on Termination of Pregnancy Act 92 of 1996 available to a public health worker refusing to assist a woman to terminate her pregnancy. This has been criticised as it 'brings to light the lack of a consistent (or principled?) approach to conscientious objection in South Africa'.[7] The Choice on Termination of Pregnancy Act was enacted to set out the circumstances in which and conditions under which the pregnancy of a woman may be terminated. It replaced the previous law on abortion as contained in the Abortion and Sterilization Act of 1975. A shortcoming with the Choice on Termination of Pregnancy Act, is that it is silent about the right to religious or conscientious objection. It is argued that this was not an oversight on the part of government, since the draft clause did in fact recognise the right to conscientious objection, subject to certain conditions. The draft bill specifically contained the following provisions:

> 1 Subject to subsection (2), no person shall be under a legal duty, whether by contract or any statutory or any other legal requirement, to participate in the termination of a pregnancy if he or she has a conscientious objection to termination of pregnancy.

6 C Ngwena 'Conscientious Objection to Abortion and Accommodating Women's Reproductive Health Rights: Reflections on a Decision of the Constitutional Court of Colombia from an African Regional Human Rights Perspective' *Journal of African Law* (2014) 58(2) 200.

7 See H Kruuse 'Conscientious Objection to Performing Same-Sex Marriage in South Africa' *International Journal of Law, Policy and the Family* (2014) 28 (2) 156.

> 2 The provisions of subsection (1) shall not affect any duty to participate in treatment which is necessary to save the life or to prevent serious injury to the health of the woman, or to alleviate pain.
> 3 Any person having an objection referred to in subsection (1) shall be obliged to refer a woman who wants her pregnancy to be terminated to a medical practitioner or a registered midwife, as the case may be, who shall terminate the pregnancy.

The bill was criticised as being unreasonable and unjustifiable in relation to the right to conscientious objection. In terms of the bill, the right to conscientious objection could not be invoked if attending to the pregnant woman was necessary to 'save the life or to prevent serious injury to the health of the woman or to alleviate pain'. The section also imposed a duty on a conscientious objector to refer the person to another healthcare professional if they invoked this right. As a result of this, government decided to omit the conscience clause.[8] Consequently, it was left to the Constitution to fill this omission and to be implicitly governed by section 15 of the South African Constitution, which implicitly accommodates the right to conscientious objection to abortion.[9] Ngwena[10] is of the view that the absence of clear guidelines addressing conscientious objection undermines the efficacy of the Act. He further submits that:

> It was a mistake for the Choice on Termination of Pregnancy Act to omit to provide for conscientious objection and set out the principles for determining its limits. Clear guidance would have served to reassure the proponents of conscientious objection to abortion, as well as the women wishing to access abortion services that their rights are acknowledged and protected. As the Act stands, it does not provide guidance on the exercise of conscientious objection.[11]

As part of the right to religious accommodation, the Religious Charter envisages that every person should have the right on the ground of their convictions to refuse to deliver, or to refer for, certain services, including medical or related (including pharmaceutical) services or procedures.[12] In practice, it may allow a medical practitioner to refuse to do abortions on religious grounds. The Charter also envisages the right of refusal to refer a patient. However, section 6 of the Act requires that a woman who requests a termination of pregnancy from a medical practitioner or a registered midwife, *shall* be informed of her rights under this Act by the person concerned. This may include that she is told of referral options, as the case may be. However, since the Act is not clear on whether it is compulsory

8 C Ngwena 'Conscientious Objection and Legal Abortion in South Africa: Delineating the Parameters' *Journal for Juridical Science* (2003) 28(1) 1–18.
9 Ngwena 2003 *Journal for Juridical Science* 4.
10 Ngwena 2014 *Journal of African Law* 194.
11 Ngwena 2003 *Journal for Juridical Science* 16.
12 Religious Charter section 2.3(b).

for medical practitioners to refer patients, it creates further confusion. Ngwena further argues that the right to conscientious objection is intended to protect the personal convictions of those who actually perform an abortion procedure and not personnel who merely assist or facilitate such a procedure.[13]

According to the World Health Organisation (WHO), conscientious objection by healthcare providers without referrals is one of the major barriers for many women seeking abortion services in public facilities in South Africa. Invoking religious or conscientious objection grounds, healthcare providers often refuse to provide abortion services. As a result of clear guidelines in the legislation, conscientious objection has remained largely unregulated and is often applied in an ad hoc manner. This creates the problem of a shortage of health facilities offering abortion services.[14] In relation to emergency medical treatment, section 27 of the Constitution may be invoked, stating that no one may be refused emergency medical treatment. Thus, Ngwena argues that 'conscientious objection cannot be invoked in an emergency or where there is no alternative healthcare provider, as failure to render treatment would pose a risk to the life of the pregnant women or would seriously endanger her health'.[15]

When healthcare professionals invoke the right to conscientious objection, they must ensure that the right is exercised in a manner that accommodates the rights of women seeking abortion services, also to ensure that substantive equality is achieved.[16] The state must ensure that abortion services are adequate and accessible. Healthcare facilities can assist conscientious objectors by setting up, for example, access to services that do not implicate those opposed on religious or conscientious belief grounds. Facilities can also provide patients with contact numbers of those who do not object to certain procedures, or create a call line or centre where a patient can be assisted or referred, in order to relieve the conscientious objector from the duty of information or referral.

Compulsory prevention or treatment of disease

Receiving or withholding medical treatment is a sensitive issue and is often related to people's religious convictions. Because of religious reasons, some individuals object to certain measures for preventing disease, such as vaccinations or inoculation. Often patients object to certain or any forms of medical treatment, such as blood transfusions, on the ground that such measures are contrary to the prescription of their religion or belief. This is particularly the case with Jehovah's Witnesses.[17] This not merely an individually held belief, but a belief held by the religious community as a whole. Where there is the likelihood of a disease that can

13 Ngwena 2014 *Journal of African Law* 201.

14 N Godi 'Strengthening Referrals: Step One to Addressing the Challenges of Conscientious Objection in Abortion Services' *Daily Maverick* (6 June 2018).

15 Ngwena 2014 *Journal of African Law* 203.

16 *Ibid.*

17 See for instance D Knapp van Bogaert and GA Ogunbanjo 'Jehovah's Witnesses and the New Blood Transfusion Rules' *South African Family Practice* (2013) 55(1) 6–9.

endanger the welfare of the community and where it is in the public interest, government can decide not to exempt members of any particular faith from the required medical treatment or measures.

The acceptance of blood transfusions by Jehovah's Witnesses is believed to be against God's will and therefore they refuse them. Section 12 of the Constitution guarantees everyone the right to bodily integrity and autonomy.[18] Read together with the right to freedom of religion, an adult member of the Jehovah's Witnesses should be entitled to refuse a life-saving blood transfusion, even if solely on religious grounds. A medical practitioner should thus respect the wishes of the patient. However, despite the wishes of the patient to refuse a blood transfusion, a medical practitioner may not refuse to treat such patient during a medical emergency and should proceed with the treatment, without administering blood.[19]

Section 7 of the National Health Act 61 of 2003 deals with consent and provides that a health service may not be provided to any person without their informed consent. Where an adult Jehovah's Witness is therefore unable to give informed consent to administer a blood transfusion, the section provides that a person who had been mandated by the patient, in writing, may give the necessary consent on behalf of the patient. Under the Health Professions Act, the Health Professions Council of South Africa (HPCSA) has published guidelines for Good Practice in the Health Care Professions that sets out the principles of good practice which all healthcare practitioners are expected to follow when seeking patient's informed consent to investigations, treatment, screening or research. In terms of these guidelines, any patient, including a Jehovah's Witness patient, can indicate their treatment preferences, in an advance statement or directive, in which the patient can set out the wish to receive a blood transfusion.[20]

In relation to children, the position is somewhat different. Section 28(2) of the Constitution states that a child's best interests are of paramount importance concerning the child. Section 27(3) further states that no one may be refused emergency medical treatment. Where parents refuse to consent to medical treatment, such as a blood transfusion, for their child, a doctor can approach the court as the guardian of minor children to overrule the parent's refusal. In the case of *Hay v B*,[21] the court held that a refusal by parents to consent to a life-saving blood transfusion for a minor child, on the grounds of religion, is unconstitutional and unlawful. In *Hay*, Dr Hay, a paediatrician, had applied to the court for an order authorising her to administer a blood transfusion to an infant against the wishes of the parents. The parents opposed the administration of the blood transfusion on the grounds that the acceptance of a blood transfusion was contrary to their religious beliefs. The court emphasised the importance of the best interests of the child and indicated that

18 The right to bodily and psychological integrity includes the right to make decisions concerning reproduction; to security in and control over their body; and not to be subjected to medical or scientific experiments without their informed consent.

19 See N Caine and K Zybrands 'The Challenges of Treating Jehovah's Witnesses' *Casebook* (2014) 22(2) 10–11.

20 *Ibid.*

21 *Hay v B* 2003 (3) SA 492 (W).

'this is the single most important factor to be considered when balancing or weighing competing rights and interests concerning children'.[22]

According to the court:

> I respect their private religious beliefs. However, in the present matter, the evidence establishes that their beliefs negate the essential content of the right in question. The applicant is adamant that baby R's best chance of survival would be by the immediate administration of a blood transfusion. The first and second respondents' concerns are understandable. However, they are neither reasonable nor justifiable. Their private beliefs cannot override baby R's right to life.[23]

The court consequently was of the view that the interests of the baby in receiving the blood transfusion outweighed the reasons advanced by the parents in opposing the administration of such transfusion. The effect of this judgment is that during a medical emergency, parents may not withhold their consent to a blood transfusion solely for religious reasons. This will violate a child's constitutional rights and, in terms of a balancing exercise, such a limitation might not be reasonable and justifiable in terms of the Constitution. McQuoid-Mason[24] argues that doctors should therefore regard such a refusal of consent as unlawful and that in these circumstances, the common law rules regarding emergency medical treatment should apply. In terms of the common law, medical treatment may be given without the necessary consent of the patient. This must be in emergency situations and provided that it does not go against the consent of the patient.

This case was, however, heard before the Children's Act 38 Of 2005 came into force. The Children's Act strengthens the requirement set out in Section 28(2) of the Constitution in that the best interests of a child are paramount in all decisions regarding children. Therefore, if a parent refuses to consent to a blood transfusion, a similar approach as advocated by McQuoid-Mason will apply. If the refusal is based solely on religious grounds, the medical practitioner may, in terms of the Children's Act, ignore such refusal and administer the blood transfusion, unless the parent can show that there is a medically accepted alternative choice available. In the absence of an emergency and where a medical practitioner disagrees with the parents' suggestions' for alternative treatments, a court should make that decision.[25]

A similar scenario came before the court in *Life Healthcare Group (Pty) Ltd and Another v JMS (as parent and guardian of the infant child MT) and Another*.[26] In

22 *Hay v B* para 494I.
23 *Hay v B* para 494C-D.
24 D McQuoid-Mason 'Parental Refusal of Blood Transfusions for Minor Children Solely on Religious Grounds — the Doctor's Dilemma Resolved' *SAMJ Forum* (2005) 95(1) 29.
25 Cane & Zybrands 2014 *Casebook* 11.
26 *Life Healthcare Group (Pty) Ltd and Another v JMS (as parent and guardian of the infant child MT) and Another* (34758/2014) [2014] ZAGPJHC 299 (20 October 2014).

this case, a young boy was admitted to a hospital for treatment. Dr Moodley, a paediatric lung specialist, was one of the medical professionals treating him. The boy's parents objected to a blood transfusion because of religious reasons and wanted to explore all alternatives to blood transfusion. However, his condition did not improve, and Dr Moodley approached the court for an order authorising her to administer a blood transfusion to the boy, should he require it. The court had to balance the child's right to life and to have his best interests inform all decisions concerning the child against the parents' right to religion. With reference to the case of *Christian Education South Africa v Minister of Education*,[27] the court held that:

> Courts throughout the world have shown special solitude for protecting children from what they have regarded as the potentially injurious consequences of their parents religious practices. It is now widely accepted that in every matter concerning the child, the child's best interest must be of paramount importance.

In granting the order, the court held that the limitation that the blood transfusion imposes on the parents' right to religion is justified by section 36 of the Constitution and that the parents' refusal to consent to blood transfusion for the child was unlawful.[28] Just recently, two more Jehovah's Witness families have been taken to the KZN High Court in Durban to force them to allow doctors to administer life-saving blood to their seriously ill children. One of the paediatricians argued:

> In as much as one respects the religious beliefs of the parents they are regrettably not acting in his best interests by not consenting to a blood transfusion which could save the minor child's life.[29]

Krishnaswami[30] has argued that it might be impossible to formulate a rule of general applicability in relation to the issue of refusing medical treatment based on religious views. Generally, according to him, 'it would be conceded that where an individual's refusal of scientific medical treatment, or his resort to unscientific treatment, endangers his life, public authorities may intervene just as they would intervene to prevent an individual from taking his own life'. Although parents also have the right to freedom of religion, our courts have held that such rights are superseded by a child's right to life in cases where the child's life is at risk. In South Africa, 'refusals of blood transfusions during medical emergencies for minor

27 *Christian Education South Africa* para 41.
28 *Life Healthcare Group* paras 15, 16.
29 See N Nair 'Three Jehovah's Witness Families Taken to Court to Save Children's Lives' *Times Live* (5 December 2018); N Nair 'Blood Transfusions are "not in the Bible", Father Tells Court' *Times Live* (5 December 2018).
30 A Krishnaswami *Study of Discrimination in the Matter of Religious Rights and Practices* 45.

children by parents solely on religious grounds are unlawful'.[31] However, the religious views of adults, who can give informed consent, should be respected. This is confirmed by the Religious Charter that emphasises the rights of every person to have their convictions taken into account in receiving or withholding medical treatment.[32] Any claim for an exemption should always be carefully balanced against the competing state interest. Religious followers will not be allowed to rely on their religious beliefs to infringe on the rights of others or important societal goals.

Taking of an oath

As a general rule evidence in court or similar proceedings is inadmissible unless the witness testifies under oath. The form of the oath is prescribed through legislation and where a witness objects to taking an oath, they are often allowed to make a solemn affirmation that he or she will speak the truth. Such an affirmation has the same legal force and effect as an oath, and there can be no refuge behind differences of religion. In relation to civil proceedings, part VII of the Civil Proceedings Evidence Act 25 of 1965 deals with oaths and affirmations. A witness in civil proceedings is permitted to take an oath in the form that most clearly conveys to him or her the meaning of the oath and which the witness considers to be binding on his or her conscience.[33] Provision has been made for persons with conscientious objections to taking the oath to make an affirmation instead.[34] An affirmation will be in the following words: 'I do truly affirm and declare that'. In terms of section 41, the taking of an oath is dispensed with altogether where the person concerned is found not to understand the nature or to recognise the religious obligation of an oath and his ignorance is shown to have arisen from youth, defective education or any other cause.

In criminal matters, the Criminal Procedure Act 51 of 1977 applies. Unlike in civil proceedings, it does not provide the same neutrality in allowing a witness to take an oath in the form that most clearly conveys to him or her the meaning of the oath and which the witness considers to be binding on his or her conscience. Rather, the Criminal Procedure Act made allowance for the Christian form of the oath only. A witness in criminal proceedings can only be examined if he is under oath, and in terms of section 162 states: 'I swear that the evidence that I shall give, shall be the truth, the whole truth and nothing but the truth, so help me God'. However, section 163[35] provides that witnesses who object to the taking of

31 McQuoid-Mason 2005 *SAMJ Forum* 30.
32 Religious Charter section 2.4.
33 As per section 39(2) of the Act.
34 In accordance with section 40.
35 '163 Affirmation in lieu of oath (1) Any person who is or may be required to take the oath and- (a) who objects to taking the oath; (b) who objects to taking the oath in the prescribed form; (c) who does not consider the oath in the prescribed form to be binding on his conscience; or (d) who informs the presiding judge or, as the case may be, the presiding judicial officer, that he has no religious belief or that the taking of

the oath in the prescribed form may make an affirmation in lieu of the oath. In terms of section 164, in cases where the witness, from ignorance arising from youth, defective education or any other cause, does not understand the nature and import of the oath or affirmation, he or she may be admitted to give evidence without taking the oath or making the affirmation. Similar provisions apply in relation to proceedings in the small claims court. The Constitution further provides for the taking of an oath or an affirmation in various instances. Before various officers (including members of the various assemblies and councils, ministers, judicial officers and so forth) take office, they must swear or affirm faithfulness to the Republic and obedience to the Constitution, in accordance with Schedule 2 of the Constitution. This can be in the form of an oath or an affirmation.

In conclusion it may be said that as a general rule no one should be compelled to take an oath contrary to the prescriptions of his religion or belief.

Military service

Under the Religious Charter, every person should have the right on the grounds of their convictions to refuse to perform certain duties, or to participate or indirectly to assist in, certain activities, such as of a military or educational nature.[36] Prior to the current Defence Act 42 of 2002, the Defence Act 44 of 1957 consolidated the law relating to the defence of South Africa. This Act had very specific provisions relating to religious objection to military service, and a few cases also came before the courts. Section 72A of the 1957 Defence Act, as amended, authorised the Minister of Manpower to appoint one or more boards for conscientious objection (to consider applications in terms of section 72B). In terms of section 72B, any person called up under the provisions of this Act to render service in the South African Defence Force could apply to the board to be classified in terms of section 72D as a conscientious objector. However, the section excluded a person who had committed himself voluntarily to any service in the South African Defence Force. Section 72D set out the different categories of conscientious objectors in terms of which an applicant could apply. Section 72D (1A) made it clear that the Board would not grant an application and classify an applicant as a conscientious objector, unless the board was satisfied that:

> (a) the applicant has conscientious objection to render military service or undergo military training under this Act;
> (b) the conscientious objection is based on moral, ethical or religious grounds and corresponds to the particulars in the application of the applicant;
> (c) the applicant's conscientious objection is sincere and deep-rooted; and

the oath is contrary to his religious belief, shall make an affirmation in the following words in lieu of the oath and at the direction of the presiding judicial officer or, in the case of a superior court, the presiding judge or the registrar of the court: "I solemnly affirm that the evidence that I shall give, shall be the truth, the whole truth and nothing but the truth".'

36 Religious Charter section 2.3(a).

> (d) the applicant's conscience does not permit him conduct, or support for conduct, which is in conflict with the reasons and grounds for his application and that he condemns crime and the pursuit or furtherance of any form of criminal violence and anarchy in or against any community or person.

In *S v Färber*,[37] the accused had been a member of the Jehovah Witnesses since 1974. When he registered for his military service, he indicated his religious affiliation as that of the Jehovah Witnesses. In accordance with section 126A of the Defence Act 44 of 1957, any person liable to render service in terms of the Act when called up to do so and refuses to render such service in the South African Defence Force, or fails to report therefor, shall be guilty of an offence. As a conscientious objector, the accused failed to report for commando duty and he had been convicted in the Magistrate's Court of failing to report for commando duty and was sentenced to 18 months' detention. However, the Act was amended and section 72B was inserted by section 9 of the Defence Amendment Act 34 of 1983, allowing someone to be classified as a religious objector. Conscientious objectors who refused to render service in the South African Defence Force were in terms of the amendments to the Defence Act no longer regarded as offenders. He took the case on review and the court held that the charge sheet in the Magistrate's Court had been incorrectly formulated in that account had not been taken of the 1983 amendments to the Defence Act. The accused had, in any event, after being called up, addressed to the commanding officer of his unit a letter, which amounted in effect to an application for exemption from further military service based on his religious objections thereto. The court, after discussing the implications and effect of the amendments to the Defence Act brought about by Act 34 of 1983, set aside the conviction and sentence.

In the case of *Hartman v Chairman, Board for Religious Objection*,[38] the applicant, a follower of Theravada Buddhism, applied in terms of s 72B(1) of the Defence Act 44 of 1957, as amended, for classification as a religious objector in terms of s 72D(1)(a)(ii) of the said Act, as:

> a religious objector with whose religious convictions it is in conflict to render any military service or to undergo any military training or to perform any task in or in connection with any armed force.

The Board for Religious Objection refused his application on the grounds that the applicant was not eligible for classification as a religious objector. He then approached the court for relief. The issue before the court was whether Theravada Buddhism, a non-theistic tradition of Buddhism, qualified as a religious conviction within the meaning of section 72. The Board was of the view that the words

37 *S v Färber* 1985 (1) SA 340 (O).

38 *Hartman v Chairman, Board for Religious Objection, and others* 1987 (1) SA 922 (O).

'religious conviction' as used in section 72D(1) should be interpreted as presupposing:

> a belief in a Supreme Being or Beings of a divine nature whose precepts are to be obeyed and actual service of and obedience to such Being or Beings in accordance with the tenets of the particular faith adhered to by the particular applicant and/or with the dictates of the personal convictions of such applicant.[39]

In the course of its judgment, the court noted that when the legislature enacted the relevant religious objection provisions of the Defence Act, they surely took note of the diversity of faiths and religions in South Africa, by acknowledging 'the recognition and protection of freedom of faith and worship'. In their view, the legislature did definitely not intend to ignore the 'sensibilities of persons who have espoused the tenets of the Buddhist faith, be it the Theravada tradition or the Mahajana branch, both of which are recognised world religions'.[40] On the assumption that the legislature was aware that Buddhism was regarded as one of the great religions of the world, even though the Theravada tradition was non-theistic, the court was of the view that 'I therefore regard it as unlikely that the Legislature intended to treat persons of one recognised religion differently from adherents of another recognised religion'.[41] The court concluded that the term 'religious convictions' included convictions based on a recognised non-theistic religion such as Theravada Buddhism and that the applicant was, accordingly, eligible for classification as a religious objector.

With the enactment of the Interim Constitution, the various statutory and non-statutory armed forces were consolidated and it provided for the establishment of the National Defence Force as the only defence force for the Republic. The 1996 Constitution left this position unaltered. In accordance with section 199 of the 1996 Constitution, the security services of the Republic consist of a single defence force, a single police service and any intelligence services established in terms of the Constitution. The defence force is the only lawful military force in the Republic and, as in the case of other security services, the defence force must be structured and regulated by national legislation, which is the Defence Act 42 of 2002. This Act provides for a defence force that consists entirely of volunteers.[42]

The Act provides for Exemption Boards, whose function it is to hear applications by members of the Regular Force or the Reserve Force for their exemption from or the deferment of the whole or any part of their training or service, as the case may be. Applications for exemption are made in accordance with section 67 and section 68 (4)(a)(vi) provides that an Exemption Board may grant an

39 *Hartman* para 942B.
40 *Hartman* para 931G-I.
41 *Hartman* para 932C-G.
42 JA Faris 'Defence' in WA Joubert and M Kuhne (eds) *LAWSA* 3 ed (2017) 13(2) para 139.

application on any justifiable ground, including that it should be granted on the grounds that the person concerned is a conscientious objector. The Act defines conscientious objection as 'an objection, against the rendering of military service or against participating in a military operation, on grounds of conscience based on compelling religious, ethical or moral beliefs'. It is thus clear that in terms of the Defence Act, the right to object to performing military or related services based on religious and conscientious objections is reasonably accommodated in the Act. Any religious objector can thus approach an Exemption Board established in terms of the Defence Act, in order to apply for religious or conscientious exemption.

Conclusion

Although there is no absolute right in all circumstances to observe one's religion, as has been illustrated in various contexts, religious freedom guarantees at least the right to have one's beliefs reasonably accommodated. Private and public institutions should create the scope within which individual believers or religious institutions can exercise their religious beliefs in a reasonable way.

The right to religious or conscientious objection, like any other fundamental right under the Constitution, is subject to the limitation clause. In relation to abortion, a balance must be struck between the interests of the healthcare worker to refuse to perform an abortion and the rights of the pregnant woman, taking into account the interests of society. Saving the life and preventing serious damage to the health of a pregnant women may serve as a legitimate limitation to the right to religious or conscientious objection. In relation to medical treatment, a refusal to consent to medical treatment on religious grounds, such as a blood transfusion, should always be balanced against the need to preserve life, particularly in the case of medical emergencies. What would be a reasonable accommodation of someone's religious rights has to be determined on the particular facts and contexts of each case. In a plural and multi-religious society, everyone should exercise their religious beliefs and convictions in a reasonable manner, with due regard to the rights of others. In order to rely on the reasonable accommodation of religious rights, religious institutions equally owe a duty of reasonable accommodation to those who may disagree with their religious views and practices.

Bibliography

Caine N and K Zybrands 'The Challenges of Treating Jehovah's Witnesses' *Casebook* (2014) 22(2) 10–11.

Faris JA 'Defence' in WA Joubert and M Kuhne (eds) *LAWSA*3 ed (2017) 13(2) para 139, South Africa: LexisNexis.

Godi N 'Strengthening Referrals: Step One to Addressing the challenges of Conscientious Objection in Abortion Services' *Daily Maverick* (6 June 2018).

Knapp Van Bogaert D and GA Ogunbanjo 'Jehovah's Witnesses and the New Blood Transfusion Rules' *South African Family Practice* (2013) 55(1) 6–9.

Krishnaswami A *Study of Discrimination in the Matter of Religious Rights and Practices* (1960) New York: United Nations Publication.

Kruuse H 'Conscientious Objection to Performing Same-Sex Marriage in South Africa' *International Journal of Law, Policy and the Family* (2014) 28(2) 156.

Lenta P 'Is there a Right to Religious Exemptions?' *South African Law Journal* (2012) 124 (2) 303–329.

McQuoid-Mason D 'Parental Refusal of Blood Transfusions for Minor Children Solely on Religious Grounds — the Doctor's Dilemma Resolved' *SAMJ Forum* (2005) 95(1) 29–30.

Nair N 'Blood Transfusions are "not in the Bible", Father Tells Court' *Times Live* (5 December 2018).

Nair N 'Three Jehovah's Witness Families Taken to Court to Save Children's Lives' *Times Live* (5 December 2018).

Ngwena C 'Conscientious Objection and Legal Abortion in South Africa: Delineating the Parameters' *Journal for Juridical Science* (2003) 28(1) 1–18.

Ngwena C 'Conscientious Objection to Abortion and Accommodating Women's Reproductive Health Rights: Reflections on a Decision of the Constitutional Court of Colombia from an African Regional Human Rights Perspective' *Journal of African Law* (2014) 58(2) 183–209.

12 Concluding remarks

For religious communities, it is particularly important that the right to believe includes the right to manifest those beliefs everywhere, also in the public sphere. According to Malherbe,[1] it is 'unnatural, impracticable and untenable' to restrict this freedom, and to ban religion from the public domain. He argues further that it is 'ultimately extremely illiberal and intolerant. Instead, the South African society is realistic, broad-minded and tolerant'. In the preceding chapters it has become clear that the degree of government regulation and interference into the affairs of religious institutions remain a complex issue. For religious institutions to function effectively in society, 'some degree of recognition of religious law and deference towards it by State courts is essential'.[2] Rivers[3] argues that in civil society we expect to find areas of exclusive religious self-government, as we also expect areas of exclusive state government. In the areas where they overlap, we find 'jointly acceptable regulation', where the extent of legitimate government regulation must be determined.

The review of the South African law and various examples in the preceding chapters suggest that it shows a commitment to religious autonomy, particularly with the dawn of the new democracy and the constitutional entrenchment of religious freedom. This is particularly apparent in relation to the issues outlined in the earlier chapters, including the recognition of the legal status of religious institutions, autonomy in relation to membership requirements and internal discipline. It is also apparent in terms of numerous religious exemptions provided for in legislation (in instances such as religious rituals, religious observances in schools, religious dress and recognition of religious marriages). However, in numerous areas, religious practices also affect other rights and can have both religious and secular significance (circumcision, religion in public institutions, ritual slaughter). This requires collaboration between various stakeholders and mutual compromise between state and religious communities.

Unfortunately, the later chapters have also outlined various developments in the last couple of years, aimed at an erosion of religious autonomy in various fields.

1 R Malherbe 'Religion in School' *NGTT* (2013) 54(4) 9.
2 J Rivers *The Law of Organized Religions* 335.
3 Rivers *The Law of Organized Religions* 337.

The extension of aspects of labour law, particularly the definition of an employee, have rendered religious appointments subject to government laws. Although religious ministers are still given the choice or not to solemnise a civil union, this is no longer the case with designated marriage officers who are civil servants. In terms of the new Civil Union Amendment Bill that was adopted by Parliament in November 2018, they may no longer object on the grounds of conscience, religion and belief in respect of solemnising same-sex civil unions, as was the case under section 6 of the Civil Union Act, which has now been repealed. Recent recommendations by the South African Revenue Service (SARS) that religious institutions should pay income tax, also points towards greater government scrutiny.

What has further emerged from the preceding chapters is reference to concepts such as neutrality, impartiality, tolerance and respect in relation to religious rights. In *Ryland v Edros*[4] the court emphasised two important values entrenched in our Constitution: the value of equality, but also the value of 'tolerance and accommodation'.[5] Farlam J supports this view when he further emphasises the importance of the values of 'equality and tolerance of diversity and the recognition of the plural nature of our society'.[6] These values are of great importance to religious communities in South Africa, both in asserting their religious rights, but also when their respective religious rights and convictions come in conflict with others.

In an European context, the European Court of Human Rights often refers to states' duty of 'neutrality and impartiality',[7] which is closely associated with 'the preservation of public order in a tolerant and pluralistic society, that is, with the legitimacy of the State'.[8] Various international law instruments refer to tolerance and respect as justification for religious freedom.[9] The United Nations Declaration on the Elimination of All Forms of Intolerance and of Discrimination Based on Religion or Belief[10] stresses the importance of promoting understanding, tolerance and respect in matters relating to freedom of religion or belief. In the UK, legislative drafters often base proposed legislation on religious tolerance, which they describe as 'an important and vital part of our society'.[11] In the South Africa context, section 185 of the Constitution establishes the Commission for the Promotion and Protection of the Rights of Cultural, Religious and Linguistic Communities, with the primary object of promoting and developing peace, friendship, humanity, tolerance and national unity among cultural, religious and linguistic communities, on the basis of equality, non-discrimination and free association.

4 *Ryland v Edros* 1997 (2) SA 690 (CC).
5 See *Ryland v Edros* para 707 H–708 I. Trengove refers to ten important constitutional principles as a manifestation of these two important values.
6 *Ryland v Edros* 708 para H.
7 See Chapter 4 with reference to *Metropolitan Church of Bessarabia v. Moldova* [2001] ECHR para. 123 .
8 Rivers *The Law of Organized Religions* 340.
9 See further N Doe N and A Jeremy 'Justification for Religious Autonomy' in R O'Dair and A Lewis (eds) *Law and Religion: Current Legal Issues* (2001) 4 423.
10 Proclaimed by General Assembly resolution 36/55 of 25 November 1981.
11 Doe & Jeremy *Law and Religion* 424.

The Religious Charter[12] also refers to issues of tolerance, but we find very little reference, in particular to religious tolerance, in other legislation. In developing legislation, government must pay attention to issues of equity, tolerance and diversity. This means respect for everyone's diverse religious traditions and advancing 'interreligious toleration and interpersonal respect among adherents of different religious or secular worldviews in a shared civil society'.[13] Legislation should give expression to the values of tolerance and respect for religion. In relation to 'tolerance' and 'the right to be different', the Constitutional Court in the words of Sachs J noted:

> Given our dictatorial past in which those in power sought incessantly to command the behaviour, beliefs and taste of all in society, it is no accident that the right to be different has emerged as one of the most treasured aspects of our new constitutional order. Some problems might by their very nature contain intractable elements. Thus, no amount of formal constitutional analysis can in itself resolve the problem of balancing matters of faith against matters of public interest. Yet faith and public interest overlap and intertwine in the need to protect tolerance as a constitutional virtue and respect for diversity and openness as a constitutional principle. Religious tolerance is accordingly not only important to those individuals who are saved from having to make excruciating choices between their beliefs and the law. It is deeply meaningful to all of us because religion and belief matter, and because living in an open society matters.[14]

The South African Constitutional Court[15] further confirmed the view that the Constitution requires the community to affirm and reasonably accommodate difference, not merely to tolerate it as a last resort. According to the court:

> The protection of voluntary as well as obligatory practices also conforms to the Constitution's commitment to affirming diversity. It is a commitment that is totally in accord with this nation's decisive break from its history of intolerance and exclusion. Differentiating between mandatory and voluntary practices does not celebrate or affirm diversity, it simply permits it. That falls short of our constitutional project which not only affirms diversity, but promotes

12 The Preamble Religious Charter recognises that the recognition and effective protection of the rights of religious communities and institutions will contribute to a spirit of mutual respect and tolerance among the people of South Africa. It states further in section 9.1 that 'every religious institution has the right in accordance with the principles of tolerance, fairness, openness and accountability to regulate its own internal affairs'.

13 Religion in Education Policy.

14 *Prince v President, Cape Law Society and Others* 2002 (2) SA 794 (CC) para 170.

15 See for instance *MEC for Education, KwaZulu-Natal and Others v Pillay* 2008 (1) SA 474 (CC)

> and celebrates it. We cannot celebrate diversity by permitting it only when no other option remains.[16]

According to Du Plessis, our Constitution was designed to impress tolerance among South Africans. He differentiates between passive tolerance and affirmative tolerance. The former means that people put up with each other, while the latter means something more. In terms of affirmative tolerance, people make an effort to understand, accept and appreciate one another. According to him 'the latter form is worth striving for, but a minimum, basic (albeit passive) tolerance is preferable to no tolerance at all'.[17] It was further held in *Minister of Home Affairs and Another v Fourie*:[18]

> The acknowledgment and acceptance of difference is particularly important in our country where for centuries group membership based on supposed biological characteristics such as skin colour has been the express basis of advantage and disadvantage. South Africans come in all shapes and sizes. The development of an active rather than a purely formal sense of enjoying a common citizenship depends on recognising and accepting people with all their differences, as they are. The Constitution thus acknowledges the variability of human beings (genetic and socio-cultural), affirms the right to be different, and celebrates the diversity of the nation. (Footnotes omitted.)[19]

Smith[20] contends that society's real choice is between tolerance and intolerance and that tolerance that attempts to give proper respect and scope to the claims of both political community and individual freedom is the only reasonable alternative to intolerance. The South African Constitutional Court in *MEC for Education, KwaZulu-Natal v Pillay*[21] appears to have followed this reasoning in what it described as 'reasonable accommodation'. The court states:

> At its core … the notion that sometimes the community, whether it is the State, an employer or a school, must take positive measures and possibly incur

16 *Pillay* para 60.
17 L du Plessis 'Freedom of or Freedom from Religion? An Overview of Issues Pertinent to the Constitutional Protection of Religious Rights and Freedom in "the New South Africa"' *Brigham Young Law Review* (2001) 442.
18 *Minister of Home Affairs and Another v Fourie and Another* 2006 (1) SA 524 (CC).
19 *Fourie* para 60.
20 SD Smith 'The Restoration of Tolerance' *California Law Review* (1990) 78: 305; See also H Cheadle and D Davis *South African Constitutional Law: The Bill of Rights* (2002) 210. 'Accommodating the variety of religions in this country would, however, be in accordance with the fundamental commitments of the Constitution to diversity and equality.' See further J Raz *The Morality of Freedom* (1986) 401–402; J Newman 'The Idea of Religious Tolerance' (1978) *American Philosophical Quarterly* 15(3) 187–195.
21 *MEC for Education, KwaZulu-Natal and Others v Pillay* 2008 (1) SA 474 (CC); See also *SACTWU v Berg River Textiles* [2012] JOL 28114 (LC).

> additional hardship or expense in order to allow people to participate and enjoy all their rights equally. It ensures that we do not relegate people to the margins of society because they do not or cannot conform to certain social norms.[22]

Cheadle[23] further takes the view that 'accommodating the variety of religions in this country would, however, be in accordance with the fundamental commitments of the Constitution to diversity and equality'. In relation to equality, Lenta[24] sees liberal multiculturalists' views on equality, in relation to the protection and accommodation of cultural and religious practices, as a principle that should take into account the different beliefs, values and commitments of the religious. Supporters of this version of equality, according to him, 'insist that uniformity of treatment should sometimes give way to accommodate the claims of members of religious minorities'.[25] This approach to equality is very different from the approach taken by the French Republic when they decided to ban the Muslim veil and all religious symbols from the public domain. Such an approach taken by the French is one that requires the 'suppression of difference and the expression of human sameness',[26] rather than accommodating difference. In *S v Lawrence*,[27] Justice O'Regan referred to the concept of even-handedness in relation to religious conviction, by stating:

> In my view, the requirements of the Constitution require more from the legislature than that it refrain from coercion. It requires in addition that the legislature refrain from favoring one religion over others. Fairness and evenhandedness in relation to diverse religions is a necessary component of freedom of religion.[28]

This approach taken by O'Regan J has been described as an approach 'conducive to the promotion of religious tolerance'. And further:

> Putting up with (often esoteric) manifestations of religious beliefs is not the hallmark of tolerating religious eccentricities. In political terms, a state's evenhanded treatment of divergent religious convictions and the realization of these convictions and their effects in societal life probably does more to evidence (and enhance) positive tolerance.[29]

22 *Pillay* para 73.
23 Cheadle & Davis *The Bill of Rights* 210.
24 P Lenta 'Muslim Headscarves in the Workplace and Schools' *South African Law Journal* (2007) 124(2) 297–298.
25 Lenta 2007 *South African Law Journal* 298.
26 See further Rivers *The Law of Organized Religions* 341.
27 *S v Lawrence; S v Negal; S v Solberg* 1997 10 BCLR 1348 (CC).
28 *S v Lawrence* para 128.
29 Du Plessis 2001 *Brigham Young Law Review* 453.

Does an accommodating, tolerant and even-handed approach to religious rights and convictions mean that there should be no government scrutiny of religious affairs? Certainly not, but within limits. The right to freedom of religion provides religious communities with the opportunity, but also the responsibility, not only to give content to this right, but also to formulate and defend their own religious identity within the limitations set by the Constitution and the law. Laws, procedures and administrative practices must be clear and generally available to those affected thereby. They must serve as regulatory measures but also provide guidance and information to religious communities and its members. These laws and procedures must further give content to the fundamental rights set out in the Constitution. Du Plessis[30] is of the view that religious groups in South Africa 'must yet learn to organize themselves for the purpose of asserting their rights under the Constitution which so generously protects them'. Religious groups and communities must assert their rights and take their concerns to court, if not able to resolve them through other means. In order to do that, religious communities must also know their rights and the legal remedies and avenues available to them. These include, but are not limited to, the common law, national legislation, local government by-laws, customary law, constitutional provisions, international law and examples of cases decide by various courts.

The role of public authorities in relation to religious freedom and the religious rights of communities, can be expressed as follows:

> Firstly, public authorities must themselves refrain from making any adverse distinctions against, or giving undue preference to, individuals or groups of individuals with regard to this right. Secondly, they must prevent any individual, or group of individuals, from making such adverse distinctions or giving such undue preferences. They may discharge these duties through the adoption of appropriate legal provisions of a preventive or remedial character — including, when necessary, penal sanctions — as well as by administrative action. In addition, they should make every effort to educate public opinion to an acceptance of the principle of non- discrimination in respect of the right to freedom of thought, conscience and religion, and to create proper leadership for this purpose.[31]

Proper leadership is essential, and here the CRL Rights Commission can play a crucial role. Instead of seeking to create more legislation, the Commission can assist religious communities by educating and informing them of their legal and constitutional rights and creating awareness of existing laws and regulations. Section 185 of the Constitution states that the functions of the CRL Rights Commission are to: (i) promote respect for the rights of cultural, religious and linguistic communities; (ii) promote and develop peace, friendship, humanity,

30 Du Plessis 2001 *Brigham Young Law Review* 464.

31 A Krishnaswami *Study of Discrimination in the Matter of Religious Rights and Practices* 53–54.

tolerance and national unity among cultural, religious and linguistic communities, on the basis of equality, non-discrimination and free association; (iii) recommend the establishment or recognition, in accordance with national legislation, of a cultural or other councils for communities in South Africa. Especially in the absence of proper processes or procedures, the Commission can play an important role. Section 185 (iv) emphasises the function of the Commission to monitor, investigate, research, educate, lobby, advise and report on issues concerning the rights of cultural, religious and linguistic communities.[32] In terms of section 5 of the CRL Act, the Commission may also facilitate the resolution of friction between and within cultural, religious and linguistic communities, receive and deal with requests related to the rights of cultural, religious and linguistic communities, and further make recommendations to the appropriate organ of state regarding legislation that impacts the rights of cultural, religious and linguistic communities. Therefore, the Commission can also act as a mediating body when religious disputes arise and assist religious institutions and members to report religious abuses to the appropriate bodies. The Commission may also establish and maintain databases of cultural, religious and linguistic community organisations and institutions. The educational and informative role of the CRL Rights Commission can particularly assist the poorer religious communities in the remote and rural areas of South Africa, where people are potentially more vulnerable to exploitation and abuse by religious leaders.[33] In its draft report, the Commission accepts this responsibility, by stating:

> Although religious organizations exist as voluntary organizations; the CRL Rights Commission should provide essential assistance in helping organizations to get their house in order and to ensure compliance with existing legislation and propose new legislation.[34]

Apart from the CRL Rights Commission, several other self-regulating organisations exist. One such organisation is the South African Council of Churches (SACC), an inter-denominational forum that unites 36 member churches and organisations. According to its vision:

> The SACC works for moral reconstruction in South Africa, focusing on issues of justice, reconciliation, integrity of creation and the eradication of poverty

32 Sections 4 and 5 of the Commission for the Promotion and Protection of The Rights of Cultural, Religious and Linguistic Communities Act 19 of 2002 repeat these notions.

33 Comments on the CRL Rights Commission's Report on the 'Commercialisation' of Religion, submitted by Freedom of Religion South Africa (FOR SA) and the South African Council for the Protection and Promotion of Religious Rights and Freedoms (28 February 2017) 62.

34 Draft Report 'An investigative Study of the Commercialisation of Religion in the Republic of South Africa' *Study commissioned by the Commission for the Promotion and Protection of the Rights of Cultural, Religious and Linguistic Communities* (August 2016) 29 para 15.4.

> and contributing towards the empowerment of all who are spiritually, socially and economically marginalised.[35]

Another organisation is the National Interfaith Council of South Africa (NICSA), a non-profit company (NPC), consisting of all faith-based organisations in South Africa. The vision of the NICSA is 'to take an inter-faith approach to building a new society with new moral values and attitudes'. They aim to 'strengthen, restore and re-build the integrity of the family and human values through interfaith dialogue and cooperation, as well as other interventions aimed at promoting national social cohesion and prosperity'.[36] There are further numerous multi-faith forums and other institutions (like FOR SA) which members of religious institutions can join or approach for assistance with various religious issues. These organisations often join important court cases as *amicus curiae* (friends of the court) in the interest of religious freedom.

The preceding chapters and numerous examples have confirmed the view that the South African Constitution never envisioned an absolute separation between the state and religion, but rather tried to interpret the right to freedom of religion as a right that encourages interaction between the state and religion, and the government and religious institutions in South Africa. It does not prohibit people from any form of religious practices in the public sphere and creates a framework for accommodating rather than suppressing religion and religious differences. According to Krishnaswami:[37]

> public authorities are under a positive duty to ensure as widely as possible freedom of thought, conscience and religion to all religions and beliefs and to their followers. Further, they have a responsibility to cut at the very roots of intolerance and prejudice by all possible means, such as educational measures and co-operation with groups willing to assist in counteracting prejudice and discrimination. Finally, they must provide adequate protection not only against discrimination itself but also, as mentioned in article 7 of the Declaration, 'against any incitement to such discrimination'.

35 South African Council of Churches, available at http://sacc.org.za/.

36 National Interfaith Council of South Africa, available at www.nicsa.org.za/. Nicsa was established to take up the challenge of moral regeneration, nation building and social and economic development; promote the recovery of the humanity (Ubuntu/Botho) and common good of all South Africans, both black and white; mobilise all faith-based organisations (FBOs) and communities for the creation of a socially cohesive South Africa in which the value of every individual citizen is measured by our common humanity; embrace the principles of inclusivity, religious tolerance and co-operation at national provincial, regional and local levels; promote social education, training and development; combat corruption and crime, be involved in HIV and AIDS programmes on prevention, care and treatment, as well as looking after orphans and the elderly; participate in legislative and other government processes to ensure that the voices of FBOs are take into account; and partner with private and public sectors for reconstruction, development and progress.

37 Krishnaswami *Study of Discrimination* 23.

South Africa follows a similar approach, where the concept of 'neutrality' is interpreted as equal recognition of all religions by the state and not a complete withdrawal of religion from the public sphere. An approach where there is interaction and cooperation between the state and religion, and where the state is expected, not only to respect and protect the rights in the Bill of Rights, but also to promote and fulfil them. What remains important is the fact that:

> religious believers cannot claim an automatic right to be exempted by their beliefs from the laws of the land. At the same time, the state should, wherever reasonably possible, seek to avoid putting believers to extremely painful and intensely burdensome choices of either being true to their faith or else respectful of the law.[38]

The South African government must thus refrain from imposing a separation between itself and religion, and must allow religion to enter the public domain on an equal basis and with respect for the rights of all religious followers.

Bibliography

Cheadle H and D Davis *South African Constitutional Law: The Bill of Rights* (2002) South Africa: Butterworth.

Doe N and A Jeremy "Justification for Religious Autonomy" in R O'Dair and A Lewis (eds) *Law and Religion: Current Legal Issues* (2001) 4422.

Draft Report 'An investigative Study of the Commercialisation of Religion in the Republic of South Africa' (Study commissioned by the Commission for the Promotion and Protection of the Rights of Cultural, Religious and Linguistic Communities) (August 2016).

Du Plessis L "Freedom of or Freedom from Religion? An Overview of Issues Pertinent to the Constitutional Protection of Religious Rights and Freedom in 'the New South Africa'" *Brigham Young Law Review* (2001) 2439–466.

Freedom of Religion South Africa (FOR SA) and South African Council for the Protection and Promotion of Religious Rights and Freedoms *Comments on the CRL Rights Commission's Report on the 'Commercialisation' of Religion* (28 February 2017).

Krishnaswami A *Study of Discrimination in the Matter of Religious Rights and Practices* (1960) New York: United Nations Publication.

Lenta P "Muslim Headscarves in the Workplace and Schools" *South African Law Journal* (2007) 124(2) 296–319.

Malherbe R "Religion in School" *NGTT* (2013) 54(4) 1–10.

Newman J "The Idea of Religious Tolerance" (1978) *American Philosophical Quarterly* 15 (3) 187–195.

Raz J *The Morality of Freedom* (1986) Oxford: Clarendon Press.

Rivers J *The Law of Organized Religions* (2010) London: Oxford University Press.

Smith SD 'The Restoration of Tolerance' *California Law Review* (1990) 78(2) 305.

38 *Christian Education South Africa v Minister of Education* 2000 (4) SA 757 (CC) para 35.

Index

For Product Safety Concerns and Information please contact our EU representative GPSR@taylorandfrancis.com
Taylor & Francis Verlag GmbH, Kaufingerstraße 24, 80331 München, Germany

www.ingramcontent.com/pod-product-compliance
Ingram Content Group UK Ltd.
Pitfield, Milton Keynes, MK11 3LW, UK
UKHW011003180926
475701UK00004B/539
9780367726966